Marx, Justice, and History

Marx, Justice, and History

A *Philosophy & Public Affairs* Reader

Edited by MARSHALL COHEN, THOMAS NAGEL,
and THOMAS SCANLON

Contributors

GEORGE G. BRENKERT

ALLEN BUCHANAN

G. A. COHEN

ALAN GILBERT

ZIYAD I. HUSAMI

RICHARD W. MILLER

STANLEY MOORE

JEFFRIE G. MURPHY

ALLEN W. WOOD

Princeton University Press
Princeton, New Jersey

L.C. Card: 79-5478
ISBN 0-691-02009-4 (paperback edition)
ISBN 0-691-07252-3 (hardcover edition)

First Princeton Paperback Printing, 1980
First Hardcover Printing, 1980
The essays in this book appeared originally
in the quarterly journal *Philosophy &
Public Affairs*, published by Princeton
University Press.

Allen W. Wood, "The Marxian Critique of
Justice," *P&PA* 1, no. 3 (Spring 1972),
copyright © 1972 by Princeton University
Press; Ziyad I. Husami, "Marx on
Distributive Justice," *P&PA* 8, no. 1 (Fall
1978), copyright © 1978 by Princeton
University Press; George G. Brenkert,
"Freedom and Private Property in Marx,"
P&PA 8, no. 2 (Winter 1979), copyright
© 1979 by Princeton University Press;
Allen W. Wood, "Marx on Right and
Justice: A Reply to Husami," *P&PA* 8, no. 3
(Spring 1979), copyright © 1979 by
Princeton University Press; G. A. Cohen,
"The Labor Theory of Value and the
Concept of Exploitation," *P&PA* 8, no. 4
(Summer 1979), copyright © 1979 by
Princeton University Press; Jeffrie G.
Murphy, "Marxism and Retribution,"
P&PA 2, no. 3 (Spring 1973), copyright
© 1973 by Princeton University Press;
Alan Gilbert, "Marx on Internationalism
and War," *P&PA* 7, no. 4 (Summer 1978),
copyright © 1978 by Princeton University
Press; Stanley Moore, "Marx and Lenin
as Historical Materialists," *P&PA* 4, no. 2
(Winter 1975), copyright © 1975 by
Princeton University Press; Richard W.
Miller, "The Consistency of Historical
Materialism," *P&PA* 4, no. 4 (Summer
1975), copyright © 1975 by Princeton
University Press; Stanley Moore, "A
Consistency Proof for Historical
Materialism," *P&PA* 5, no. 3 (Spring 1976),
copyright © 1976 by Princeton University
Press; Allen Buchanan, "Revolutionary
Motivation and Rationality," *P&PA* 9, no. 1
(Fall 1979), copyright © 1979 by Princeton
University Press; G. A. Cohen, "Karl Marx
and the Withering Away of Social Science,"
P&PA 1, no. 2 (Winter 1972), copyright
© 1972 by Princeton University Press.

Printed in the United States of America
by Princeton University Press
Princeton, New Jersey

CONTENTS

INTRODUCTION

The struggles of the late 1960s stimulated among English-speaking academic philosophers a new interest in applying moral philosophy to the problems of contemporary society. They also stimulated a search for critical perspectives on Marx and Marxist thought, long neglected even by social philosophers working in the Anglo-American analytic tradition. Since its inception, *Philosophy & Public Affairs* has sought, among other things, to provide a forum for both of these endeavors and to publish articles that would help bridge the gap between contemporary analytic moral philosophy and Marxist social theory.

Viewed from either side, this task is not an easy one. From its forebears in both German logical positivist and British ordinary language philosophy, contemporary analytic philosophy has inherited an attitude of suspicion and sometimes of complacent superiority toward the terminology and philosophical style of the Hegelian tradition. On the other hand, from a Marxist point of view, much of mid-twentieth-century analytic political philosophy is viewed as an almost perverse recreation of those traditions of eighteenth-century political thought which, in the opinion of many Marxists, Marx had definitively criticized and even Hegel had already surpassed.

Moving beyond this condition of mutual ignorance and suspicion requires both education and theoretical development. Some contributions to the process have taken the form of a new Marxist scholarship influenced by the techniques of contemporary analytic philosophy. Others have attempted to explore points of contact between the two traditions: to interpret and assess Marx's treatment of problems of moral and political philosophy, and to show how Marxist criticism and social theory bear on contemporary analytic moral philosophy and contemporary moral problems. The present volume includes contributions of both these sorts. Those in the first section concentrate on Marx's attitude toward morality in general, and toward the use of particular moral concepts in the evaluation of societies and social institutions. In the second section the emphasis shifts to Marx's theory of historical change and development, and to the theory of revolution.

The first essay in the collection, Allen W. Wood's "The Marxian Critique of Justice," opens a discussion, which proceeds through the next three essays, on the role of justice and of other moral notions in Marx's philosophy. According to Wood, and contrary to much received opinion, Marx does not condemn capitalism for being unjust or, indeed, for failing to exhibit or promote any other moral or social ideal or principle. According to Wood's interpretation, justice is not a standard by which human reason in the abstract measures human actions, institutions, or other social phenomena. It is, rather, a standard by which each mode of production—feudal, capitalist, or socialist —measures itself and only itself. In particular, the appropriation of surplus value, in the view of many the characteristic injustice of capitalism, is not unjust and the new, revolutionary mode of production will be no more just than the old one. Disguised exploitation, unnecessary servitude, economic instability and declining productivity are characteristics of capitalism and they provide good reasons for condemning it. But, in Wood's view, these reasons do not derive from a moral theory and Marx never tried to give a philosophical account of why these features (among others) constitute good reasons for condemning a system that possesses them.

Ziyad I. Husami argues, to the contrary, that in employing language like the language of exploitation, which is typically used in philosophical discourse about justice, Marx certainly seems to be condemning capitalism for its injustice. Husami denies that standards of justice are relative to modes of production. He suggests that Wood is collapsing Marxian moral theory into Marxian sociology of morals, and confusing the explanation of a phenomenon like surplus value with the evaluation of it. For Husami it is entirely appropriate for the proletariat and its spokesmen to criticize the abstract, juridical standards of capitalist justice, whose function it is to disguise the exploitation of labor by invoking proletarian and post-capitalist standards of justice. For Marx the socialist concept of justice, which is closely linked to the concept of equality, is plainly superior to the capitalist conception, but it still regards man simply as a worker, and fails to take account of what Marx calls "the whole man." It is the communist conception of distributive justice which adopts the Hegelian view that man's ultimate need is for self-realization and therefore makes the satisfaction of needs (from each according to his ability, to each according to his needs) its fundamental principle. This, for Marx, is the true standard of justice.

George G. Brenkert offers a mediating view. According to him Marx does, indeed, have an underlying moral reason for opposing the capitalist institution of private property. Brenkert agrees with Wood that for Marx the capitalist conception of justice is merely juridical and appropriate only for judging phenomena that arise within the capitalist mode of production. He argues, however, that what is true of justice is not necessarily true of freedom. For freedom is related to the mode of production in a significantly different way. Brenkert argues, therefore, that Marx's criticism of private property is a moral one, but one founded on the principle of freedom and on the effect private property has on the development of individuality and personality. Unlike justice, freedom provides a transcultural standard and possesses an ontological dimension that justice lacks. The basic criterion of freedom, by which all societies can be judged, is the degree to which they foster the self-development of man and society through their development of the productive forces of society.

In his reflections on the preceding discussion, Wood reiterates his view that Marx is not offering a moral critique of society. For Wood he is, like Nietzsche, a critic of morality itself. The question whether capitalist society engages in exploitation and is unjust is a question that can be raised and answered only relative to capitalist society's own legal conceptions of right and justice. By these standards, exploitation is, in fact, just. Wood agrees with Brenkert, however, that Marx condemns capitalism because it limits man's freedom as well as upsetting his security and comfort. But Wood argues that goods such as freedom and security are non-moral goods and that, unlike justice, they need not be judged relative to the mode of production. As Wood sees it the value of these non-moral goods is sufficient, quite aside from appeals to our love of virtue or our sense of guilt, to convince any reasonable person to favor the overthrow of any social order that frustrates them unnecessarily. In Wood's view Marx's critique of morality may be too harsh and it may well be that present-day Marxists ought to develop a moral critique of capitalism. He continues to believe, however, that Marx himself did not undertake to provide one.

The first section of the volume concludes with three studies of particular aspects of Marx's views on justice. G. A. Cohen argues that the real basis of Marx's charge that the capitalist mode of production systematically and "unjustly" exploits the worker is neither the labor theory of value (which holds that socially necessary labor time determines value) nor its popular surrogate (which holds that labor creates value). It is, contrary to the usual view, the fairly obvious truth that labor creates what has value. In his view, this clarification of the charge that capitalism exploits labor should facilitate a proper evaluation of this central Marxist claim. For, Cohen argues, the claim that labor creates value is not only unnecessary to the charge of exploitation, but false as well. In "Marxism and Retribution," Jeffrie G. Murphy explores some remarks of Marx's on the theory of retributive justice or punishment. Marx appears to believe that a retributive theory of punishment of the sort developed by Kant and Hegel is (as opposed to a utilitarian theory) at least formally correct. But Marx rejects the retributive theory, which justifies state coercion on the ground that it is a product of each man's rational will, because it presupposes a view of all men, including criminals, as autonomous participants in a system of mutually beneficial relations which the Marxist analysis of society shows to be materially incorrect. In Marx's view, the concepts employed by the retributive theory present themselves as derivations from some eternal and ahistorical concept of rational autonomy when they are, in fact, mere reflections of class ideology and the *embourgoisement* of language. In Murphy's view, it is immoral to apply the retributive theory to situations in which its empirical presuppositions are false. If we wish to develop a morally defensible institution of punishment, we must first create a society in which autonomous persons do in fact derive mutual benefit from their social relations. Murphy suspects that in such circumstances there would be far less need for institutions of punishment. Alan Gilbert, in his essay "Marx on Internationalism and War," turns to the subject of distributive justice in the context of international relations. According to Gilbert, the actual social and political relations between at least the elites in the rich countries and the citizens of the poor countries offers little hope that any obligation to redistribute wealth will in fact be honored. He suggests that on a Marxian view the interests of most people—at least of working people—in the rich nations coincide with those of a majority of people in the poor nations and not with the elite of their own state. He argues that this view provides an alternative strategy for achieving distributive justice. After reviewing Marx's discussion of the relevant historical evidence Gilbert explains its contemporary implications. He concentrates attention on cases of colonial wars waged by capitalist countries against independence or radical social movements and on the immigration of individuals from poor countries to rich ones. He believes that an internationalist political strategy based on a Marxist analysis of class interests provides the best hope for rectifying the injustice of unequal distribution between poor and rich nations.

In the second section, the emphasis of the essays moves from Marx's themes of justice and morality to his doctrines of sociology and history. According to Stanley Moore, Marx's claim to provide an empirical and descriptive version of socialism, as opposed to the speculative and prescriptive version offered by the utopian socialists, is unjustified. According to Wood, both tendencies are present in Marx's own version of socialism which in fact inconsistently combines a sociology of change with a dialectic of liberty. According to the sociology of change revolution is to be explained as a consequence of a conflict between the forces and relations of production. It occurs when property relations become "fetters" impeding the development of technology. By contrast, Marx's dialectic of liberation explains revolution as the result of class conflict. In Moore's view, this mode of explanation is incompatible with Marx's materialism and with his sociology of change. According to his sociology of change, in the transition from feudalism

to capitalism, economic transformation precedes political revolution
and it is this analysis which provided revisionists such as Bernstein and
Jaurès with the starting point for opposing the revolutionary pattern
of socialist transformation. According to Marx's dialectic of liberation,
however, in the transition from capitalism to socialism, political revolution precedes economic transformation. In Moore's view this doctrine is, however, incompatible with Marx's own historical analysis
and with the facts of recent history. And it is the element in Marx's
utopian dialectic of liberation which provides the foundation for the
kind of despotic elitism manifested in Leninism and Stalinism. In
Moore's view, the liberationist element in Marx's thought should be
rejected in favor of a revisionist program based on his scientific sociology of change. Then the long ascent to social justice and individual
freedom can be put on a sound basis. In a reply, "The Consistency of
Historical Materialism," Richard W. Miller argues that if Marxian texts
are approached with the same generosity that is normally accorded
other great philosophers, a consistent interpretation of Marx is available. The explanation of historical change in terms of the conflict of
the forces and relations of production can be reconciled with its explanation in terms of class conflict. If such crucial terms as "productive force," "relation of production," "feudalism," and "capitalism" are
properly interpreted it can also be seen that, contrary to Moore,
Marx's view is that through an extended process of political struggle
the bourgeoisie transformed the English economy from a predominantly feudal one to a classic example of the capitalist mode of production. Miller therefore rejects Moore's claim that Marx's view of the
transition from capitalism to socialism is incompatible with his view
of the transition from feudalism to capitalism. He also rejects Moore's
claim that the Marxist view of the development of capitalism has been
refuted by the historical facts. In Miller's view, Marx presents a consistent theory whose truth or falsity remains an open empirical question.

In his essay, "Revolutionary Motivation and Rationality," Allen
Buchanan poses a different problem for Marx's theory of revolutionary
change. Buchanan argues that even if revolution is in the best interests
of the proletariat and every member of the proletariat realizes this and

acts rationally, the proletariat will not achieve concerted revolutionary action. This conclusion rests on the premise that concerted revolutionary action is for the proletariat a public good in the technical sense. By a public good is meant any benefit which, if it is available to any member of a group, is available to all members of the group including those free-riders who do not share the costs of producing it. According to Buchanan, Marx's theory of revolutionary motivation is undermined by the free-rider problem, for each member of the proletariat, if he acts rationally, will refrain from joining the revolutionary struggle. Buchanan claims that his analysis of Marx's doctrine helps to explain two phenomena that adherents of Marx's theory of proletarian motivation find difficult to account for: the revolutionary's use of violence against members of the proletariat and his reliance on what Marx calls "obsolete verbal rubbish" about justice and rights. These are strategies for trying to overcome the free-rider problem. But Marx himself does not provide a theory of revolutionary motivation which is able to explain the transition from capitalism to socialism. In the final essay, G. A. Cohen argues that according to Marx, one of the desirable features of the triumph of socialism would be the withering away of social science. "If there were no difference between essence and appearance, there would be no need for science," Marx wrote. Under feudalism and capitalism the discrepancy between essence and appearance is necessary, for these societies are held together by mechanisms that disguise their basic anatomies. If serfs knew that the community of the manor was a sham, they would not knowingly surrender a part of their produce to the lord. Under capitalism, if factory workers knew they were not compensated for all their labor, they would cease working for the capitalists, since their sole motive for doing it is self-interest. When the proletariat is made aware of the truths of Marxist social science and penetrates the veil of social appearances, it will revolt. With the advent of socialism, the relations of man to man in society will at last become transparent and visible. There will be no difference between appearance and essence. Engels said that the German working-class movement was the rightful heir to German philosophy. Cohen thinks he meant that the proletariat would fulfill in practice what philosophers had attempted in theory: the project of making the world intelligible. While Cohen believes that a reduced reliance on social science is desirable, he argues that it is futile to hope for the total transparency and freedom from epistemological alienation that Marx envisions as a culmination of the dialectic of history. The unity of theory and practice cannot be achieved in precisely the manner Marx and Engels envisaged. The point of philosophy will remain not only to change the world but also to interpret it. We agree that this is, indeed, the complex fate of philosophy and of society.

M.C., T.N., T.S.

PART I

MARX'S VIEWS ON JUSTICE AND OTHER FUNDAMENTAL ETHICAL IDEAS

ALLEN W. WOOD   The Marxian Critique
                                           of Justice

When we read Karl Marx's descriptions of the capitalist mode of production in *Capital* and other writings, all our instincts tell us that
these are descriptions of an unjust social system. Marx describes a
society in which one small class of persons lives in comfort and idle-
ness while another class, in ever-increasing numbers, lives in want
and wretchedness, laboring to produce the wealth enjoyed by the first.
Marx speaks constantly of capitalist "exploitation" of the worker, and
refers to the creation of surplus value as the appropriation of his
"unpaid labor" by capital. Not only does capitalist society, as Marx
describes it, strike us as unjust, but his own descriptions of it themselves seem to connote injustice.

When we look in the writings of Marx and Engels for a detailed
account of the injustices of capitalism, however, we discover at once
that not only is there no attempt at all in their writings to provide
an argument that capitalism is unjust, but there is not even the
explicit claim that capitalism is unjust or inequitable, or that it violates anyone's rights. We find, in fact, explicit denunciations and sustained criticisms of social thinkers (such as Pierre Proudhon and
Ferdinand Lassalle) who did condemn capitalism for its injustices
or advocated some form of socialism as a means of securing justice,
equality, or the rights of man. We even find, perhaps to our surprise,
some fairly explicit statements to the effect that capitalism, with all
its manifold defects, cannot be faulted as far as justice is concerned.
Whatever else capitalism may be for Marx, it does not seem that it is
unjust.

The fact that Marx does not regard capitalism as unjust has been noted before.[1] But Marx's reasons for holding this view, and the concept of justice on which it rests, have been less frequently understood. It is of course true that Marx and Engels do not say much about the manner in which social or economic justice may be actualized, and that they do not concern themselves greatly with the ways in which just social institutions may be distinguished from unjust ones. And if, as I wish to argue, the attainment of justice does not, in itself, play a significant role in either Marxian theory or Marxist practice, these omissions are neither serious nor surprising. Nevertheless, Marx and Engels did take seriously the concept of justice and did have a place for it in their conception of society and social practice. Both were in fact highly critical of what they took to be the misuse of this concept in social thought, its "mystification" and ideological "glorification." This Marxian critique of justice may be viewed as an attempt to clarify the role of the concept of justice in social life and to prevent its ideological abuse. Much can be learned, I think, by tracing this critique to its roots in the Marxian conceptions of society and social practice, and viewing it in relation to Marx's own reasons for denying that capitalism is unjust while at the same time calling for its revolutionary overthrow.

I

The concept of justice has traditionally played an important role in theories of the rational assessment of social institutions. It is commonly felt that justice is the highest merit any social institution can possess, while injustice is the gravest charge which could ever be lodged against it. It seems to be no exaggeration to say that to both the philosopher and the common man justice has often appeared, as Engels once put it, "the fundamental principle of all society, . . . the standard by which to measure all human things, . . . the final judge to be appealed to in all conflicts."[2] Why is such importance attached

1. Most recently by Robert C. Tucker, *The Marxian Revolutionary Idea* (New York, 1969), pp. 37-48. Cf. Tucker, *Philosophy and Myth in Karl Marx* (Cambridge, Eng., 1961), pp. 18-20, 222f. (See also pp. 272-275, below.)
2. *Marx Engels Werke* (Berlin, 1959), 18: 274. Cf. Karl Marx and Friedrich Engels, *Selected Works* (Moscow, 1951), I, 562. (All translations in the text are my own.)

to the concept of justice? "Justice" (*Gerechtigkeit*), according to Marx and Engels, is fundamentally a juridical or legal (*rechtlich*) concept, a concept related to the law (*Recht*) and to the rights (*Rechte*) men have under it. The concepts of right and justice are for them the highest rational standards by which laws, social institutions, and human actions may be judged from a juridical point of view.[3] This point of view has long been regarded as being of particular importance for the understanding and assessment of social facts. It is not too much to say that the traditional Western conception of society is itself a fundamentally juridical conception. The social whole, according to this tradition, *is* the "state" or "body politic," the framework within which human actions are regulated by legal and political processes. The study of society in this tradition has been, above all, the study of these processes; the ideal society, since Plato's time, has been conceived of as the ideal *state*; and social practice, in its highest form, has been thought to be the skillful fashioning of a state through the giving of just laws, or the regulation of the actions of citizens by a wise government. The social life of man, according to this tradition, is his life in relation to the political state; man as a social being is man in relation to those powers which promulgate laws, guarantee rights, and issue juridical commands. Granted this conception of society, it is quite understandable that right and justice should be taken as the fundamental social principles, the highest measure of all social things.

The source not only of Marx's critique of justice, but also of the fundamental originality of his social thought, is his rejection of this political or juridical conception of society. Marx tells us in his preface to *A Contribution to the Critique of Political Economy* that the origins of his social thought lay in the discontent he felt with this conception as a student of law and the philosophy of law, and particularly of Hegel's *Philosophy of Right*. His critical reflections, he tells us—and we can see it for ourselves in the articles and manuscripts produced by Marx in the course of the year 1843—"led to the result that juridical relations [Rechtsverhältnisse], like forms of the state, are to be grasped neither through themselves nor through the so-called universal development of the human spirit, but rather are rooted in the material rela-

---

3. *Werke*, 18: 276. Cf. *Selected Works*, I, 564.

tions of life, whose totality Hegel . . . comprehended under the term 'civil society.' "[4] The social whole, the fully concrete unity of social life was, in Hegel's view, to be found in the political state; the sphere of men's material activities and interests, civil society, was treated by Hegel as a system of social processes taking place *within* the political whole and dependent on it. Marx reversed this relationship. Human society, he maintained, is a developing system of collective productive activity, aimed at the satisfaction of historically conditioned human needs; its institutions, including juridical and political ones, are all aspects of this productive activity. As early as 1844 Marx tells us that "Religion, the family, the state, the law [Recht], morality, science, art, etc., are only particular modes of production and fall under its general law." And in the *German Ideology* Marx and Engels reject "the old conception of history which neglects real relationships and restricts itself to high-sounding dramas of princes and states."[5]

The key to Marx's transformation of Hegel's concept of society is found in the Marxian conception of human practice. Human society, according to the Marxian view, is a fact of nature. But it is nevertheless characterized throughout by the essential quality of man as a natural phenomenon, by productive activity or labor, which distinguishes man from the rest of the natural world. "Men begin to distinguish

4. *Werke*, 13: 8. Cf. *Selected Works*, I, 328.
5. *Werke*, Ergänzungsband I, Teil 537. Cf. Karl Marx, *Early Writings*, trans. and ed. T. B. Bottomore (New York, 1964), p. 156; *Marx/Engels Gesamtausgabe* (Berlin, 1932), I/5, 25; *Writings of the Young Marx on Philosophy and Society*, trans. and ed. Loyd Easton and Kurt Guddat (Garden City, N.Y., 1967), p. 428. But for Marx the relation between civil society and the state was never something that could be reduced to simple formulas. Shlomo Avineri has argued convincingly that in Marx "the political never appears as a mechanistic or automatic reflection of the economic" (*The Social and Political Thought of Karl Marx* [Cambridge, Eng., 1968], p. 41). The political state, Avineri notes, is not only a "reflection" of civil society, but an alienated and distorted "projection" of it (*ibid.*, p. 52). Marx's transformation of the Hegelian concept of society, therefore, is not intended to provide a theory of political behavior, but to make one possible, by removing the illusion that political and juridical institutions themselves constitute an autonomous standpoint from which social reality can be understood. Since the political state is an alienated projection of civil society, even the rationality of juridical institutions is not transparent from the juridical or political standpoint, and must be understood from the standpoint of production. This fact will be seen later on to have important implications for the notion of justice.

themselves from animals when they begin to *produce* their means of life, a step conditioned by their bodily organization."⁶ "The animal," says Engels, "merely *uses* external nature and brings about changes in it merely by his presence in it; man makes it serviceable to his ends through such changes, he *masters* it. This is the final and essential distinction between men and other animals, and it is labor which effects this distinction."⁷ The essential feature of labor for Marx and Engels is its purposiveness, the fact that it is the expression of *will*. Labor, says Engels, is that by which men "impress the stamp of their will upon the earth."⁸ Man alone, Marx points out, "makes his life-activity itself an object of his will and consciousness."⁹ And again, in *Capital*, he says: "What distinguishes the worst architect from the best of bees is that he raises his structure in his head before he builds it in wax. At the end of the labor process a result comes about which at the beginning was already in the representation of the laborer, which was already present ideally."¹⁰ But human productive activity, according to Marx, always takes place in particular historical circumstances. At a given point in human history, men are possessed of determinate methods and capacities for subjecting nature to their will—methods and capacities which they have inherited from previous generations through a specific process of historical development. These productive forces (*Produktivkräfte*), as Marx calls them, correspond to, and are expressed in, determinate relationships between men, within which alone these forces, in their historically given form, can be applied to nature. These relationships Marx calls production relations (*Produktionsverhältnisse*). Because men are not free to choose the degree of their mastery over nature at a given stage in history, they are also not free to choose the form these production relations will take. Hence production relations are, in Marx's words, "necessary and independent of their will."¹¹

Human productive activity, however, not only transforms nature; it

6. *Gesamtausgabe*, I/5, 10. Cf. *Writings of the Young Marx*, p. 409.
7. *Werke*, 20: 452. Cf. *Selected Works*, II, 82.
8. *Ibid.*
9. *Werke*, Erg. 1, Teil 516. Cf. *Early Writings*, p. 127.
10. *Werke*, 23: 193. Cf. Karl Marx, *Capital*, trans. Samuel Moore and Edward Aveling (New York, 1968), I, 178.
11. *Werke*, 13: 8. Cf. *Selected Works*, I, 328.

also transforms man himself.[12] In altering nature and in developing his productive forces, man acts on himself as well. Human history, for Marx, consists above all in the development and transformation of human nature. The activity of labor itself is for Marx essentially man's self-production.[13] This is because the employment of productive forces is not just a means to human ends, but is rather "a determinate kind of activity of individuals, a determinate way of expressing their life, a determinate *mode of life*. As individuals express their life, so they are. What they are is bound up with their production, and *what* they produce with *how* they produce."[14] Men produce by adopting determinate modes of collective activity, modes which in turn act upon them and change them. As they satisfy their needs by productive activity, therefore, they are at the same time producing new forms of activity and new needs. "The production of new needs," say Marx and Engels, "is the first historical act."[15]

Human productive activity, therefore, is a complex historical process composed of many interdependent factors acting upon and reacting with one another. Men's needs, their productive forces, their production relations are all decisive moments in it, but none of them is independent of the others. At a given stage in history these interdependent factors form a whole, a complex system of human activity with a kind of relative stability. Such a historically conditioned system of productive activity has its own characteristic forms of social and cultural life, and within it men have a characteristic human nature, distinguishing this system from the preceding system of activity out of which it arose historically and from the succeeding system into which it will eventually pass over. Such a historically conditioned social whole is called by Marx a "mode of production" (*Produktionsweise*).

The Marxian conception of society is sometimes described as "economic determinism." By this it is often meant that Marx's theory takes one aspect of social life (the "economic" aspect) to be the crucial one on which all others depend. Marx, according to this account, either reduces all of social life to economics, or he regards the rest of

12. *Werke*, 23: 192. Cf. *Capital*, I, 177.
13. *Werke*, Erg. 1, Teil 574. Cf. *Early Writings*, p. 202.
14. *Gesamtausgabe*, I/5, 11. Cf. *Writings of the Young Marx*, p. 409.
15. *Gesamtausgabe*, I/5, 18. Cf. *Writings of the Young Marx*, p. 420.

social life as an epiphenomenon of economics, or else as a series of effects proceeding entirely from "economic" causes. This interpretation of Marx, it seems to me, is fundamentally mistaken. There is no space here to deal with this issue in the depth it deserves, but I would like at least briefly to suggest why it seems to me wrong to understand Marx's "determinism" in this simplistic way. In the first place, Marx did not regard himself primarily as a political economist; he thought of himself rather as a *critic* of political economy, attempting to preserve what was valuable in classical political economy within a more comprehensive theory of society and history. He criticizes political economists for the one-sidedness of their approach to social phenomena, for their failure to see the interconnection between the different factors in social life. When Marx refers to production relations as "economic" relations, he does not mean to isolate one "aspect" of social relations as the crucial one, but simply to emphasize that all such relations are *forms* of human productive activity, and should be viewed in their connection with production.

Marx does say that "the mode of production conditions social, political, and spiritual life-processes." He also says that "it is not men's consciousness which determines their being, but on the contrary their social being which determines their consciousness."[16] But he does not mean to reduce social, political, and spiritual processes to processes of production, as some philosophers have tried to reduce mental phenomena to physical ones. Nor does Marx mean to say that "production," regarded as one factor among others in the social process, is in general the *cause* of the remaining social institutions. Marx's point here can best be understood if we keep in mind that his conception of society is a transformation of Hegel's conception, and can best be brought out by looking at Hegel's own anticipation of it early in the *Philosophy of Right*. Hegel is speaking about the function of legislation in the state, and says: "Legislation must not be considered abstractly and in isolation, but rather must be seen as a dependent moment in one totality, in its connection with all the other determinations which make up the character of a nation and an epoch."[17] Legislation, according to Hegel, is one of the "determinations" (*Bestimmungen*)

16. *Werke*, 13: 8f. Cf. *Selected Works*, I, 329.
17. Hegel, *Philosophie des Rechts* (Hamburg, 1955), sec. 3, p. 22.

which make up a nation and an epoch, one of the dependent moments
in a totality. To be properly understood, therefore, it must not be
treated as something independent of this totality, or something intelligible on its own, but rather must be viewed as a partial process
within the total process. The totality of national life in a given epoch
could, in this sense, be said by Hegel to determine and to condition
the laws of the nation. It would, however, be either incorrect or unintelligible to say that for Hegel legislation could be *reduced* to the
totality of national life. Hegel is not reducing legislation to anything;
he is rather attempting to appreciate its richness by noting its connection with other factors in national life. Nor is it at all plausible to
attribute to Hegel the view that legislation is a mere "epiphenomenon"
of national life. Legislation, in Hegel's view, might very well be said
to be caused by specific factors within the totality of national life, but
this is a result of the fact that legislation is itself a determination or
dependent moment within this organic totality.

The organic whole of social life in a given historical epoch is of
course not for Marx a nation or political state, but a mode of production. This whole is called a mode of *production* because human life is
essentially productive activity. And Marx explicitly distinguishes "production" in this comprehensive sense from "production in its one-sided
form" as one of the elements or "determinations" of the total process.[18]
Not only human needs, modes of commerce and exchange, and property relations, but also men's political life, religion, morality, and philosophical thought are moments, phases, determinations of human productive activity. Like the more narrowly "economic" categories of
exchange and consumption, they are "elements in a totality, distinctions within a unity. . . . There is an interaction between the various
moments. This is the case with every organic whole."[19] Legal and

18. *Werke*, 13: 631. Cf. David Horowitz, *Marx and Modern Economics* (New
York, 1968), p. 39.
19. *Werke*, 13: 630f. Cf. *Marx and Modern Economics*, pp. 38f. Compare the
following passage from the *German Ideology*: "This interpretation of history
depends on setting forth the actual process of production, proceeding from the
material production of life itself, and interpreting the form of interaction connected with and created by it, that is by civil society in its various stages, as the
basis of all history; at the same time setting forth [civil society] in its action as
state and tracing all the various theoretical products and forms of consciousness,
religion, philosophy, ethics, etc., in their genesis from it. Then the matter can

political structures are therefore called "superstructures" by Marx; they are structures which are dependent on and hence "built upon" the mode of production within which they operate as regulative institutions.[20] These institutions owe their existence and their form to the mode of production within which they operate, to the specific manner in which they regulate existing production relations and serve the needs of given individuals. Law and politics may indeed affect and condition these other moments of the social process, but they are also affected and conditioned by them. They "mirror" or "reflect" the productive social life they regulate.[21] The task of comprehending them is not that of reducing political or juridical facts to economic facts, but that of discovering empirically the "connection [Zusammenhang] of the social and political structure with production."[22]

I have been claiming that Marx's conception of society is founded on a reversal of the Hegelian relationship between social production (civil society) and the political state. I have argued that just as for Hegel civil society was a partial process within the totality of national political life, so for Marx the state was a partial process reflecting the life of civil society. This claim needs to be clarified and qualified, however. For it was not an "eternal truth" for Marx (nor, *mutatis mutandis*, for Hegel) that the political life and productive activity of man stand in this relationship to one another. Marx did not believe, in fact,

---

be presented in its totality (and thus also the reciprocal effects of these various sides on one another)" (*Gesamtausgabe*, I/5, 27; cf. *Writings of the Young Marx*, p. 431).

20. *Werke*, 13: 9. Cf. *Selected Works*, I, 329.

21. *Werke*, 23: 99: "This juridical relation [of exchange] . . . is a relation of wills in which the economic relation is mirrored [sich widerspiegelt]." Here as elsewhere terms suggesting "mirroring" or "reflection" (such as "sich widerspiegeln," "Reflexion," "reflektiren") have sometimes been seriously mistranslated using the English word "reflex." Thus Moore and Aveling translate the above as: "This juridical relation . . . is a relation of two wills, and is but the reflex of the real economic relation between the two" (*Capital*, I, 84). This translation suggests that the juridical relation is like a knee jerk produced by an economic hammer-tap, or the mechanism of a Pavlovian dog emitting juridical saliva in response to economic stimuli. Such an impression is entirely the result of mistranslation, and has nothing to do with Marx's view of the matter. Marx's "mirroring" terminology is of course derived from Hegel (cf. *Werke*, 25: 58; *Capital*, III, 48 and *Werke*, 23: 640; *Capital*, I, 612).

22. *Gesamtausgabe*, I/5, 15. Cf. *Writings of the Young Marx*, p. 413.

that the identification of the social whole with the political state was necessarily false under all historical circumstances. In the *Grundrisse* he distinguishes three general types of society, the tribal, the oriental, and the ancient, which because they were rooted in the common ownership of means of production by the political whole or its representative involved no separation of the political state from civil society. In such societies the productive and political life of man was an immediate unity, and the productive activity of the individual was indistinguishable from his participation and membership in the political *Gemeinwesen*, the tribe, state, or polis. Thus from a Marxian viewpoint ancient political science, such as we find in Plato's *Republic* or Aristotle's *Politics*, cannot be faulted for conceiving of the social whole as identical with the laws, customs, and institutions of the polis. In ancient society, the social life of man was his political life, and it was quite correct to say, as Aristotle did, that the "way of life" of a people was its *politeia*.

The differentiation of the political state from civil society was made historically possible, Marx believed, by the introduction of commodity exchange into the productive life of society, and the resulting opposition between the form of common property corresponding to the tribal *Gemeinwesen* and the form of private property corresponding to the exchange of commodities. This opposition, present already in the oriental and ancient productive modes, made possible in Marx's view the alienation of the state from civil society which characterized feudal production, and which reaches its extreme form in the fragmented life of capitalist civil society. Here the state, which began in immediate unity with the process of social production, has become a distinct institution operating within this process, which nevertheless still claims to represent society in its totality. The existence of the political state as a determination and alienated reflection of man's productive life is therefore not an eternal truth about the nature of society, but a historical truth about those European societies which have passed through feudal to capitalist production.

The importance of human productive activity in the Marxian conception of society, however, transcends this historical process, or rather represents a principle of social life which emerges with increasing clarity from it. Only when the sphere of human productive activity as such emancipates itself from the limiting regulatory forms of political life can the universal character of man's social being as cooperative labor become apparent to him. Hence it was Marx's view that social production, the true basis of all society, could not be appreciated as such by the ancient world, and only emerged with clarity in the economic life of the capitalist mode of production. This is why Marx repudiated the tendency of other thinkers, such as Rousseau and Hegel, to idealize the political life of the ancient world and to long for its restoration or to conceive of the modern state as a principle of social unity to be imposed on the fragmented world of capitalism. Instead, Marx saw implicit in the modern emancipation of civil society from the state the possibility of establishing men's cooperative labor itself as the basis of a new form of *Gemeinwesen*. It is this notion of the replacement of the political state by a new form of community based on labor which lies at the root of Marx's belief that in communist society the state will be abolished and transcended (*aufgehoben*).

II

The concept of justice, as we have seen, is in the Marxian account the highest expression of the rationality of social facts from the *juridical* point of view. This point of view, however, is always the point of view of one of the dependent moments of a given mode of production, the sphere of political authority or *Staatsrecht*. Marx, as we have seen, rejected the Hegelian notion that the organic unity of society is to be in any sense identified with the regulatory functions of the political state. Just as little is the state a power acting on the mode of production from outside, determining its form and controlling its historical destiny. The political state is rather a power acting *within* the prevailing mode of production, it is one of the instruments of production fashioned by the historical past and employed in the present by given individuals to satisfy their historically conditioned needs. The state is an expression, a determination, of the prevailing mode of production. Its point of view, the juridical one, and the conceptions of right and justice which express this point of view, are rationally comprehensible only when seen in their proper connection with other determinations of social life and grasped in terms of their role within the prevailing productive mode.

For all his detailed study of social reality and his profound concern with the rational assessment of it, we find no real attempts in Marx's writings to provide a clear and positive conception of right or justice. This relative neglect of juridical concepts and principles does not derive from a personal aversion to "moral preaching" or from an "amoral" attitude toward social reality, as some have suggested. It is due rather to Marx's assessment of the role of juridical conceptions in social life. Because Marx regarded juridical institutions as playing only a supporting role in social life, he attached considerably less importance to juridical conceptions as measures of social rationality than most previous social thinkers were inclined to do. The juridical point of view, for Marx, is essentially one-sided, and to adopt it as the fundamental standpoint from which to judge all social reality is to adopt a distorted conception of that reality. But it is not true that Marx tells us nothing about justice as a rational social norm. In *Capital* he says: "The justice of transactions which go on between agents of production rests on the fact that these transactions arise as natural consequences from the relations of production. The juristic forms in which these economic transactions appear as voluntary actions of the participants, as expressions of their common will and as contracts that may be enforced by the state against a single party, cannot, being mere forms, determine this content. They merely express it. This content is just whenever it corresponds to the mode of production, is adequate to it. It is unjust whenever it contradicts that mode. Slavery, on the basis of the capitalist mode of production, is unjust; so is fraud in the quality of commodities."[23]

This passage by no means amounts to a clear statement of a Marxian "theory of justice," but it is nevertheless quite illuminating. For although Marx speaks in the passage only of the justice of "transactions," the account he gives is general enough to apply to actions, social institutions, even to legal and political structures. And what he says about the justice of transactions does suggest several important theses regarding the concept of justice and its proper function in social theory and practice.

First, as we should expect, Marx views the concept of justice in

23. *Werke*, 25: 351f. Cf. *Capital*, III, 339f.

terms of its function within a given mode of production. The employment of this concept by human thought and its application to social
practice are always dependent moments of the process of production.
The rational validity of any such employment is, for Marx, always
measured in terms of the prevailing mode of production. The political
state and the concepts of law and right associated with the public
regulation of society are for Marx both determinations of the prevailing mode of production and alienated projections of it. They mirror
or reflect production, but in a distorted and mystified way. The state
gives itself out as the true representative of society, and *Rechtsbegriffe*
pretend to constitute the foundation for the rationality of social practice, based either on the autonomous rationality of the state or on
unconditioned rational principles of "right" or "justice" beyond which
no rational appeal can be made. But in Marx's view the real *raison
d'être* of juridical institutions and concepts can be understood only
from the more comprehensive vantage point of the historical mode of
production they both participate in and portray. Justice, therefore, as
a *Rechtsbegriff*, always requires explication from beyond "juristic
forms." A determination of the justice of transactions or institutions
demands, rather, an appreciation of their function in production.
When Marx says that a just transaction is one that corresponds to the
prevailing mode of production, he means, I think, that it is one which
plays a concrete role in this mode, one which functions as an actual
moment in the productive process. Just transactions "fit" the prevailing mode, they serve a purpose relative to it, they concretely carry forward and bring to actuality the process of collective productive activity
of human individuals in a concrete historical situation. The judgment
whether a social institution is just or unjust depends, then, on the
concrete comprehension of the mode of production as a whole, and
on an appreciation of the connection between this whole and the institution in question. This is perhaps why Engels says that "social justice
or injustice is decided by the science which deals with the material
facts of production and exchange, the science of political economy."[24]

Secondly, then, justice is not a standard by which human reason in
the abstract measures human actions, institutions, or other social

24. Marx and Engels, *Kleine Ökonomische Schriften* (Berlin, 1955), p. 412.

facts. It is rather a standard by which each mode of production measures *itself*. It is a standard present to human thought only in the context of a specific mode of production. Hence there are no general rules or precepts of "natural justice" applicable to any and all forms of society. The ownership of one man by another, for example, or the charging of interest on borrowed money are not in themselves just or unjust. Under the ancient mode of production, the holding of slaves was, as Aristotle argued, both right and expedient. Usury, on the other hand, was essentially foreign for the most part to this mode of production; and where it involved simply making a profit on the momentary distress of another, it was certainly unjust. Under capitalist production, however, direct slavery is unjust; while the charging of interest on borrowed capital is perfectly just.

Thirdly, it is clear that Marx followed Hegel in rejecting a formal conception of justice. For Marx, the justice or injustice of an action or institution does not consist in its exemplification of a juridical form or its conformity to a universal principle. Justice is not determined by the universal compatibility of human acts and interests, but by the concrete requirements of a historically conditioned mode of production. There *are* rational assessments of the justice of specific acts and institutions, based on their concrete function within a specific mode of production. But these assessments are not founded on abstract or formal principles of justice, good for all times and places, or on implicit or hypothetical contracts or agreements used to determine the justice of institutions or actions formally and abstractly. Abstracted from a concrete historical context, all formal philosophical principles of justice are empty and useless; when applied to such a context, they are misleading and distorting, since they encourage us to treat the concrete context of an act or institution as accidental, inessential, a mere occasion for the pure rational form to manifest itself. But the justice of the act or institution is its concrete fittingness to *this* situation, in *this* productive mode. The justice of transactions, Marx says, is not a matter of form, but a matter of content. The justice of an institution depends on the particular institution and the particular mode of production of which it is a part. All juridical forms and principles of justice are therefore meaningless unless applied to a specific mode of production, and they retain their rational validity only as long as the content they possess and the particular actions to which they apply arise naturally out of and correspond concretely to this productive mode.[25]

Finally, the justice of acts or institutions does not depend for Marx on their results or consequences. We might think, for instance, that just acts and institutions would tend to make people happier than unjust ones. But this is by no means necessary. For if a mode of production rests on the exploitation of one class by another, then it seems likely that just institutions under that mode will tend in general to satisfy the needs of the oppressors at the expense of the oppressed. But if this is Marx's view, we might at least be tempted to think that he would agree with Thrasymachus that justice is what is in the interest of the stronger, i.e., of the ruling class. And we may be inclined to think also that he would agree with Hume that those acts and institutions are just which contribute to the preservation, stability, and smooth functioning of society, i.e., of the prevailing mode of produc-

---

25. This is not to deny, of course, that there has been a certain continuity in philosophical treatments of the concept of justice. The discussions of this concept in Plato's *Republic* and in Book 5 of the *Nichomachean Ethics* pose many of the same philosophical problems we meet with today. And Kant was quite correct, in the Marxian view, when he said that a universal resolution of the question "Was ist Recht?" is *the* perennial task of the jurist (*Gesammelte Schriften*, Akad. Ed. [Berlin, 1914], 6: 229). But in the Marxian view these facts point to the fundamental inadequacy of the tradition of social philosophy and jurisprudence based on the political or juridical conception of society. Jurisprudence, according to Engels, "compares the legal systems of different peoples and different times, not as the expression of their respective economic relations, but as systems having their foundation in themselves. The comparison presupposes that there is something common to them all, which the jurists set forth by a comparison of legal systems under the name 'natural right.' But the standard used to measure what is and is not natural right is just the most abstract expression of right itself, namely *justice*, . . . *eternal* justice" (*Werke*, 18: 276f.; cf. *Selected Works*, I, 564f.). By this procedure, it is possible to ask abstract questions about the nature of social institutions from an abstract, juridical standpoint, and to provide equally abstract answers to them, seeking a single formal and universal answer to a set of questions which can only be answered in concrete circumstances. The apparent unity in their philosophical concept of justice, as Engels goes on to point out, has not prevented men from maintaining the greatest conceivable diversity in "just" practices, and the common acceptance of universal philosophical principles of justice is even compatible with quite serious disagreement as to what sorts of actual social arrangements are just and unjust. "The conception of eternal justice," he says, "therefore belongs among those things by which . . . 'everyone understands something different'" (*ibid.*).

tion. For, we might argue, if a transaction is to arise naturally out of the existing production relations, to correspond to the prevailing mode of production and play a concrete role in it, then it must serve, or tend to serve, the interests of the ruling class under that mode, and it must contribute, or tend to contribute, to the security and stability of the existing order of things. Now in the short run this may very well be so, and just transactions may even be carried on in many cases with the conscious intention of furthering the interests of a certain class or maintaining the stability of the existing order. But if, as Marx believes, there is an inherent tendency in each mode of production itself toward mounting instability, increasing social antagonism and conflict, and ultimately toward its own eventual overthrow and abolition, then in the long run those very transactions which are most just, which are most intimately a part of a specific mode of production, must also contribute in an essential way to its instability and eventual destruction. For Marx, a transaction is just on account of its function within the whole, and not on account of its consequences for the whole.

There is no reason, it seems to me, to regard the Marxian concept of justice as a relativistic one. It is true that whether a given transaction or institution is just or unjust will depend for Marx on its relationship to the mode of production of which it is a part, and that some institutions which are just in the context of one mode of production would be unjust in the context of another. But one does not have to be a relativist to believe that the justice of an action depends to a great extent on the circumstances in which the action is performed, or that the justice of an institution depends on its cultural setting. A relativist, as I understand it, is someone who believes that there are or can be certain kinds of fundamental conflicts or disagreements between peoples, cultures, or epochs about whether certain specific actions are or would be right or wrong, just or unjust, and that there is no rational way of resolving such disagreements, no possible "correct answer" to them. The Marxian concept of justice, however, involves no view of this kind. If, for example, a historical analysis of the role of slavery in the ancient world could show that this institution corresponded to, and played a necessary role in, the prevailing mode of production, then in the Marxian view the holding of slaves by the ancients would be a *just* practice; and the claim that ancient slavery was unjust, whether it is made by contemporaries of the institution or by modern men reading about it in history books, would simply be wrong. When Marx and Engels remark that men at different times and places have held diverse views about the nature of "eternal justice," they are not espousing the relativistic position that different views are "right" at different times and places. They are rather arguing that all glorified, ideological conceptions of justice are in some respects false and misleading, since their applicability is limited as regards time and place, and also because they often express a one-sided view even of those institutions to which they do apply.

III

I want to turn now to the question whether the appropriation of surplus value by capital is for Marx an injustice. A number of socialists in Marx's day argued that capitalism involved an unequal (and hence unjust) exchange of commodities between worker and capitalist. Their argument was based on Ricardo's principle, later adopted in a slightly modified form by Marx himself, that labor is the sole creator of exchange value and that "the value of a commodity . . . depends on the relative quantity of labor necessary for its production."[26] The worker, these socialists pointed out, hires himself out to the capitalist for a definite wage, and is supplied by the capitalist with tools and raw materials—what Marx calls "means of production" (*Produktionsmittel*)—whose value is consumed by use in the process of labor. At the end of this process, however, the worker has produced a commodity of greater value than the combined values of the wages paid him and the means of production consumed. That this value, which Marx was to call surplus value (*Mehrwert*), should be appropriated by the capitalist is an injustice, according to these socialists. For, according to Ricardo's principle, the worker's labor was responsible not only for the value paid him in wages, but for the surplus value as well. Hence surplus value must have arisen because the capitalist paid the worker less in wages than what his labor was worth. If the capitalist had paid

26. David Ricardo, *Principles of Political Economy*, ed. Piero Sraffa (Cambridge, Eng., 1951), I, 11. Cf. *Werke*, 21: 176 and Marx, *The Poverty of Philosophy* (New York, 1963), p. 8.

the worker the full value of his labor, no surplus value would have resulted, and the demands of strict justice would have been satisfied.[27]

Marx, however, rejected both this account of the origin of surplus value and the claim that surplus value involves an unequal exchange between worker and capitalist. He thought that this explanation of surplus value was at bottom no different from the one given by Sir James Steuart and others before the physiocrats, that surplus value originated from selling commodities above their value.[28] These socialists merely turned things around and explained surplus value by supposing that labor was purchased below its value. Both explanations made surplus value appear the result of mere accident, and were therefore inherently unsatisfactory.

The flaw in the argument that surplus value involves an unequal exchange, as Marx saw it, relates to the phrase "the value of labor." Human labor itself, the creative exertion of the human mind and body, is strictly speaking not a commodity at all in capitalist society. "Labor," says Marx, "is the substance and immanent measure of value, *but has itself no value.*"[29] In the socialists' argument, the phrase "value of labor" is in fact used to refer to two very different things. On the one hand, it is used to refer to the value *created by* labor, the value present in the commodity over and above the value of the means of production consumed in producing it. It is in this sense that the capitalist pays the worker less than "the value of his labor." But, Marx points out, it is not the value created by labor which the capitalist pays for. He does not buy finished commodities from the worker, less the amount of his means of production consumed; rather, he buys, in the form of a commodity, the worker's capacity to produce commodities for him. What he purchases from the worker is not the worker's products, but rather what Marx calls his "labor power" (*Arbeitskraft*). It is this *power* which is sold as a commodity for wages. In the capitalist labor process, the capitalist merely makes use of what he has bought antecedent to the process. "As soon as [the worker's] labor begins," says

27. *Werke*, 4: 98-100. Cf. *The Poverty of Philosophy*, pp. 69-72.
28. *Werke*, 26: I, 7-11. Cf. Marx, *Theories of Surplus Value*, trans. Emile Burns (Moscow, 1954), part I, pp. 41-43.
29. *Werke*, 23: 559. Cf. *Capital*, I, 537.

Marx, "it has already ceased to belong to him; hence it is no longer a thing he can sell."[30]

The value of labor power, Marx points out, like the value of any other commodity, depends on the quantity of labor necessary for its production (or, according to the Marxian "law of value," the average labor time socially necessary for the production of commodities of that kind). In other words, the value of labor power depends on the quantity of labor necessary to keep the worker alive and working, or to replace him if he should die or quit. Marx does not hold, however, that this is necessarily the same as the worker's "bare subsistence," whatever that phrase is supposed to mean in general. The value of labor power depends on what is *socially* necessary: it therefore "contains a historical and moral element."[31] In China, it might consist of a bowl of rice a day; in affluent America, it might include the means necessary to supply the worker with a late-model automobile, a color television set, and similar depraving and debilitating necessities of life. The value of labor power, like the value of any other commodity, depends on the level of development of productive forces and on the concrete production relations to which they correspond. It can go up or down, but it cannot be just or unjust.

Now according to Marx, the wage worker *is* generally paid the full value of his labor power. He is paid, in other words, what is socially necessary for the reproduction of his life-activity as a worker. This is, according to the Ricardian formula and the strictest rules of commodity exchange, a *just* transaction, an exchange of equivalent for equivalent.[32] Surplus value, to be sure, is appropriated by the capitalist without an equivalent.[33] But there is nothing in the exchange requiring him to pay any equivalent for it. The exchange of wages for labor power is the *only* exchange between capitalist and worker. It is a just exchange, and it is consummated long before the question arises of selling the commodity produced and realizing its surplus value. The capitalist has bought a commodity (labor power) and paid its full value; by using, exploiting, this commodity, he now creates a greater value than he began with. This surplus belongs to him; it never

30. *Ibid.*   31. *Werke*, 23: 185. Cf. *Capital*, I, 171.
32. *Werke*, 23: 190. Cf. *Capital*, I, 176.
33. *Werke*, 23: 609. Cf. *Capital*, I, 583.

belonged to anyone else, and he owes nobody a penny for it. "This circumstance," says Marx, "is peculiar good fortune for the buyer [of labor power], but no injustice at all to the seller."[34] The appropriation of surplus value by capital, therefore, involves no unequal or unjust exchange.

Nevertheless, it might still seem that Ricardo's principle could be used to argue that the appropriation of surplus value by capital is an injustice to the worker. Ricardo's principle says that labor is the sole creator and indeed the very substance of value, that the means of production do not increase in value except as they are productively consumed by labor and incorporated in its products. It would seem to follow that this entire increase ought to go to the worker, since it is through his labor alone that it comes about. "The labor of a man's body, and the work of his hands," as Locke put it, "are properly his."[35] The full value of the commodity, exclusive of the means of production consumed in producing it, seems to belong by right to the worker. In appropriating a portion of that value without equivalent, the capitalist may not be engaging in an "unequal exchange" with the worker in the strict sense, but he is reaping the fruits of the worker's unpaid labor; he is exploiting him, taking from him what is justly his. Hence capitalism is unjust. It is really this argument, I think, that we attribute to Marx when we take his denunciations of capitalism as a system based on "exploitation" and "unpaid labor" to be denunciations of it for its injustice.

The argument is based on two assumptions. The first is that surplus value arises from the appropriation by capital of part of the value created by labor for which the worker receives no equivalent. The second is that each man's property rights are based on his own labor, so that every man has a right to appropriate the full value created by his labor, and anyone who deprives him of any part of this value may be said to have done him an injustice. Now Marx plainly accepts the first of these two assumptions. Does he accept the second? He recognizes, of course, that the notion that property rights are based on one's own labor is common among bourgeois ideologists, and he even sees

34. *Werke*, 23: 208. Cf. *Capital*, I, 194.
35. John Locke, *Second Treatise on Government* (Indianapolis, Ind., 1952), p. 17, par. 27.

reasons why this notion should seem plausible. "Originally," he says, "property rights appeared to us to be based on one's own labor. At least this assumption must be made, since only commodity-owners with equal property rights confronted each other, and the only means of appropriating an alien commodity was by alienating one's own commodities, which could only be replaced by labor."[36] In a mode of production in which each individual producer owns his own means of production and exchanges the commodities he produces with other individual producers, property rights would be based entirely on a man's own labor. This simple, noble, petty-bourgeois ideal of production Marx sometimes calls the system of "individual private property."[37] Under this system, the laborer would appropriate the full value of his product, and anyone who deprived him of part of this value (by a fraudulent exchange, say, or by robbery) would have done him an injustice. But in Marx's view, capitalist production differs from this idyllic *mutualité* in several important ways.[38] In capitalist production, men are engaged in cooperative labor, using jointly the same means of production (as in a factory, for example). More importantly, capitalism is predicated on the separation of labor from the means of production, on the division of society into a class which owns the means of production and a class which owns only labor power. Marx describes in *Capital* how this separation arose historically, and he argues that this class separation aids capitalist development while itself becoming more and more pronounced as a result of this development.

Now in a society based exclusively on individual private property, surplus value would not exist. But the reason for this would be simply that since every individual owns the means of production he employs, labor power would not be among the commodities traded in that society. In capitalism, however, labor power does appear as a commodity on an ever-increasing scale, owing to the form taken by the productive forces and the historical tendency toward the separation of labor from the means of production. But labor power, like any commodity,

36. *Werke*, 23: 609f. Cf. *Capital*, I, 583f.
37. *Werke*, 23: 791. Cf. *Capital*, I, 763.
38. Cf. P. J. Proudhon, *Système des contradictions économiques, ou la philosophie de la misère* (Paris, 1850), II, 397.

is only purchased to be *used*, and it cannot function as a commodity unless it is useful to its purchaser. If the entire value of the commodity produced by the wage laborer were expended in wages and means of production, the capitalist would have received no use from the labor power he purchased, and he would have done better simply to convert the value of his means of production into commodities he could consume. If he realized no surplus value, the capitalist would have no incentive to develop the forces of production, and no occasion to exercise that prudent abstinence for which he is rewarded by God and man alike. Hence the appearance of labor power as a commodity, according to Marx, brings about a "dialectical reversal" of the previously assumed foundation of the right of property: under the system of *capitalist* private property, "property turns out to be the right on the part of the capitalist to appropriate alien unpaid labor or its product, and on the part of the worker the impossibility of appropriating his own product. The separation of property from labor has become the necessary consequence of a law that apparently originated in their identity."[39]

The justice of the transactions in capitalist production rests on the fact that they arise out of capitalist production relations, that they are adequate to, and correspond to, the capitalist mode of production as a whole. The justice of property rights based on labor in a system of individual private property arises from the fact that these rights correspond to the production relations of individual producers each owning the means of production he uses. By the same token, then, the reversal of these property rights under capitalism is equally just. Capitalism is made possible by the existence of labor power as a commodity, by its use as a commodity to produce surplus value and expand capital. Labor power could not even appear as a commodity if there were no surplus value created by it for capital. Therefore, if there were no surplus value, if workers performed no unpaid labor and were not exploited, the capitalist mode of production would not be possible. Under a capitalist mode of production the appropriation of surplus value is not only just, but any attempt to deprive capital of it would be a positive injustice. Marx rejected slogans like "a just wage" and

39. *Werke*, 23: 610. Cf. *Capital*, I, 584.

"a fair day's wages for a fair day's work" because in his view the worker
was already receiving what these slogans were asking for. A "just
wage," simply because it is a wage, involves the purchase of labor
power by capital. The worker is exploited every bit as much when he
is paid just wages as when he is paid unjust ones. Thus in response
to the Lassallean demand for "a just distribution of the proceeds of
labor," Marx asks: "What is a 'just' distribution? Do not the bourgeois
assert that the present distribution is 'just'? And isn't it in fact the
only 'just' distribution based on the present mode of production? Are
economic relations ruled by juridical concepts [Rechtsbegriffe] or do
not juridical relations arise on the contrary out of economic ones?"[40]

One of the reasons neoclassical economists repudiated the labor
theory of value was the fact that this theory, especially in its Ricardian
form, had been used by social malcontents to argue that profits on
capital constitute an injustice to the worker. And on this point, at
least, the neoclassical position was not merely a piece of shabby apologetics. The economists saw that the profits on invested capital were
an essential part of the existing economic process, and that this process could not possibly function without them. They therefore rejected
any view which made profits appear to originate merely from unjust
exchanges or arbitrary practices of distribution, as a misunderstanding of the nature of the economic system and the role played in it by
profits. For this and other reasons, they were content not only to
repudiate much of what classical economics had accomplished but
even to abdicate many of the traditional responsibilities of the science
of political economy in order to free themselves from the labor theory
of value. Marx's analysis of capitalism, however, shows that the notion
that profits are unjust does not derive from the labor theory of value
alone, but follows only when this theory is combined with the labor
theory of property, a natural rights doctrine often mistakenly associated or identified with it. Marx thought, moreover, that the labor
theory of value could be used to advance criticisms of capitalism
which did not depend for their force on the application to capitalism
of juridical principles alien to it, but derived simply from a correct
understanding of the organic functioning of capitalism and the suc-

40. *Werke*, 19: 18. Cf. *Selected Works*, II, 20.

cessive stages of development marked out for it by its nature as a mode of production. Those who insist on finding in Marx's critique of capitalism some "principles of justice" analogous to the labor theory of property are therefore only shifting Marx's critique back to the level on which he found the question in the socialist writings of his own day, and from which he did his best to remove it.

We might be tempted at this point to think that whether capitalism should be called "unjust" or not is merely a ve.bal issue. Marx did, after all, condemn capitalism, and he condemned it at least in part because it was a system of exploitation, involving the appropriation of the worker's unpaid labor by capital. If Marx chose to call these evils of capitalism not "injustices" but something else, they still sound to most of us like injustices, and it seems that we should be free to apply this term to them if we like. The difference between Marx and ourselves at this point, we might suppose, is only that his application of the term "justice" is somewhat narrower than ours.

It is extremely important to see why such an attitude would be mistaken. When Marx limits the concept of justice in the way he does, he is not by any means making a terminological stipulation. He is basing his claim on the actual role played in social life by the concept of justice, and the institutional context in which this term has its proper function. His disagreement with those who hold that capitalism is unjust is a substantive one, founded on his conception of society and having important practical consequences.

"Justice," as we have seen, is a *Rechtsbegriff*, a concept related to "law" and "right." And although Marx never tries to tell us precisely what the scope of the class of *Rechtsbegriffe* is, it is clear that the central role of all these concepts has to do with political or juridical (*rechtlich*) institutions, institutions whose function is the regulation of the actions of individuals and groups through socially imposed sanctions of some kind, whether civil, criminal, or moral in nature. These institutions include those promulgating, applying, or administering laws, those in which collective political decisions are made or carried out, and those regulating the actions and practices of individuals by generally accepted norms of conduct. When something is called an "injustice," or when it is claimed that a practice violates someone's "rights," some sort of appeal is being made to juridical institutions, to the manner in which they regularly do act or the manner in which they should act if they are to fulfill their proper social function.

When capitalist exploitation is described as an "injustice," the implication is that what is wrong with capitalism is its mode of *distribution*. When the appropriation by capital of the worker's unpaid labor is thought of as "unjust," the claim being made is that the worker is being given a smaller (and the capitalist a larger) share of the collective product of society than he deserves, according to the juridical or moral rules and practices which govern distribution, or at least, which *should* govern it. It is therefore being suggested that the answer to capitalist exploitation is to be found in the proper regulation of distribution by means of the promulgation and enforcement of laws, the taking of political decisions, and the stricter adherence by individuals to correct and appropriate moral precepts.

Such a conception of what is wrong with capitalist exploitation is, however, entirely mistaken according to Marx. Distribution, he argues, is not something which exists alongside production, indifferent to it, and subject to whatever modifications individuals in their collective moral and political wisdom should choose to make in it. Any mode of distribution is determined by the mode of production of which it is a functional part.[41] The appropriation of surplus value and the exploitation of labor are not *abuses* of capitalist production, or arbitrary and unfair practices which happen accidentally to be carried on within it (like fraud, for instance, or smuggling, or protection rackets). Exploitation of the worker belongs to the essence of capitalism, and as the capitalist mode of production progresses to later and later stages of its development, this exploitation must in Marx's view grow worse and worse as a result of the laws of this development itself. It cannot be removed by the passage or enforcement of laws regulating distribution, or by any moral or political reforms which capitalist political institutions could bring about. Moreover, any "reforms" of capitalist production which proposed to take surplus value away from capital and put an end to the exploitation of the worker would themselves be injustices of a most straightforward and unambiguous kind. They

41. *Werke*, 13: 620-631; cf. Horowitz, *Marx and Modern Economics*, pp. 27-39. *Werke*, 25: 884-891; cf. *Capital*, III, 877-884.

would violate in the most obvious way the fundamental property rights derived from the capitalist mode of production, and constitute the imposition on it of a system of distribution essentially incompatible with it. It is a mystery how such well-meaning reformers could expect to keep their scheme of "just" distribution working once it had been set up. (One is reminded of Aristotle's remark that any system, no matter how misconceived, can be made to work for a day or two.)

But this is not all. Even if revolutionary practice should put an end to capitalist exploitation, and even if an important aspect of this practice should consist in a change in the juridical rules governing distribution, it would still be wrong to say that the end to exploitation constitutes the rectification of "injustice." Revolutionary politics does not consist, for Marx, in the imposition on society of whatever moral or juridical rules or "principles of justice" the revolutionary politician should find most commendable. It consists rather in the adjustment of the political or juridical institutions of society to a new mode of production, of a determinate form and character, which has already taken shape in society. Unless a fundamental change of this kind in the mode of man's productive activity is already taking place in society of its own accord, any attempt at a truly revolutionary politics would be irrational, futile, and, to use Marx's own word, mere "Donquichoterie."[42] This is what Marx and Engels mean when they say in the *German Ideology* that "Communism is for us not a *state of affairs* to be brought about, an *ideal* to which reality must somehow adjust itself. We call communism the actual movement which is transcending [aufhebt] the present state of affairs. The conditions of this movement result from presuppositions already existing."[43]

Political action, therefore, is for Marx one subordinate moment of revolutionary practice. Political institutions do not and cannot create a new mode of production, but can only be brought into harmony with a mode of production that men themselves are already bringing to birth. They can only set the juridical stamp of approval, so to speak, on whatever form of productive activity historical individuals are creating and living. If revolutionary institutions mean new laws, new

42. Marx, *Grundrisse zur Kritik der Politischen Oekomonie* (Berlin, 1953), p. 77. Cf. *The Grundrisse*, trans. and ed. David McLellan (New York, 1971), p. 69.
    43. *Gesamtausgabe*, I/5, 25. Cf. *Writings of the Young Marx*, p. 426.

standards of juridical regulation, new forms of property and distribution, this is not a sign that "justice" is at last being done where it was not done before; it is instead a sign that a new mode of production, with its own characteristic juridical forms, has been born from the old one. This new mode of production will not be "more just" than the old, it will only be just in its own way. If the new is higher, freer, more human than the old, it would be for Marx both entirely inaccurate and woefully inadequate to reduce its superiority to juridical terms and to commend it as "more just." Anyone who is tempted to do this is a person still captivated by the false and inverted political or juridical conception of society, since he insists on interpreting every crucial change in it as a change whose meaning is fundamentally political or juridical in character. He is treating the old mode of production as if it were merely one of the determinations of a mystical juridical structure of society, whereas in reality the actual juridical structure of society is a dependent moment of the prevailing productive mode. He is also treating the social whole as if he, in his sublime rationality, could measure this whole against some ideal of right or justice completely external to it, and could then, standing on some Archimedean point, adjust social reality to this ideal. He is removing social reality from his theory, and his social practice from reality. In Marx's view, when anyone demands an end to capitalist exploitation on the ground of its "injustice" he is employing an argument carrying no rational conviction to urge action with no practical basis toward a goal with no historical content.

Someone might think that capitalism could be condemned as unjust by applying to it standards of justice or right which would be appropriate to some postcapitalist mode of production. No doubt capitalism could be condemned in this way, but since any such standards would not be rationally applicable to capitalism at all, any such condemnations would be mistaken, confused, and without foundation. The temptation to apply postcapitalist juridical standards (however they may be understood) to capitalist production can only derive, once again, from the vision of postcapitalist society as a kind of eternal juridical structure against which the present state of affairs is to be measured and found wanting. The Marxian conception of society and social change, as we have seen, repudiates any vision of this kind. In the *Critique of the Gotha Program* Marx points out that postcapitalist society itself will have different stages of development, to which different standards of right will correspond. And in the long run, of course, Marx believes that the end of class society will mean the end of the social need for the state mechanism and the juridical institutions within which concepts like "right" and "justice" have their place. If, therefore, one insists on saying that Marx's "real" concept of justice is the one he would deem appropriate to a fully developed communist society, one's conclusion probably should be that Marx's "real" concept of justice is no concept of it at all.

For Marx, justice is not and cannot be a genuinely revolutionary notion. The revolutionary who is captivated by the passion for justice misunderstands, in the Marxian view, both the existing production relations and his own revolutionary aspirations. He implies, by his use of juridical conceptions, that his protest against the prevailing mode of production is a protest against evils which can and should be remedied by moral, legal, or political processes, which in fact are only dependent moments of that mode of production itself. He views his revolutionary aspirations as a kind of ideal juridical structure underlying the existing society, an ideal or hypothetical contract or set of natural rights or rational principles of right, which are being violated, concealed, or disfigured by the rampant "abuses" and "injustices" of the present society. He thus treats the *essence* of the actual production relations as arbitrary and inessential, as a set of mere "abuses"; and he regards the social conflicts and antagonisms to which these relations give rise as unfortunate by-products of social abnormalities, rather than as the driving force behind his own revolutionary consciousness. His "revolutionary" aim is therefore not really to overthrow the existing society, it is only to correct the abuses prevalent in it, to rectify its tragic and irrational injustices, and to make it live up to those ideals of right and justice which are, or ought to be, its genuine foundation. Our determined revolutionary, in other words, animated by his passion for justice, is already equipped to deliver the keynote address at the next Democratic Convention.

Marx's call to the revolutionary overthrow of capitalist production therefore is not, and cannot be, founded on the claim that capitalism is unjust. Marx in fact regarded all attempts to base revolutionary practice on juridical notions as an "ideological shuffle," and he dismissed the use of terms like "equal right" and "just distribution" in the working-class movement as "outdated verbal trivia."[44] It is simply not the case that Marx's condemnation of capitalism rests on some conception of justice (whether explicit or implicit), and those who attempt to reconstruct a "Marxian idea of justice" from Marx's manifold charges against capitalism are at best only translating Marx's critique of capitalism, or some aspect of it, into what Marx himself would have consistently regarded as a false, ideological, or "mystified" form.[45]

There can be no doubt that for Marx it was of the utmost practical importance that the worker's movement not be sidetracked by a preoccupation with the attainment of "justice" and "equal rights." But his insistence on the justice of capitalism was not motivated by tactical considerations. It is regarding this point that Tucker seems to me to go astray.[46] He argues persuasively that Marx did not criticize capitalism for injustice and in fact did not believe it to be unjust. But he seems to me to be mistaken as to Marx's reasons for holding that capitalism is unjust, and to give an inadequate account of them.

Tucker says that the "underlying issue" for Marx in his refusal to condemn capitalism for injustice was his opposition to the position, held by Proudhon and others, that the solution to the social problems posed by capitalist production must consist in striking an equitable balance between the antagonistic interests of different social agents of production. Marx, in Tucker's view, believed not in the equilibrium of antagonisms but in their abolition through the revolutionary overthrow of the capitalist mode of production. Marx sought, he says, not a balance between interests but a harmony of interests. Thus, according to Tucker, Marx rejected the view that capitalism is unjust because

44. *Werke*, 19: 22. Cf. *Selected Works*, II, 23.

45. A good example of this insistence on finding an idea of "justice" implicit in the Marxian critique of capitalism is to be found in Ralf Dahrendorf, *Die Idee des Gerechten im Denken von Karl Marx* (Hanover, 1971). The same sort of misunderstanding has led Dahrendorf elsewhere to view Marx's analysis of class conflict as involving a conception of class "based essentially on the narrow, legal conception of property" (*Class and Class-Conflict in Industrial Society* [Stanford, Cal., 1959], p. 21). If the argument of the earlier part of this paper is correct, this estimate could not be farther from the truth.

46. Tucker, *The Marxian Revolutionary Idea*, pp. 48ff.

"justice" and similar notions connote "a rightful balance in a situation where two or more parties or principles conflict." Marx believed, however, that the antagonism between capital and labor should not be compromised or turned into a harmony, but rather abolished through the revolutionary destruction of capital as a social force. Thus Tucker regards Marx's insistence that capitalism is not unjust as an expression of his fear that "the distributive orientation ultimately pointed the way to abandonment of the revolutionary goal."[47] Marx denied that capitalism is unjust, then, in order to persuade the workers' movement to take a revolutionary rather than a reformist direction. Following Tucker's account, Marx's critique of justice appears to be fundamentally a tactical stance, motivated by the fear that the workers' movement might abandon its revolutionary aspirations for some less radical program of social reform.

Now I do not want to deny that Marx believed that social antagonisms in general and the antagonism between capital and labor in particular should be abolished rather than balanced or compromised. This seems to me to have been Marx's view, and also his major reason for disagreeing with Proudhon and others like him on many points. But I do not think this view by itself accounts for Marx's insistence that capitalism is not an unjust system. In the first place, while it may seem to Tucker that the term "justice" always connotes a rightful balance between conflicting interests, I see no particular reason to think that Marx believed this. For him, justice is the rational measure of social acts and institutions from the juridical point of view. In a class society the administration of juridical relations will normally involve some mode of dealing with the antagonistic interests generated by the contradictions inherent in the mode of production. And while justice in this regard should consist in handling these antagonisms in a way which corresponds or is adequate to the mode of production, there is no reason to think it will do so by striking a "rightful balance" between opposing interests. Capitalist justice, for instance, which involves treating men as equals insofar as they are property owners, will presumably involve some sort of balance between the conflicting interests of two large capitalists, for example, but it can only handle

47. *Ibid.*, p. 51.

conflicts between the interests of capital and labor by forcibly promoting the former and ruthlessly suppressing the latter. From a Marxian standpoint, this would be the only thing that justice as a "rightful balance" of opposing interests could mean under capitalism, and the phrase does not sound particularly appropriate.

But secondly, even if we grant that for Marx justice connoted a rightful balance between conflicting interests, Tucker's account is still not satisfactory. What Tucker says might then explain why Marx did not dwell on the injustices of capitalism, and also why he would have criticized those who did. But it could not explain why Marx positively denied that capitalism was unjust. For if justice connotes a "balance" between conflicting interests, Marx might very well have agreed that no such balance is being struck between capital and labor, and admitted that capitalism is unjust, but he might have urged at the same time that injustice is not the primary defect of the capitalist mode of production and insisted that the workers would be misled if they devoted all their energies to rectifying these injustices. It would have been of questionable tactical value, it seems to me, for Marx to go further than this and positively deny that capitalist exploitation is unjust, unless he thought he had good independent grounds for doing so. Marx also seems to me not to have been as worried as Tucker thinks about the danger of the distributive orientation undermining the revolutionary character of the workers' movement. At any rate he was not afraid that the long-range goals of the proletariat would be altered by such petty-bourgeois nonsense. Whether or not we think subsequent history has proven him wrong, Marx was always convinced that the situation of the proletariat could never be made tolerable to the proletarians themselves by anything short of a revolutionary transformation of production. His real worry was only that the widespread acceptance of false notions about the defects of capitalism and the conditions for their removal would delay this transformation and make it more painful. Marx's fundamental objection to the rhetoric of justice was not that it was bad propaganda, but that it presupposed a theory of society which he believed he had shown to be false. Speaking of the distributive orientation espoused by the Lassalleans, he says: "Vulgar socialism (and from it again a part of democracy) took over from the bourgeois economists the consideration and treatment of distribution as independent of the mode of production and hence the presentation of socialism as turning principally on the question of distribution. But after the real relation has long been made clear, why retrogress again?"[48]

IV

If Marx did not criticize capitalism for being unjust, the question naturally presents itself: Why *did* Marx condemn capitalism? But it would be extremely naïve to suppose that there could be any single, simple answer to such a question. The only genuine answer to it is Marx's comprehensive theory of capitalism as a concrete historical mode of production; for it was *as a whole* that Marx condemned capitalism, and his condemnation was based on what he believed was a unified and essentially complete analysis of its inner workings and its position in human history. Capitalism, in Marx's view, had performed a valuable historical task in developing social forces of production. He even speaks of this development as the historical "justification" of capital.[49] But this development had taken place at enormous human cost. Not only had it impoverished the physical existence of the mass of workers whose labor had brought about the development of productive forces, but the intellectual and moral lives of men had been impoverished by it as well. The rapidity of social change under capitalism had created a permanent state of instability and disorder in social relationships which had taken away from human happiness perhaps more than was added by the increase in human productive capacities. But the capitalist era itself, in Marx's view, was drawing to a close. Marx argued that the capacity of capitalism further to develop the forces of production was meeting with increasing obstacles, obstacles resulting from the organic workings of the capitalist system of production itself. At the same time, and partly as a result of these same obstacles, the human cost of capitalism was growing steadily greater. The interests and needs of fewer and fewer were being served by its continuation, and its preservation was being made more and more difficult by the cumulative effects of its own essential processes.

48. *Werke*, 19: 22. Cf. *Selected Works*, II, 23f.
49. *Werke*, 25: 271. Cf. *Capital*, III, 259.

Within Marx's account of the essential irrationality and eventual breakdown of capitalism, the concept of the "exploitation" of labor by capital plays an important role. And since it is the Marxian charge that capitalism is essentially a system of exploitation which has done most to create the impression that Marx condemned capitalism for injustice, I would like to try briefly to explain what role I think this charge actually plays in Marx's critique of capitalism.

Human society, according to some philosophers, is founded on the harmony of human interests, the fact that social relationships are of mutual benefit to those participating in them. In the Marxian view, however, past societies have equally been founded on conflicts of interest, and on the forced labor of one class for the benefit of another. All society, Marx believes, involves an "exchange of human activity" between agents of production;[50] but one of the essential forms of such exchanges is the social relation of dominion and servitude. This relation, in Marx's view, constitutes the foundation of class conflicts and of the historical changes wrought by them.

The essence of servitude for Marx consists in the fact that servitude is a specific form of human productive activity: it is, namely, productive activity which, by means of the loss and renunciation of its products, is itself alienated from the producer and appropriated by someone or something external to him, standing over against him as the independent aim and object of his production. Dominion, as Marx points out, involves not merely the appropriation and enjoyment of things, but "the appropriation of another's will."[51] When the master enjoys the slave's services or the fruits of his labor, he enjoys them as the result of the slave's productive activity, as something into which the slave has put his will and realized his purposes. The appropriation of the slave's products by the master, therefore, necessarily involves for the slave their renunciation, the alienation of the slave's own life-activity and the immediate frustration of his productive will. The labor of servitude is, as Hegel said, essentially "inhibited desire."[52] In

---

50. *Werke*, Erg. 1, Teil 450. Cf. *Writings of the Young Marx*, p. 271.

51. *Grundrisse*, p. 400. Cf. *Pre-Capitalist Economic Formations*, ed. Eric Hobsbawm (New York, 1965), p. 102.

52. Hegel, *Phänomenologie des Geistes* (Hamburg, 1952), p. 149. Cf. Hegel, *Phenomenology of Mind*, trans. J. B. Baillie (New York, 1967), p. 238.

its essence, such labor is, in Marx's words, "not voluntary but coerced, it is *forced* labor, . . . a labor of self-sacrifice, of mortification."[53]

In capitalist production, according to Marx, these relations of dominion and servitude are disguised. The capitalist and the worker appear to be independent owners of commodities, exchanging their goods as free individuals. The exchanges between them are entirely just and their equal rights as property owners are strictly respected throughout capitalist production relations, thus giving rise to the illusion that these relations themselves are entirely the result of a voluntary contract between independent persons. In fact, however, since the capitalist mode of production is founded on the sale of labor power by one class to another, capitalist production rests essentially on the appropriation by capital of a part of the worker's product in the form of surplus value. Capital, by its very nature as capital, that is, by its function in capitalist production relations, necessarily exploits the worker by appropriating and accumulating his unpaid labor. And as Marx argues in *Capital*, the end result of the wage laborer's activity is always the further accumulation of capital, of his own product in an alien and autonomous form, which becomes both the necessary condition and the independent aim of his labor, of his life-activity itself.

This exploitation of the laborer by capital is not a form of injustice, but it is a form of servitude. "Capital obtains surplus labor," according to Marx, "without an equivalent, and in essence it always remains

53. *Werke*, Erg. 1, Teil 514. Cf. *Early Writings*, p. 125. The concept of the alienation (*Entfremdung*) of labor is not something confined to Marx's early writings, as is sometimes believed. Marx continued to use both the term *Entfremdung* and the concept throughout his analysis of capitalist production, and he continued to compare the accumulation of social wealth in the alienated form of capital to Feuerbach's theory of religion as the alienated essence of man conceived by man as an independent object. Consider, for example, the two following passages from *Capital*: "The laborer, on leaving the labor process, is what he was on entering it—a personal source of wealth, but destitute of all means to actualize this wealth for himself. Since before entering the labor process his own labor is alienated [entfremdet] from him, and appropriated and incorporated by the capitalist, it objectifies itself during the labor process in the form of an alien [fremdem] product. . . . The laborer therefore produces objective wealth in the form of capital, of a power alien to him [ihm fremde] which dominates and exploits him" (*Werke*, 23: 595f.; cf. *Capital*, I, 570f.). "As in religion man is dominated by a work of his own head, so in capitalistic production he is dominated by a work of his hand" (*Werke*, 23: 649; cf. *Capital*, I, 621).

forced labor, however much it appears to result from a free contractual agreement."[54] Capitalist exploitation is not a form of fraudulent exchange or economic injustice, but it is a form of concealed dominion over the worker. Capitalism is a system of slavery, and a slavery the more insidious because the relations of dominion and servitude are *experienced* as such without being *understood* as such. The fundamental character of the capitalist relation is even hidden from political economy, in Marx's view, so long as it fails to solve the riddle of surplus value. By solving this riddle, Marx believes he has unmasked the capitalist relation and made it possible for the workers to understand their condition of poverty, frustration, and discontent for what it is: a condition of servitude to their own product in the form of capital.

It bears repeating that although this servitude is a source of misery, degradation, and discontent to the worker, it is *not a form of injustice.* Those who believe that the notion of servitude necessarily "connotes" injustice are the victims of prejudices which many men of less enlightened ages (Aristotle, for example) did not share. And for Marx the appearance of such prejudices in capitalist society is largely the result of the bourgeois ideology which praises capitalism for having done away with direct slavery and feudal serfdom, and for having replaced these "injustices" and "human indignities" with an open society of free men meeting in a free market. The actual servitude which hides behind this mask of universal liberty is, however, neither more nor less just than its predecessors in Marx's view. The servitude of the wage laborer to capital is rather an essential and indispensable part of the capitalist mode of production, which neither the passage of liberal legislation nor the sincere resolve by bourgeois society to respect the "human rights" of all its members can do anything to remove. Nor is the mere fact that capitalism involves servitude a sufficient ground for the workers to rise against it. It is not Marx's belief that servitude as such is an unqualified wrong, an evil to be abolished at all cost with an attitude of *fiat justitia, pereat mundi.* The servitude of capitalism, according to Marx, and even the direct slavery involved in capitalist colonies, have been necessary conditions for the develop-

54. *Werke*, 25: 827. Cf. *Capital*, III, 819.

ment of modern productive forces.[55] To condemn this servitude unqualifiedly would be to condemn all the productive advances of modern society, which Marx was not about to do. Condemning a relation of servitude when it results from historical limitations on productive forces is for Marx about as rational as condemning medical science because there are some diseases it cannot cure.

A historically potent demand, a genuine and effective *need* for emancipation arises in an oppressed class only under certain conditions. This need does not appear merely as a social ideal, but always as an actual movement within the existing production relations toward concrete historical possibilities transcending them. And it arises, according to Marx's theory, only where there is a disharmony or antagonism between the productive forces and the existing production relations. Within a given mode of production, men develop and change the forces of production. In this way they bring about new historical possibilities, and with them new human desires and needs. These new possibilities cannot be actualized, however, and these new needs satisfied, within the existing production relations. The productive forces have, so to speak, outgrown the production relations and have become antagonistic to them. It is this antagonism which, in Marx's view, supplies the conditions for an epoch of social revolution. And it is only in terms of this antagonism that an effective need for emancipation on the part of an oppressed class can take shape. "Humanity," says Marx, "only sets itself tasks it can solve": "A form of society never perishes before all the productive forces for which there is room in it have developed; and new, higher relations of production never come forth before the material conditions for their existence have taken shape in the womb of the old society itself."[56]

Capitalism itself, Marx believed, systematically creates the forces which will eventuate in its revolutionary overthrow and historical transcendence. It is the inherent tendency of capitalist production to increase the rate of surplus value, to accumulate an ever-larger supply of social wealth in the form of capital. This historical tendency of capitalism leads, as Marx argues in *Capital*, to the mounting instability of capitalist production in a number of different but related ways.

55. *Werke*, 4: 131f. Cf. *The Poverty of Philosophy*, pp. 111f.
56. *Werke*, 13: 9. Cf. *Selected Works*, I, 329.

Prominent among these tendencies to instability is the increasing burden of servitude placed on the workers by capitalist accumulation.
Marx does not think that as capital accumulates, the wages of the
worker will necessarily decrease. Indeed, he holds that in general those
conditions under which capital expands most rapidly relative to labor
are likely to be the most favorable for the worker's material situation.[57]
But the accumulation of capital does mean that the *dominion* of capital over the worker, and the "golden chain" the worker forges for himself, which fetters him to capital, tend to grow heavier and heavier.[58]
The slave's peculium may possibly increase, but his servitude necessarily grows more and more burdensome.[59]

According to the Marxian theory, then, capitalist production accumulates on the one side an ever-growing supply of social wealth, an
ever-expanding set of productive forces; but on the other side it creates
at the same time a class of restless slaves, constantly growing in numbers and in discontent. It expands the capacities for the satisfaction
of human needs, while at the same time cutting men off in steadily
increasing numbers from the means of appropriating and making use
of these capacities. And it expands the forces of production by means
of the forced labor of precisely those who are alienated from them.
Thus capitalism itself produces both the need on the part of the
workers to overcome and abolish capitalist production and the material forces which make the abolition of capitalism a genuine historical
possibility. It produces at once an ever-growing burden of servitude
and an ever-greater capacity for emancipation. In this way, the
productive forces it has created become increasingly antagonistic to
the production relations by means of which it has created them. This
does not mean, however, that for Marx capitalism is bad or irrational
because its downfall is inevitable. On the contrary, Marx thought that
its perpetuation of a condition of unnecessary servitude, its extension
of this condition to the great majority of men, and its creation of
human desires and opportunities which cannot be satisfied within a
capitalist framework were precisely the sorts of defects which would

57. *Werke*, 6: 416. Cf. *Selected Works*, I, 91.
58. *Werke*, 23: 646; cf. *Capital*, I, 618. *Werke*, 6: 416; cf. *Selected Works*,
I, 91.
59. *Werke*, 19: 26. Cf. *Selected Works*, II, 27.

bring about its downfall. Capitalism, in Marx's view, was breaking down because it was irrational, and not the reverse. The irrationalities in capitalism were for Marx at once causes of its downfall and reasons for its abolition.

But if Marx viewed the workers' desire for emancipation as an important reason why capitalism should be abolished, it still seems to me almost as mistaken to say that Marx's critique of capitalism is founded on a "principle of freedom" as it is to say that it is founded on a "principle of justice." I think it would be wrong, in fact, to suppose that Marx's critique of capitalism is necessarily rooted in *any* particular moral or social ideal or principle. It has sometimes been claimed that Marx was fundamentally a utilitarian, because he believed the overthrow of capitalism would bring about greater human happiness. Others have argued that Marx was really a Kantian, since the servitude and exploitation of capitalism to which he objected involve the treatment of men as means only, rather than as ends in themselves. Still others have seen in Marx's hope for an expansion of man's powers under socialism an implicit "self-realization" theory. But of course it is quite possible for someone to value human happiness without being a utilitarian, to object to the treatment of men as mere means without being a Kantian, and to favor the development of human powers and capacities without subscribing to any particular moral philosophy. So there is no good reason, it seems to me, for the adherents of any particular position in moral philosophy to claim that Marx is one of their number. At any rate, Marx seems to me no more a subscriber to any particular moral philosophy than is the "common man" with whose moral views nearly every moral philosopher claims to be in agreement.

Marx's own reasons for condemning capitalism are contained in his comprehensive theory of the historical genesis, the organic functioning, and the prognosis of the capitalist mode of production. And this is not itself a *moral* theory, nor does it include any particular moral principles as such. But neither is it "merely descriptive," in the tedious philosophical sense which is supposed to make it seem problematic how anything of that sort could ever be a reason for condemning what is so "described." There is nothing problematic about saying that disguised exploitation, unnecessary servitude, economic instability, and declining productivity are features of a productive system which constitute good reasons for condemning it. Marx's theory of the functioning and development of capitalism does argue that capitalism possesses these features (among others), but Marx never tried to give any philosophical account of why these features would constitute good reasons for condemning a system that possesses them. He was doubtless convinced that the reasons for condemning capitalism provided by his theory were good ones, and that whatever information moral philosophers might or might not be able to give us about the nature of condemnations of social systems and the nature of reasons for them, no special appeal to philosophical principles, moral imperatives, or evaluative modes of consciousness would be needed to show that his own reasons for condemning capitalism were good and sufficient ones. That he was correct in these convictions is indicated by the fact that no serious defender of capitalism has ever disputed his critique solely on the grounds of moral philosophy. It has been argued in defense of capitalism that Marx's theory of capitalist production rests on unsound economic principles, that it distorts or misinterprets the relation between capital and labor, and that it gives an inaccurate, one-sided, or incomplete picture of capitalism. It has also been claimed that Marx's account of the genesis of capitalist production is historically inaccurate, and that his predictions about its future have been largely falsified by events which have happened since his time. But no one has ever denied that capitalism, understood as Marx's theory understands it, is a system of unnecessary servitude, replete with irrationalities and ripe for destruction. Still less has anyone defended capitalism by claiming that a system of this sort might after all be good or desirable, and it is doubtful that any moral philosophy which could support such a claim would deserve serious consideration.

ZIYAD I. HUSAMI   Marx on Distributive
Justice

Capitalism, Marx thought, had made stupendous technical progress—
its development of productive forces far surpassing that of all earlier
social formations. That aside, no social system has ever been condemned more radically, indicted more severely, and damned more
comprehensively than capitalism was by Marx. It is a system of domination of men by men, of men by things, and of men by impersonal
forces. The exploitation associated with private property in the means
of production sets class against class; competition turns capitalist
against capitalist and worker against worker. In their social relations
and in the state, men are afforded only a spurious community. Labor
and the means of labor are separated; they devolve on different
classes. Yet material production, the basis of social life, requires their
union. Capitalism thereby locks the social classes, which represent the
elements of the production process, in an antagonistic interdependence, an interdependent antagonism.

Capitalism also creates a society in which man is subordinated to
production rather than production to man. Production is impelled by
profit, not by the satisfaction of human needs. The worker is used as
means for the generation of material wealth—wealth that is wielded
against him. Bourgeois society expands material wealth and contracts
human possibilities; it fosters outer wealth and inward poverty.

Capitalism is a system of contradictions between the social process
of production and the private mode of appropriation; between the
planning and rationality of the individual production units and the
anarchy of social production at large; between the unrestricted de-

velopment of wealth in the form of commodities and the restricted power of society to consume; between professed ideals and actuality. Its spokesmen preach liberty, equality, fraternity, representative government, and the greatest happiness for the greatest number. Capitalism engenders servitude, inequality, social antagonism, unrepresentative government for society, "autocratic rule," and "barracks discipline" in the workplace. It achieves the greatest misery for the greatest number.

Did Marx consider capitalist society just? Did he condemn it, at least in part, on the grounds of its injustice? His *direct* and *explicit* statements on this subject are few and far between but, in numerous passages throughout his works, Marx employs the sort of language typically used in philosophical discourse on justice and seems to be condemning capitalism for its injustice. A few illustrations are in order.

The *Communist Manifesto*, while pointing out the deficiencies of the petty-bourgeois socialism typical of Sismondi, praises it because it "dissected with great acuteness the contradictions in the conditions of modern production. It laid bare . . . the concentration of capital and land in a few hands . . . , the misery of the proletariat . . . , the crying inequalities in the distribution of wealth."[1]

The *Holy Family* states that the proletariat is dehumanized. Its "life situation" is the negation of its "human nature." Through wage labor, the proletariat class is forced into "creating wealth for others and misery for itself." In the *Poverty of Philosophy*, we are told that the bourgeois are "indifferent . . . to the sufferings of the proletarians who help them acquire wealth." The *German Ideology* states that the proletariat "has to bear all the burdens of society without enjoying its advantages." *Capital*, vol. 1, says that "the capitalist gets rich, not like the miser in proportion to his personal labor and restricted consumption, but at the same rate as he squeezes out the labor power of others, and enforces on the laborer abstinence from all life's enjoyments." *Capital*, vol. 3, speaks of "coercion and monopolization of so-

---

1. Marx and Engels, Manifesto of the Communist Party, in *Selected Works*, vol. 1 (Moscow: Foreign Languages Publishing House, 1962), p. 57. Hereafter cited as *CM* and *SW*.

cial development (including material and intellectual advantages) by one portion of society at the expense of the other."[2]

The preceding and similar passages yield the picture of a society with extreme inequalities of wealth. This wealth is produced by one class and enjoyed by another which is indifferent to the poverty, suffering, and misery of the producers. One class monopolizes material and intellectual advantages such as access to education and culture at the expense of another class which is coerced into shouldering all the burdens of society. The capitalists do not amass their wealth and its attendant material and cultural enjoyments from their own labor but by exploiting the labor power of the workers.

The attempt to deduce from such passages a Marxian conception of justice may be considered objectionable on the ground that Marx did not necessarily consider a society that fits this description unjust. Without prejudging the case, it should be noted at the outset that, especially with Marx, one must avoid rending a passage from its immediate context, textual or theoretical. Some of Marx's interpreters, such as Robert C. Tucker and Allen W. Wood, assert that Marx considers capitalism just.[3] They base this opinion largely on the strength of a single passage in which Marx seems to be saying that the appropriation of surplus labor—that is, the exploitation of labor power—is "a piece of good luck for the buyer [of labor power, the capitalist], but by no means an injustice (*Unrecht*) to the seller [the worker]."[4]

To be sure, Tucker and Wood admit that Marx considered capitalism exploitative, but they ascribe to him the view that capitalist exploitation does not exclude capitalist justice. Actually, the passage on which

2. Marx and Engels, *The Holy Family*, in *Writings of the Young Marx on Philosophy and Society*, ed. and trans. Loyd Easton and Kurt Guddat (New York: Doubleday, 1967), p. 368. Marx, *The Poverty of Philosophy* (Moscow: Foreign Languages Publishing House, n.d.), p. 118. Marx and Engels, *The German Ideology* (Moscow: Progress Publishers, 1964), p. 85. Marx, *Capital*, vol. 1, (Moscow: Progress Publishers, 1965), p. 651. Marx, *Capital*, Vol. 3 (Moscow: Progress Publishers, 1966), p. 819.

3. Robert C. Tucker, "Marx and Distributive Justice" in *The Marxian Revolutionary Idea* (New York: Norton, 1969), chap. 2; Allen W. Wood, "The Marxian Critique of Justice," above, pp. 3-41.

4. *Capital*, 1: 194. The English translation of Moore and Aveling renders *Unrecht* as "injury." Tucker cites this passage on p. 45; Wood on p. 22.

they rely is bogus—it occurs in a context in which Marx is plainly satirizing capitalism. Marx, immediately after the passage in question, characterizes the appropriation of surplus labor as a "trick." He writes:

> Our capitalist foresaw this state of things [the appropriation of surplus value] and that was the cause of his laughter. . . . The trick has at last succeeded [*Das Kunststück ist endlich gelungen*]; money has been converted into capital. [*Capital*, 1:194]

Tucker and Wood sunder the bogus passage from its context and, in consequence, fail to ask what Marx means by the "trick" of exploiting labor power. Marx elsewhere uses identical and far more explicit language when he characterizes exploitation as "robbery," "usurpation," "embezzlement," "plunder," "booty," "theft," "snatching," and "swindling." For instance, in the *Grundrisse*, he speaks of *"the theft [Diebstahl] of alien labor time* [that is, of surplus value or surplus labor] *on which the present wealth is based."*[5] If the capitalist *robs* the worker, then he appropriates what is not rightfully his own or he appropriates what rightfully belongs to the worker. Thus there is no meaningful sense in which the capitalist can simultaneously rob the worker and treat him justly. But Tucker and Wood, having failed to take note of the "trick" and its meaning, roundly—and falsely—declare that the worker, though exploited, is not cheated or robbed or treated unjustly.

Having suspended judgment on the suitability of deducing a conception of justice from relevant or seemingly relevant passages in the Marxian corpus, I shall proceed to formulate the problem of capitalist injustice within the Marxian theoretical framework. My concern in this essay is to ascertain Marx's position on this question, but not to assess its validity.

THE PROBLEM

Marx, in his mature works, develops at length his empirical theory of the distribution of wealth and income under capitalism.[6] He says that

5. Marx, *Grundrisse: Foundations of the Critique of Political Economy* (*Rough Draft*), trans. with a Foreword by Martin Nicolaus (London: Allen Lane with New Left Review, 1973), p. 705, emphasis in the original.

6. See especially the introduction to *Grundrisse* and *Capital*, vol. 3, chap. 51, "Distribution Relations and Production Relations."

every mode of production involves a corresponding mode of distribution. Actually every mode of production involves two basic types of distribution: (1) the distribution of the means of production (or of productive wealth) and (2) the distribution of the annual product of society (or of the annual income) among the population. Marx holds that the distribution of wealth and of income are related by the dialectical category of reciprocal action (*Wechselwirkung*) or bilateral causation.[7] Given a certain distribution of productive wealth in, for example, class society, there results a certain distribution of income among the various classes. And, reciprocally, the distribution of income reacts upon and reinforces the prevailing distribution of wealth. It should be emphasized that the distribution of income cannot be considered separately from the distribution of wealth—except "in the shallowest conception" (*Grundrisse*, p. 96). Under capitalism, the empirical problem of income distribution resolves itself into the determination of the conditions, processes, and economic laws according to which the annual product is divided into generic class shares: wages for the proletarians who do not own productive wealth and surplus value for the propertied classes. This surplus value is divided into profit, interest, and rent for the owners of the means of production (industrial capitalists, finance capitalists, and landowners, respectively). I shall concentrate on the distribution of income between workers and owners (or capitalists).

Distributive justice is concerned with the moral evaluation of particular distributions. Its standards define *inter alia*, how wealth and income ought to be distributed or measure the moral desirability of actual distributions. The *locus classicus* of Marx's treatment of distributive justice is the *Critique of the Gotha Program*. In the context of discussing what the just distribution of the proceeds of labor (that is, the annual product) consists in, Marx advances two principles of distributive justice: distribution according to labor contribution and distribution according to needs. These criteria are presented as proletarian or as suitable for adoption by a proletarian party. Marx also indicates that they will be realized in post-capitalist society.

The problem of determining whether or not Marx regarded capi-

7. *Wechselwirkung* is also a category of Hegelian logic. Cf. Hegel, *Science of Logic*, trans. A. V. Miller with a Foreword by J. N. Findlay (London: Allen & Unwin, 1969), pp. 554-571.

talism as just seems, at first, to be a matter of evaluating the capitalist distribution of wealth and income in terms of these distributive standards. But the Marxian sociology of morals suggests that morals are somehow specific to their social context. We wonder whether it is good Marxian doctrine to evaluate capitalist practices by post-capitalist, or by proletarian, standards. Within this problem, two questions may be discerned.

First, can Marx, consistent with his sociology of morals, use proletarian or post-capitalist standards in evaluating capitalist distribution? Second, does Marx—his consistency notwithstanding—explicitly or implicitly use these standards in evaluating capitalist distribution?

The Marxian Sociology of Morals and the Marxian Moral Theory

The sociology of morals is a part of Marx's historical materialism and purports to account for the social origin of moral outlooks in historical perspective.

According to Marx, elements of the superstructure—whether forms of consciousness such as ideas on politics, law, and morality, or institutions such as the state—have *two* levels of determination. One is the mode of production (or type of society) in which they occur; the other is the class interests which they represent. Moral outlooks change as modes of production change. Within any mode of production, the variety of moral outlooks is anchored in, and explained by, the class structure of society. Thus to account for a norm sociologically, one must specify, first, the mode of production in which it occurs and, secondly, the social class in that society with which the norm is associated.

Within a given mode of production, a social class generally attains, in the course of its development, a style of life and forms of consciousness which are determined by the conditions of its social existence and, particularly, by its class interests. The owning class lives under conditions of existence which differ significantly from the conditions of the non-owning class. Accordingly, the forms of consciousness of these classes, including their moral outlooks, differ. The ruling class, through its control of the means of socialization, endeavors to make its ideas the ruling ideas in society. The ideas of the ruling class express its class interests; they are the "ideas of its dominance."[8] The ruling class fails in maintaining the hegemony of its ideas when the oppressed class develops from a class in-itself to a class for-itself; when it comes to an awareness of its life situation and articulates its class interests. The proletariat, for example, develops its own critical and revolutionary consciousness. Given the division of labor in society and its separation of mental and material labor, intellectuals act as thinkers and spokesmen for the various classes. Marx says that intellectuals belonging to the bourgeoisie may move over to the proletariat when they reflect on the latter's life situation (*German Ideology*, p. 85; *CM* in *SW*, 1:43). The socialists and communists are the theorists of the proletariat (*Poverty of Philosophy*, p. 120).

Every mode of production has a corresponding mode of distributing burdens and benefits. The ruling class regards as just the mode of distribution which benefits itself at the expense of the non-owning class. It espouses a norm of distributive justice that expresses its class interests and prevails over other conceptions. In general, every ruling class conceives of its interests as the social or general interest and proclaims the norms expressive of them as "naturally" just or as just in some absolute sense. Marx points out that such interests and norms are social, not natural; sectional, not general. They are historically developed and historically surmountable. If the spokesmen for a class justify their values by maintaining that their moral outlook is independent of historical development or of class interests, then they maintain false beliefs about their morality. Such false beliefs are called "ideological illusions." The moral outlook itself, on that count alone, is not considered illusory.

The distributive arrangements of a society can be evaluated by means of a standard different from the prevailing (or ruling) standard of justice. The exploited class, for example, the proletariat, develops a conception of justice different from the prevailing one and arrives at a negative evaluation of the existing distribution of productive wealth and income. Similarly, the bourgeoisie has conceptions of freedom and equality that reflect its own interests and class situation. But the proletariat and its intellectual spokesmen arrive at different

8. *German Ideology*, p. 60. Most of my account of Marx's sociology of morals derives from the section on Feuerbach.

conceptions of equality and freedom. Despite the tendency of the ruling class to establish the hegemony of its ideas and ideals, social
criticism by means of a different set of ideas and ideals remains possible.

Thus it is valid, on Marx's showing, for the proletariat and its
spokesmen to criticize capitalist distribution using proletarian standards of justice. Marx, as will be shown, offers such a critique.

Furthermore, Marx neither states nor implies that the existential
determination of moral standards entails a logical limitation on their
use in evaluative contexts. To put it differently, in accounting for the
social origin and historicity of norms, the Marxian sociology of morals
does not state or imply that a norm arising in, or pertaining to, one
mode of production cannot be validly used in the *evaluation* of another mode. Rather, the existential determination of moral standards
implies existential constraints or existential prerequisites for their
realization. For instance, proletarian norms of justice can be validly
used in evaluating earlier societies but these norms cannot be realized
in any or all societies. The realization of these norms requires, in
addition to their subjective acceptance, relevant existential and
institutional prerequisites (for example, the social ownership of the
means of production or material abundance). Were Marx to be asked
why it is that people often evaluate earlier societies from the perspectives of later societies, he would probably say (as he says in a
different context) that people have consciousness and, therefore, they
think. They reflect, comparatively and evaluatively, on their past,
present, and future. Marx engages in such reflection, as he does in the
Manuscripts when he asks: "What in the evolution of mankind is the
meaning of this reduction of the greater part of mankind to abstract
[that is, one-sided] labor?"[9] The answer to this question requires the
application of a normative conception of labor to the various historical forms of labor. Such evaluations, Marx points out, are frequently
made during periods of social instability and of social transition. The
rising class, as the harbinger of the new society, embodies the future
outlook, the outlook that will become dominant. In its struggle with

9. Marx, *The Economic and Philosophic Manuscripts of 1844*, trans. Martin
Milligan, ed. with an introduction by D. J. Struik (New York: International
Publishers, 1964), p. 72. Hereafter cited as *EPM*.

the declining class, it criticizes the declining society in terms of the would-be ruling norms. Class conflicts are reflected in conflicts of ideas. This happened in all countries where the bourgeoisie struggled for power against the feudal nobility. Similarly, as capitalist contradictions intensify and proletarian consciousness develops, the proletariat and its spokesmen criticize the bourgeois order from the standpoint of the future society and its norms. In the *German Ideology*, Marx says that individuals "seem freer" under the domination of the bourgeoisie than before but "in reality . . . they are less free because they are more subjected to the violence of things" (pp. 93-94). It is clear that a judgment is being made in terms of a standard considered valid for the evaluation of capitalism and earlier modes of production. In *Capital*, Marx evaluates pre-communist systems from the standpoint of communist society and points out the "absurdity" of class societies. Under slavery, he says, some men own other men and use them as means of production; under capitalism, some men acquire a monopoly on land and derive revenue from doing so. Such institutions are judged to be absurd from the standpoint of a higher—communist—form of society.

> From the standpoint of a higher economic form of society, private ownership of the globe by single individuals will appear quite as absurd (*abgeschmacht*) as private ownership of one man by another. Even a whole society, a nation, or even all simultaneously existing societies taken together, are not the owners of the globe. They are only its possessors, its usufructuaries, and, like *boni patres familias*, they must hand it down in an improved condition. [*Capital*, 3: 776]

Wood and Tucker misconstrue the Marxian sociology of morals by failing to note that elements of the superstructure, such as conceptions of justice, have *two* levels of determination. By focusing only on the *social* determination of norms to the exclusion of their *class* determination, they are led to believe that, for Marx, a norm is just when it accords with a mode of production and unjust when it discords with that mode. They overlook Marx's relation of moral conceptions within the same mode of production to the opposed social classes.

In so doing, Tucker and Wood collapse the Marxian moral theory into the Marxian sociology of morals and ascribe to Marx, by implication, a variant of moral positivism. They hold that, for Marx, the *only* standard that may be validly used in evaluating the justice of the institutions of a mode of production is the one that accords with this mode. Tucker states that "the only applicable norm of what is right and just is the one inherent in the existing economic system. Each mode of production has its own mode of distribution and its own form of equity, and it is meaningless to pass judgment on it from some other point of view."[10] Wood argues that "if, for example, a historical analysis of the role of slavery in the ancient world could show that this institution corresponded to, and played a necessary role in, the prevailing mode of production, then in the Marxian view the holding of slaves by the ancients would be a *just* practice; and the claim that ancient slavery was unjust, whether it is made by the contemporaries of the institution or by modern men reading about it in history books, would simply be wrong."[11]

10. Tucker, "Marx and Distributive Justice," p. 46. Tucker relies on the following passage from Marx's *Critique of the Gotha Program* (in *SW* 2: 24): "Right can never be higher than the economic structure of society and its cultural development conditioned thereby." This statement is offered by Marx to explain why the producer's right under socialism is proportional to his labor contribution but not to what would satisfy his needs. The material abundance that the distribution according to needs presupposes does not obtain, and this places a constraint on the producer's reward. Having said this, Marx, nonetheless, proceeds to criticize the "defects" of socialist justice, as will be shown in the next section, by means of communist justice (the failure to satisfy needs). This confirms my interpretation that, for Marx, the existential prerequisites for the realization of norms do not entail a logical limitation on the use of norms in evaluative contexts. The absence of necessary prerequisites prevent the norm of distribution according to needs from being realized in socialist society, but does not prevent Marx from using this norm to evaluate socialist society. The passage cited by Tucker does not entail, explicitly or implicitly, a logical limitation on the evaluative use of conceptions of right, and its context does not support Tucker's claim.

11. Wood, "Marxian Critique of Justice," pp. 18-19, emphasis in the original. Wood bases his claim on a passage from *Capital*, 3: 339-340. Marx, here, is commenting on a statement by the economist Gilbart that the payment of interest on borrowed money is a "self-evident principle of natural justice." Marx tells him that this is not a matter of "natural" justice; it is conditioned by production relations. A transaction, Marx adds, "is just whenever it corresponds to the mode of production. . . . It is unjust whenever it contradicts that mode."

From the accounts of Tucker and Wood, it follows that Marx considered the institutions of slavery, serfdom, and wage labor as necessarily just institutions in the ancient, feudal, and capitalist social formations, respectively. What is more, it would have been invalid and irrational for an ancient slave, as it is for a modern proletarian, to claim that his conditions of existence are unjust since these conditions are, in the main, determined by the institutions of slavery and wage labor, and these institutions are congruent with their respective modes of production.

The interpretation of Wood and Tucker makes it impossible for the oppressed to criticize the injustice of their life situations, but the Marxian sociology of morals makes such criticism possible and comprehensible. Furthermore, Tucker and Wood state that Marx criticized capitalism, at least in part, for its inequality and unfreedom. But if the *only* applicable norm of justice is the one that accords with the capitalist mode of production then, similarly, the only applicable norms of equality and freedom must be the ones that accord with this mode of production. Consequently, the position taken by Tucker and Wood implies that Marx could not have validly criticized capitalist freedom as unfreedom and capitalist equality as inequality. For him

---

Wood, having been persuaded by the bogus passage (see fn. 4 above and related text), takes this statement to be Marx's assessment of capitalism. The fact is that Marx's statement is strictly sociological; it does not contain his evaluation of capitalist transactions, or of interest in particular. Marx is explaining how it is that transactions come to be considered just, or how certain conceptions of justice become dominant. When he says that the justice of transactions consists in their correspondence to a mode of production, he is saying in shortened form that they also correspond to the interests of the propertied class and this is how the matter is viewed from the standpoint of that class. It is unreasonable to expect Marx to restate his whole sociology of morals every time he uses it. Wood, instead of inquiring how Marx's remark on Gilbart fits into Marx's sociology of morals, reformulates Marx's sociology to fit this passage. He fastens on it, lifts it out of its theoretical context, generalizes it, and presents it to us as further confirmation of the bogus passage. When Wood (p. 16) ascribes to Marx the view that the charging of interest on borrowed money is not in itself "just or unjust," and that under capitalism, "it is perfectly just" he makes an utterly false claim. On the subject of usury, Marx was fond of quoting approvingly and at length Luther's harsh—in fact, savage—condemnation of it as the most criminal robbery. See *Capital*, 1: 592-593 and *Theories of Surplus Value*, vol. 3 (Moscow: Progress Publishers, 1971), pp. 528-529.

to have done so presupposes the use of standards of freedom and equality that are incongruent with the capitalist mode of production. But neither Wood nor Tucker detect any inconsistency in Marx on this score. And, in fact, there is none. The problem lies in their view that Marx relates norms only to modes of production when in fact he relates them also to the various social classes within a mode of production.

In his reply to Proudhon, Marx says that the institutions Proudhon recommends will not do away with social classes and with the social antagonism that attends them in bourgeois society because the propertied class takes advantage of the non-propertied class. It is the bourgeoisie that considers such a class-divided society just.

> There is thus no individual exchange without the antagonism of classes. But the respectable conscience refuses to see this obvious fact. So long as one is a bourgeois, one cannot but see in this relation of antagonism a relation of harmony and eternal justice, which allows no one to gain at the expense of another. For the bourgeois, individual exchange can exist without any antagonism of classes. For him, these are quite unconnected things. [*Poverty of Philosophy*, p. 75]

It is the bourgeois who sees justice in the midst of exploitation, not Marx or the class-conscious proletarian. The normative component in the consciousness of the oppressed classes, whether they are the slaves of antiquity or the proletarians of capitalism, contributes to the subjective conditions (aside from the objective conditions) which undermine and lead to the overthrow of these social systems. In the *Grundrisse*, Marx says that "with the slave's awareness that he *cannot be the property of another*, with his consciousness of himself as a person, the existence of slavery becomes a merely artificial, vegetative existence, and ceases to be able to prevail as the basis of production" (p. 463). That is to say, the slave evaluates his situation in life by means of a norm, by means of a concept of a person that does not accord with the mode of production in a slave-owning society or with the interests of the slave owners, because it tells him that he, as a person, is equal to the slave owner and that there is no legitimate ground for him to be the property of another man. The proletarian, as his class consciousness develops, also evaluates capitalism by means of a standard that does not accord with this mode of production. He judges that the separation of his labor capacity from the means or conditions of its realization (the means of production) forced on him by the system of private property is "improper," and that the product of his labor is his own product. This judgment helps in bringing about the doom of capitalism. Marx, in *Grundrisse* (p. 463), speaks of the proletarian's labor capacity:

> The recognition [*Erkennung*] of the products as its own, and the judgment that its separation from the conditions of its realization is improper—forcibly imposed—is an enormous [advance in] awareness [*Bewusstsein*], itself the product of the mode of production resting on capital, and . . . the knell to its doom.

The proletarian's judgment declares the distributional arrangements of society (both of productive wealth and of the product or of income) to be improper. The slave, too, objects to a system based on private property not only in things but in human beings and this objection goes to the heart of the distributional arrangements of slave society.

A great deal more might be said about Marx's sociology of morals but I must confine myself to two points only. First, elements of the superstructure, including moral outlooks, are not epiphenomenal. The *German Ideology*, where historical materialism receives its first and most comprehensive, though incomplete, formulation, states explicitly that the superstructure reacts upon the base. Here, again, we have reciprocal action (*Wechselwirkung*), the Marxian dialectical category *par excellence* (*German Ideology*, pp. 49-50). The mere absence of the existential or institutional prerequisites for the realization of norms does not in itself reduce these norms to insignificance. The Marxian norms of self-realization, humanism, community, freedom, equality, and justice are not reduced to insignificance merely because the institutional framework they require is absent under capitalism. Such norms serve a critical function in transforming the consciousness of the proletariat, conferring on it the power of the negative or making it the agency of revolutionary change.

The weapons of criticism obviously cannot replace the criticism of weapons. Material force must be overthrown by material force. But theory also becomes a material force once it has gripped the masses. . . .

As philosophy finds its material weapons in the proletariat, the proletariat finds its intellectual weapons in philosophy.[12]

Marx's statement that the counter-norms of the slave and proletarian—superstructural elements—undermine the respective substructures follows from his theory and exemplifies *Wechselwirkung*.

Second, although Marx does not explicitly deal with the relation between the social origin of ideas and values and their truth, validity, or moral desirability, his theoretical praxis makes clear that he did not confuse these two matters.[13] For instance, he adopted the labor theory of value from the bourgeois economists (mostly from Ricardo) and made it a cornerstone of his political economy. Had he thought that the bourgeois origin of this theory invalidates it, he would not have accepted it. Further, in the *Theories of Surplus Value* (the fourth volume of *Capital* which deals with the "literary history" of political economy), Marx devotes nearly two thousand pages to thorough analyses of theories advanced mostly by bourgeois economists. Again, he would not have undertaken such analyses had he thought that the exposure of the social origin of these theories is sufficient to invalidate them. His procedure makes clear that whether a theory is acceptable or unacceptable must be settled by rational argument. Typically, Marx explores the logical cogency of a theory, its presuppositions and consequences, and its adequacy to account for the relevant observed phenomena.

He states clearly in the *German Ideology* that the truths of science are established empirically.[14] Marx also seems to have held that the acceptability of a moral outlook is settled by argument. He adopted

12. Marx, *Toward the Critique of Hegel's Philosophy of Law: Introduction*, in *Writings of the Young Marx*, pp. 257, 263.

13. H. B. Acton, *The Illusion of the Epoch: Marxism-Leninism as a Philosophical Creed* (London: Cohen & West, 1962), pp. 205 ff., accuses Marx of such confusion.

14. For example in *German Ideology*, p. 31, he says that the premises of historical materialism "can thus be verified in a purely empirical way."

(and adapted) from Hegel the values of self-realization and of freedom as self-determination. Hegel himself admits that his views on
self-realization, the transition from the in-itself (*Ansichsein*) to the
for-itself (*Fürsichsein*), are Aristotelean in inspiration—they correspond to potentiality and actuality. His views on freedom are largely
Lutheran. The sources of these Hegelian values were probably known
to Marx. But even if they were not, Marx did not consider Hegel's endorsement of them a reason for their moral rejection; and whatever
else Hegel was, he was not a proletarian spokesman. We may conclude that, for Marx, the desirability of principles of justice should be
settled by argument. Consistent with his sociology of morals, Marx
can validly use proletarian or post-capitalist standards, including
standards of justice, in evaluating capitalism. I shall turn now to an
examination of his principles of justice.

THE MARXIAN PRINCIPLES OF DISTRIBUTIVE JUSTICE

In the early phase of communist society ("socialist society" in Marxist
literature), the principle of distributive justice can be stated thus: to
each according to his labor contribution. As Marx puts it:

> The right of the producers is proportional to the labor they sup-
> ply.
> The same amount of labor which he [the producer] has given to
> society in one form he receives back in another. [*Critique of Gotha*,
> SW, 2:23]

Every producer receives from society—after certain deductions are
made—consumption goods embodying an amount of labor equal to
the amount of labor he contributed. Marx emphasizes that what is
distributed as individual income is not the total social product.
Socialist society could not maintain itself if it were to distribute and
consume all that it produces. This implies that the producer's reward
is not the arithmetical equivalent of his labor contribution, and Marx
proceeds to explain why this disparity between labor contribution and
reward is not unjust. From the total social product, several deductions
must be made for the general purpose of reproduction; that is, (1)

for the replacement of the means of production that were used up, (2) for the expansion of future production to meet the demands of an increased population, and (3) for reserves or for an insurance fund against emergencies and natural disasters. The remaining portion of the social product would be allotted for consumption but this consumption fund is divided into two main portions: the first portion goes into *social consumption* and includes funds for the satisfaction of "social needs," such as education and health services; and welfare funds for "those unable to work," such as the very young, the old, and the infirm. The remainder of the consumption fund would be allotted to *individual consumption* and would be divided among the producers in accordance with their labor contribution.

According to Marx, the deductions for future production and for reserves are a matter of economic necessity and not of equity. For him, they involve no injustice.

The deductions from the consumption fund for social services do not conflict with just distribution according to labor contribution because such services redound to the advantage of the producer: ". . . what the producer is deprived of in his capacity as a private individual benefits him directly or indirectly in his capacity as a member of society" (*Critique of Gotha*, SW, 2:22). Nor do the deductions for welfare expenditures diminish the justice of rewards in socialist distribution, because they satisfy the demands of human solidarity.

The distributive justice of the first phase involves two principles: (1) a formal principle of equal right or equality of treatment, and (2) a material principle of proportioning reward to labor contribution. All individuals are treated alike as workers. But different individuals being unequal in their physical and mental endowments make unequal productive contributions and receive unequal rewards. However, from this inequality of reward one should not conclude that Marx is elevating inequality, as such, to the level of a moral principle. He says that with the abolition of classes in socialist society, "all social and political inequality arising from them would disappear" (*Critique of Gotha*, SW, 2:30). Socialist society is said to eliminate the inequality of social and political power. And even though the rewards of the producers are not arithmetically equal, income differentials are not likely to be great because society will fulfill such social needs as education and health care, and the deduction from the social product for these needs "grows considerably in comparison with present-day society and it grows in proportion as the new society develops" (*Critique of Gotha*, SW, 2:22). Further, this deduction for social needs precedes consumptive (or income) distribution. Marx clearly does not favor the creation of wide income differentials since these would result in a form of social stratification which, he contended, should be eliminated from the structure of society. Thus a socialist society departs from the Marxian norm of a just socialist society to the extent that it permits wide income differentials favoring its ruling elites at the expense of social needs.

Socialist distributive justice marks an "advance" over the capitalist distribution of wealth and income but, adds Marx, it is an advance marred by "defects" (*Critique of Gotha*, SW, 2:23, 24). The advance is, at least, twofold. First, by abolishing the private ownership of the means of production, socialism establishes the principle of equal right by removing the asymmetrical power relations or inequalities associated with social classes and their attendant privileges. Socialism "recognizes no class differences, because everyone is a worker like everyone else" (*Critique of Gotha*, SW, 2:24). The producers derive income by virtue of their productive contribution and no one derives income—as under capitalism—by virtue of ownership of means of production. ". . . No one can give anything except his labor . . . nothing can pass to the ownership of individuals except individual means of consumption" (*Critique of Gotha*, SW, 2:23). Second, socialism ends class exploitation. The deductions that are made from the social product are made by the associated producers in the interests of the associated producers for the common satisfaction of their needs. These deductions redound to the producers in a modified form. Under capitalism, deductions from the social product are made by the private owners of the means of production who use them as they see fit, in their own interests, and at the expense of the producers. The associated producers establish rational and collective control over the means of production and over the social product and use them for socially beneficent purposes. This termination of exploitation may be explicated in another way. Under socialism, the producer is treated justly because his reward is proportional to his labor contribution. Under capitalism, the producer is treated unjustly because his reward—as I shall show in the next section—is not proportional to the *labor* he supplies but, at best, to the value of his *labor power* (a lesser quantity). Accordingly, the labor he contributes in one form does not return to him in another form. The capitalist appropriates part of the worker's labor and this is why the worker is exploited under capitalism.[15] Socialist society, according to Marx, ensures its variant of justice by excluding exploitation.

Socialist justice, according to Marx, leaves much to be desired. In establishing equal rights for every producer, socialist justice applies the same standard—labor contribution—to all producers. But different individuals, being unequal in their physical and mental endowments, make unequal productive contributions and are differentially rewarded. Thus equal rights applied to unequal individuals issue in

15. The labor theory of value states that the value of a commodity is determined by the socially necessary amount of labor (or labor time) expended in its production or reproduction. Economic theory in Marx's time treated "labor" as the commodity that the worker sells. Marx asks: what is the value of a ten-hour working day viewed as a commodity? According to the theory, it is the labor time incorporated in it, which yields the tautology: the value of a ten-hour working day is ten hours. This, says Marx, is not illuminating. Further, if labor is the commodity that the worker sells and if he were to receive the value of his commodity, then he would receive as wages the value of his product. But this is contrary to fact since the product belongs to the capitalist. Were the worker to receive the value of his product, then one cannot account for the capitalist's profits. Hence, Marx introduces a distinction between labor as the measure of value and labor power as the capacity to work. The commodity that the worker sells is labor power, not labor. Wages are the compensation for labor power, not for labor. The value of labor power during a day is the socially necessary labor time expended in its maintenance, or expended on the commodities required for its maintenance. In a portion of the working day, the worker contributes the equivalent of the value of his labor power, and in the remainder of the working day he contributes surplus labor or surplus value to the capitalist. Marx *explains* how the capitalist appropriates this surplus value in accordance with capitalist property relations and their juridical expression. The capitalist contracted for labor power, and the labor contract entitles him to its use for the duration of the specified working day. This use yields him surplus labor which cost him nothing and is the source of his profit. Marx, then, *evaluates* this appropriation as an act of plunder, as robbery of the worker. Marx says, evaluatively, that the labor contract is a juridical fiction, a *"fictio juris"* (*Capital*, 1:540).

material inequality. Moreover, different individuals have unequal needs. Even for individuals making equal labor contributions and receiving equal rewards, material inequality would still result because of their unequal expenditures occasioned by their unequal needs. The upshot is that one will be richer than another; one's needs will be better satisfied than another's. In addition, socialist justice favors those who are gifted by nature, and penalizes those who are not; it treats natural talents as entitlements to relative social advantages. Marx is saying, in other words, that the just comparative treatment of individuals should not discriminate on the basis of natural differences for which the individuals themselves are not responsible.

Socialist justice treats human beings one-sidedly as workers and ignores their individuality. They are "regarded only as workers and nothing more is seen in them, everything else being ignored" (*Critique of Gotha*, SW, 2:24). To appreciate this criticism, it should be noted that the Marxian method of ethical thinking consists primarily in the moral evaluation of social institutions such as private property, social classes, and the division of labor. It examines their consequences for the human individuals living under them and then measures these consequences against the Marxian conception (or ideal) of man. The conception of man presupposed by certain social institutions or systems (for example, the egoistic man of modern civil society) is delineated and then measured against Marx's own conception. Either implicitly or explicitly, this method is concerned with what type of man and what type of interpersonal relations certain social institutions produce and whether these types are morally desirable. The socialist principle of distributive justice, and the institutions associated with it, by regarding man simply as a worker fail to take into account what Marx calls "the whole man" (*totaler Mensch*). A human being is more than a worker, he is also a person with a plenitude of material and spiritual needs.[16] His ultimate need is for self-realization (*Selbstverwirklichung*). To conceive of man simply as worker is to

16. In *EPM*, p. 144, Marx says that the "rich human being" is one "in whom his own realization exists as an inner necessity, as *need*." In the *Excerpt-Notes of 1844, Writings of the Young Marx*, p. 273, he says that the need of an object is proof "that the object belongs to my nature," or that it is necessary to "the realization of my nature."

conceive of him as an "abstract man." The term "abstract" which Marx adopts from Hegelian terminology means "one-sided" or "poor in content." The distributive justice of developed communist society makes the satisfaction of needs—hence the full development of individuality—its guiding principle. To overcome these defects, the principle of distributive justice in communist society states: "From each according to his ability, to each according to his needs" (*Critique of Gotha*, SW, 2:24).

The realization of this distributive principle of justice presupposes material abundance which results, on the one hand, from a high level of development of productive forces and, on the other hand, from a transformation of the nature and conditions of work and the attending change in the attitude toward work. The productive forces develop because the social relations of production, especially the social mode of appropriating and distributing the produce, is in harmony with the social mode of producing. But the inequality of reward remains because the needs of different individuals are unequal. Marx rejects the arithmetic equality of rewards because some people would receive less than they need for the free, all-round development of individuality he advocates. He rejects inequality which creates privilege, and accepts only that inequality which allows for the development of individuality. In the communist conditions of abundance, the unequal or proportional distribution according to needs is not thought to result in a sinister social hierarchy.

It is not uncommon in moral philosophy for conceptions of justice to be linked to other moral conceptions. For Marx, socialist justice is closely linked to equality and communist justice to self-realization. The two principles of justice exclude exploitation by abolishing private property and affirm the crucial importance of the rational and collective control over the conditions of social existence. This control is an aspect of freedom.

CAPITALISM AND DISTRIBUTION ACCORDING TO LABOR CONTRIBUTION

I argued that Marx can validly employ the socialist principle of justice in evaluating capitalist institutions. The transaction between capitalist and worker exemplifies the manner in which capitalism systematically violates the principle of compensation according to labor contribution. According to Marx, the worker would be treated unjustly even if he did get the full value of his labor power, because what this labor power produces exceeds in value the value of the labor power itself. The value of his labor power invariably embodies an amount of labor less than the amount of labor he is forced to contribute. The worker is despoiled of this excess, of his surplus labor which creates surplus value. Capitalist injustice consists in this non-equivalence of contribution and reward, in the despoliation or exploitation of labor power. However, the worker does not even get the value of his labor power and this involves further non-equivalence and injustice.

According to Marx's economic theory, the worker produces the equivalent of his wages in a portion of the working day, and in the remaining portion he renders "surplus," "unpaid," or "alien labor"— that is, surplus value to the capitalist. ". . . Wages *only* express *paid labor*, never all labor done" (*Grundrisse*, pp. 570-571). This extraction of surplus labor or surplus value from the worker and its appropriation by the capitalist without compensation is called "exploitation." The worker is exploited or made to render uncompensated labor even when he receives the full value of his labor power. ". . . Surplus value—and capitalist production is based on it—is value which cost no equivalent" (*Theories of Surplus Value*, 3:523). ". . . Capital obtains this surplus labor without an equivalent, and in essence it always remains forced labor—no matter how much it may seem to result from free contractual agreement" (*Capital*, 3:819).

Clearly, then, capitalism violates the principle of reward according to labor contribution. The labor contract is unjust even when the worker receives the full value of his commodity (labor power) because he receives no equivalent for his surplus labor. By contrast, in socialist society, the freely associated producers decide on the deductions to be made from the social product, and the deductions for social needs (which are the only deductions relevant to equity of distribution), return to the producers in a modified form. Marx's implicit application of the socialist principle of justice to capitalist institutions is evident from his ethical rejection of capitalist property rights. The appropriation of surplus labor, made legitimate by these rights, is considered theft and embezzlement by Marx. The *Grundrisse* maintains that present wealth is based on the theft of surplus labor (p. 705).

Capital is stored, unpaid labor, the portion of surplus value that was capitalized. "The greater part of the yearly accruing surplus product, embezzled, because abstracted without return of an equivalent . . . is thus used as capital . . ." (*Capital*, 1:611).

Adam Smith speaks of capital as command over labor and as stored-up labor. Marx says that capital is also the command over unpaid labor; it is "the power to appropriate alien labor without exchange, without equivalent, but with the semblance of exchange" (*Grundrisse*, p. 551; *Capital*, 1:534). Having ethically rejected both the right of the capitalist to appropriate surplus labor (theft, embezzlement) and the institution of private property ("present wealth") which makes such appropriation feasible and comprehensible, Marx rejects the typical claims made in justifying surplus value or gross profit as the capitalist's reward. It is claimed that capitalist profit is justified because

(1) it is the reward for superintendence (or wages for management);

(2) it is the reward for "abstinence" (Nassau Senior); the capitalist deservedly earned his profit because he abstained from consuming. He denied himself the enjoyments attending upon consumption by saving and investing his capital;

(3) it is the reward or premium on risk—the capitalist risks his capital and deserves to be rewarded.

Marx's rejection of these claims is a consequence of his rejection of the institution of private property. In rejecting some of them, he resorts to both serious argument and satire. In these contexts, we get a chance to read Marx not merely as philosopher, sociologist, economist, and historian but also as man of letters, a satirist, and ironist to boot.[17]

17. Edmund Wilson, *To the Finland Station*, with a new introduction (New York: Farrar, Straus, and Giroux, 1972), p. 340, writes: ". . . Another element of Marx's genius is a peculiar psychological insight: no one has ever had so deadly a sense of the infinite capacity of human nature for remaining oblivious or in-

In rejecting the first claim, Marx points out that the capitalist demands his profit because he is a capitalist, an owner of capital, and not because he is a manager. To be sure, some capitalists act as managers, and this was generally the case in early capitalism, but their profits are not proportional to their managerial functions. Profit is the privilege that derives from ownership. In the cooperative enterprises owned collectively by workers, Marx notes, the rewards of the managers are not equal to the profits of the enterprise. Furthermore, capitalist enterprises tend to separate ownership and management: the capitalists hire professionals to act as managers. This renders the capitalist increasingly superfluous; the social task of managing the productive facilities of society can be undertaken without him. This separation provides an even stronger reason to dispense with capitalist ownership and to reject any justification of profit as a fair reward to the capitalist.

Marx rejects the second claim, the abstinence argument for the legitimacy of profit, by pointing out that modern capitalism makes it possible for the capitalist to enjoy consumption and to save.[18] The two are not necessarily mutually exclusive. It is a crude apologetic to claim that the capitalist, in forbearing from consuming his income, makes painful sacrifices for which he must be rewarded. His income level enables him to save without making such sacrifices. Profit is his reward as a result of his ownership of means of production, and not as a result of his abnegation. Given the level of his income, the capitalist, in saving and investing, does not deny himself enjoyments or opportunities in life necessary to his well-being, but in appropriating surplus value he denies the worker comparable enjoyments and opportunities in life. Then Marx turns to satire. He wonders what is meant by "abstinence." Does it mean that if the corn is not all eaten, but part of it is sown, that the capitalist has abstained? Or, if the wine is not

different to the pains we inflict on others when we have a chance to get something out of them for ourselves. In dealing with this theme, Karl Marx became one of the great masters of satire. Marx is certainly the greatest ironist since Swift, and he has a good deal in common with him."

18. The "abstinence theory" of Nassau Senior is discussed in *Capital*, 1:591-598. Alfred Marshall used "waiting" instead of "abstinence" in *Principles of Economics*, 8th ed. (London: Macmillan, 1938, pp. 232 ff).

all drunk, but some of it is left to mature, that the capitalist has abstained? How can the capitalists consume their capital? Can they eat the steam-engines, cotton, and railways? This, adds Marx, would be an enormous feat and the manner of realizing it is a secret that vulgar political economy has not divulged. If the world still "jogs on," it must be because of this "modern penitent of Vishnu, the capitalist" (*Capital*, 1:597). To be sure, the capitalist is under great pressure to accumulate. "Accumulate, accumulate! This is Moses and the prophets" (*Capital*, 1:595). And capitalism offers him numerous enticements to consume. In his breast there is a "Faustian conflict" between the passion to accumulate and the desire for enjoyment. Marx is so moved that he comes to the aid of the capitalist but, alas, with a socialist solution that the capitalist dreads the most.

> The simple dictates of humanity therefore plainly enjoin the release of the capitalist from this martyrdom and temptation, in the same way that the Georgian slave-owner was lately delivered, by the abolition of slavery, from the painful dilemma, whether to squander the surplus product, lashed out of his niggers, entirely in champagne, or whether to reconvert a part of it into more niggers and more land. [*Capital*, 1:597 598]

Marx's rejection of the third claim, the risk argument, should not be paraphrased.

> All economists, when they come to discuss the prevailing relation of capital and wage labor, of profit and wages, and when they demonstrate to the worker that he has no legitimate claim to share in the risks of gain, when they wish to pacify him generally about his subordinate role *vis-à-vis* the capitalist, lay stress on pointing out to him that, in contrast to the capitalist, he possesses a certain fixity of income more or less independent of the great adventures of capital. Just as Don Quixote consoles Sancho Panza with the thought that, although of course he takes all the beatings, at least he is not required to be brave. [*Grundrisse*, p. 891]

Marx rejects the claim that the worker is guaranteed income while the capitalist bravely takes risks. The worker has no security of employment, especially because of the capitalist tendency to generate an industrial reserve army.

There are two aspects of the transaction between capitalist and worker that exemplify the capitalist violation of the principle of compensation according to labor contribution. One aspect belongs to the sphere of circulation (the marketplace) where the purchase and sale of labor power is concluded in a labor contract. The other aspect belongs to the sphere of production, where labor power is used and made to contribute surplus labor. The non-equivalent transaction between capital and labor is not transparent. The sphere of circulation and its labor contract is the sphere of phenomenal appearances which shows the opposite of the actual relation. Marx, with partly suppressed irony, calls the marketplace "a very Eden of the innate rights of man, which satisfies the rights of freedom, equality, and property" (*Capital*, 1:176). He describes the phenomenal appearances of the market as follows: the capitalist as owner of a commodity (money or the commodities that money can buy) meets the worker as owner of another commodity called labor. Each of them is a free person. They enter into a contractual relationship which satisfies the right to freedom because the contracting parties are constrained only by their own free wills. Their contract satisfies the right of equality because each of them contracts with the other as a commodity owner. The capitalist offers to pay the worker a wage which is purportedly the monetary equivalent of the value of his labor. The worker accepts. Equivalents are exchanged for equivalents and this further ensures equality. Wages appear as the value or price of labor. A day's wage appears as the monetary compensation for a full day's work. Property rights are satisfied because each disposes only of what is his own, of his own commodity. The exchange between worker and capitalist resembles the buying and selling of all other commodities. This, indeed, seems to be the best of all possible deals. Marx's theory turns on showing that the rights of the labor contract are "formal" and explains how the phenomenal appearances are the direct opposite of the actual relation. True, the worker, unlike the slave, is free in that he owns his person or his faculties but, Marx adds with sarcasm, he is also free in another sense: free from property (*Capital*, 1:714). Deprived of the

ownership of means of production and means of livelihood, he is
forced (not free) to sell his labor power to the capitalist. That both
capitalist and worker are owners of commodities does not place them
on a footing of equality. The worker sells his capacities, and his
human worth is reduced to the level of a thing, while the capitalist
commands the labor power of the worker and uses it to augment his
capital. Even though the exchange between capitalist and worker appears "in the same guise as the buying and selling of all other commodities," it is not a typical exchange of commodities because labor
power is a very "peculiar commodity" that yields values greater than
its own (*Capital*, 1:540). And wages are not the compensation for the
labor contributed but for labor power (that is, for the capacity to
work). A day's wage is the monetary compensation for a portion of the
working day and not for the full working day. The freedom, equality,
and equivalent exchange of the labor contract turn into unfreedom,
inequality, and non-equivalent exchange for the worker because of the
unequal economic power of the capitalist and the worker. The capitalist labor contract and the capitalist legal system mask the true nature
of the wage relation because they treat labor—not labor power—as a
commodity and consider the worker fully compensated for his labor
or for the entirety of the working day. What lends credence to this
mystification is the fact that the worker gives his day's labor for wages.
The impression that a day's work is fully compensated is enhanced
whenever the worker bargains over his hourly rate.

Wood, in examining what the presumed justice of capitalism consists in relies on the passage about innate rights and misses its ironic
tone. He turns Marx's statement on the formal equality of the exchange into a statement on what the justice of exchange is for Marx.
Wood claims that "according to Marx, the worker is generally paid
the full value of his labor power. . . . This is . . . a *just* transaction,
an exchange of equivalent for equivalent" ("Marxian Critique of
Justice," p. 21).

The terms "justice" and "just exchange" nowhere appear in the
passage to which Wood refers. But even if we grant Wood his paraphrase of the passage in question, its ironic tone should have alerted
him to the "formal" character of this justice. Like formal equality and

freedom, this justice would produce and perpetuate its own opposite. Wood proceeds to show, with textual support, that the worker receives the value of his commodity or that equivalents are exchanged in the marketplace, and concludes that capitalism, according to Marx, is "entirely just," or perfectly just.[19] This perfection, Wood fails to note, is the perfection of a simplifying assumption which Marx introduces, and rigidly adheres to, in the major part of volume 1 of *Capital*, where he explains the origin of surplus value. Marx assumes that all commodities, including labor power, exchange at their value, and proceeds to show that surplus value does not arise in the sphere of circulation or in the marketplace (by buying cheap and selling dear) but in the sphere of production where labor power is forced to render surplus labor. The payment to the worker of the full value of his labor power does not guarantee justice because wages are part of the surplus value filched from the workers. Wood's and Tucker's claim to the contrary is conclusively refuted by Marx's text. It bears repeating that since the worker is defrauded when he is exploited, exploitation cannot be just. Wood is mistaken in claiming that "capitalist exploitation is not a form of fraudulent exchange" ("Marxian Critique of Justice," p. 37). Marx says that wages are part of the "tribute annually exacted from the working class by the capitalist class. Though the latter with a portion of the tribute (*Tributs*) purchases the additional labor power —even at its full price, so that equivalent is exchanged for equivalent,

19. Wood, pp. 36, 16. Wood also writes (p. 3): "When we look in the writings of Marx and Engels for a detailed account of the injustices of capitalism, however, we discover at once that not only is there no attempt at all in their writings to provide an argument that capitalism is unjust, but there is not even the explicit claim that capitalism is unjust or inequitable, or that it violates anyone's rights." Although I am limiting my discussion to Marx, Wood's false assertion regarding Engels should not go uncontested. Engels in *Karl Marx*, SW, 2:166, says that the appropriation of surplus value is the appropriation of the unpaid labor of others. The exposure of this appropriation, Engels adds, "removed the last justification for all the hypocritical phrases of the possessing classes to the effect that in the present social order right and justice, equality of rights and duties and a general harmony of interests prevail, and present-day bourgeois society, no less than its predecessors was exposed as a grandiose institution for the exploitation of the huge majority of the people by a small, ever-diminishing minority." For Engels, too, justice and exploitation are mutually exclusive.

yet the transaction is for all that only the old dodge of every conqueror who buys commodities from the conquered with the money he has robbed them of."[20]

In fact, Marx tells us that the equality, freedom, and property rights of the marketplace provide the standard by which vulgar political economy evaluates capitalist society. According to Marx, vulgar political economy, in contradistinction to the scientific political economy of, say, Ricardo, deals with phenomenal appearances and ends up with little more than theoretical superficiality and ideological apologies for the capitalist system.[21] Marx always treated this vulgar political economy dismissively. Thus it is ironic that Wood, a sympathetic interpreter of Marx, should have turned the equivalent exchange of the marketplace into a Marxian standard for evaluating capitalism when Marx considers it the standard with which vulgar political economy evaluates capitalism. ". . . This sphere of simple circulation or of exchange of commodities [i.e., the market and its equivalent exchange etc.], . . . furnished the 'Free-trader Vulgaris' with his views and ideas, and with the standard by which he judges a society based on capital and wages" (*Capital*, 1:176).

So far Marx has assumed that the worker receives the full value of his labor power and shown that, under this condition, the transaction between capital and labor is unjust because it is a transaction of non-equivalents in which the worker is defrauded. Now Marx

20. *Capital*, 1:582. Regarding Marx's simplifying assumption, see, for example, *Capital*, 1:599: "In the chapters on the production of surplus value it was constantly presupposed that wages are at least equal to the value of labor power. Forcible reduction of wages below this value plays, however, in practice too important a part, for us not to pause upon it. . . ." Marx repeatedly reminds his readers of this assumption—see, for example, *Capital*, 1:166, n.1; 314, and 519. He says that he is studying the "ideal average" (*idealer Durchshnitt*) and the "general type" (*allgemeinen Typus*) of capitalist relations in *Capital*, 3:142-143, 173-175. On Marx's methodology, see Paul Sweezy, *The Theory of Capitalist Development* (New York: Monthly Review Press, 1964), chap. 1; Louis Althusser, "Sur la 'moyenne ideale' et les formes de transition" in his book (with E. Balibar), *Lire le Capital*, vol. 2 (Paris: Maspero, 1968), pp. 72 ff.

21. See, for example, *Capital*, 1:307: "Vulgar economy . . . here as everywhere sticks to appearances in opposition to the law which regulates and explains them." *Capital*, 3:844: "The well-meaning desire to discover in the bourgeois world the best of all possible worlds replaces in vulgar economy all need for love of truth and inclination for scientific investigation."

relaxes this assumption and tells us that wages generally tend to sink below the value of labor power, involving even more disparity between labor contribution and reward and furthering injustice. Some, but not all, of the main reasons for the deviation between wages and the value of labor power are as follows.

(1) Workers displaced by machinery form the bulk of what Marx calls the "industrial reserve army." This army of unemployed human beings increases the supply of labor power relative to the demand for it, thereby depressing wages below the value of labor power. "That portion of the working class, thus by machinery rendered superfluous . . . swamps the labor market and *sinks the price of labor power below its value*" (*Capital*, 1:431, emphasis added). The formation of the industrial reserve army is a necessary defense mechanism for the capitalist system, and not an accidental aberration.

(2) The value of labor power is determined by two criteria; first, physical subsistence requirements and, second, a sociohistorical element pertaining to the desired standard of living in a certain society at a certain time. The first criterion defines the minimum wage because, in general, it is not in the interest of the capitalist to pay the workers less than their physical subsistence requires. He wants to extract the maximum amount of labor from them and to do so, he must make sure they are capable of working. But the second criterion, says Marx, may be "expanded, or contracted, or altogether extinguished so that nothing remains but the physical limit" (*Wages, Price and Profit*, SW, 1:422).

Left to its own inner dynamic, the capitalist system with its drive for profits tends to disregard the sociohistorical element that enters into the determination of the value of labor power, or to make wages *less* than the value of labor power. Hence, capitalism is bent on injustice.

(3) If labor power is a commodity and its purchaser has the right to use it, there must be a limit to the duration or intensity of its use if the worker is to receive its full value. For a given wage, the capitalist tends to maximize his profit by lengthening the working day or by intensifying labor (for example, by speeding up the production line) to the utmost working capacity of the worker, which means that he pays the worker for one day's labor power and extracts from him more than one day's expenditure of labor power. In one of the scenarios of *Capital*, the proletarian tells the capitalist that this violates the labor contract and the law of exchanges:

> By an unlimited extension of the working day, you may use up a quantity of labor power greater than I can restore in three. . . . You pay me for one day's labor power, whilst you use that of 3 days. That is against our contract and the law of exchanges. I demand, therefore, a working-day of normal length . . . because I, like every other seller, demand the value of my commodity. [*Capital*, 1:234]

In unmistakably prescriptive language, Marx says that the workers have a "duty to themselves" to set limits on the "tyrannical usurpations of capital" by struggling for a rise in wages, "a rise not only in proportion to the surplus time exacted, but in a greater proportion" (*Wages, Price and Profit, SW*, 1:439). Their duty is not only to secure the value of their labor power but also to make inroads into the surplus value of the capitalist.

(4) Capitalist production moves through periodic cycles. The capitalists, whenever they can, try to pay the workers less than the value of their labor power. When the business cycle is on the downswing and wages tend to decline, the capitalists try to reduce wages disproportionately; and when the cycle is on the upswing and wages tend to rise, the capitalists resist raising wages proportionately. "If, during the phases of prosperity, when extra profits are made, he [the worker] did not battle for a rise of wages, he would, taking the average of one industrial cycle, not even receive his average wages, or the value of his labor [power] (*Wages, Price and Profit, SW*, 1:440).

(5) When the value of money depreciates, the worker's standard of living deteriorates if he does not secure a proportionate rise in wages. But the capitalists under such circumstances resist such a rise; they try to make wages less than the value of labor power. "All past history proves that whenever such a depreciation of money occurs the capitalists are on the alert to seize this opportunity for defrauding the workman" (*Wages, Price and Profit, SW*, 1:437).

On Marx's showing, the worker is invariably defrauded whether or not he receives the full value of his labor power because he is exploited in either case.

Capitalism and Distribution According to Needs

I argued earlier that Marx can validly employ the principle of just distribution according to needs to evaluate capitalism. On his showing, capitalism is unjust because it systematically violates this principle. Marx does not consider capitalism unjust because the technical base of its productive system does not generate the material abundance necessary for satisfaction of needs. Rather, he considers capitalism unjust because it does not satisfy human needs within its own productive possibilities and thus violates the principle of distribution according to need. He objects, not to the technical base, not to the productive forces, but to the social mode of their employment; that is, the social relations of production and particularly in the mode of appropriating and distributing the annual product.

In order for a society to satisfy its needs, it must allocate the available labor time at the prevailing level of productivity to the production of the requisite goods and services. But capitalism has "no conscious regulation of production" (*SW*, 2:462). Capitalism is characterized by a contradiction between the rational planning of production in individual production units and the anarchy of social production. It is not a planned system that reconciles supply and demand (including needs) *ex ante* but, at best, *ex post* and quite imperfectly. Where supply exceeds demand, human labor and material wealth are wasted; when demand exceeds supply human needs are left unsatisfied. More generally, during economic crises which result largely from unplanned social production, capitalism is wasteful of human resources and productive capacity. Such wastefulness militates against the satisfaction of needs. The lack of conscious planning is not only a condition of injustice but also of unfreedom since to be free, men must rationally and collectively control the conditions of the common life, including the conditions of material production.

Capitalism is directly oriented, not to the satisfaction of human needs, but to the generation of surplus value. It is profit, not need satisfaction, that determines what goods are to be produced and in what quantities, and what services are to be provided and in what manner.

Capitalism is ridden with contradictions but "the fundamental contradiction" is between the unrestricted development of wealth in the form of commodities and the restricted consuming power of society. The "consuming power of society" is based "on antagonistic conditions of distribution" which restrict the consumption of the great mass of the population (*Theories of Surplus Value*, 3:56). Money, says the young Marx, is the intermediary between "man's needs and the object, between his life and his means of life" (*EPM*, 165-166). Should one lack money, one's needs are reduced to chimeras. Inadequate income frustrates one's needs by frustrating the possibility of their gratification.

The foregoing makes clear that *capitalist exploitation* and its attendant income distribution *violate not only the socialist principle of justice but also the communist principle* by denying the workers an adequate income for the satisfaction of their needs. The claim of Tucker and Wood that, for Marx, exploitation and injustice are disjunctive is not tenable. Exploitation is incompatible with justice. Communist justice is conducive to self-realization; capitalist injustice makes it impossible.

REDISTRIBUTIVE MEASURES

Marx held that the income of the working class increases—and the degree of its exploitation decreases—only within limits that are ultimately determined by the need to maintain the capitalist system and, in particular, the accumulation of capital. "It cannot be otherwise in a mode of production in which the laborer exists to satisfy the needs of self-expansion of existing values, instead of, on the contrary, material wealth existing to satisfy the needs of development on the part of the laborer" (*Capital*, 1:621).

But despite the systemic limitations on the increase of the workers' income, Marx advocated measures for the redistribution of income under capitalism. He rejected the all-or-none principle as a strategy informing the political action of the working class. Such a principle, which he associated with the anarchists, amounted to "indifference to politics" or to "abstention from politics."[22] Its practical

22. Marx, "Der politische Indifferentismus" in Marx and Engels, *Werke*, vol. 18 (Berlin: Dietz Verlag, 1962), pp. 299-304. See also Marx and Engels "Ficti-

implication is to maintain the exploitation of the working class, un-diminished, until the revolution. Marx, in contrast, advocated struggles for reforms which would culminate in revolution. Aware of its situation in life, of the nature of the system under which it lives, and of its historical role, and armed with its independent trade unions and a party organization, the working class can struggle for reforms without becoming reformist; that is, without losing sight of its ultimate objective in the "abolition of the wages system." The *Communist Manifesto*, written nearly 100 years before the birth of the welfare state, prescribes a ten-point transitional program, including redistributive measures such as a heavy progressive or graduated tax, the abolition of all right of inheritance, and universal education (*SW*, 1:53-54). In *Wages, Price and Profit*, Marx strongly advocates collective bargaining to ensure that the workers will receive, at least, the value of their labor power (*SW*, 1:440 ff.). In the *Address of the Central Committee to the Communist League*, he calls for the continual enlargement of the public sector at the expense of the private sector; for a change in the distribution of wealth so that "the utmost productive forces, means of transport, factories, railways, etc.," will be concentrated in "the hands of the state" (*SW*, 1:116).

Almost all of the measures Marx recommended to redistribute wealth and income are aimed at the foundation of capitalism, at reducing the exploitation of the working class or the extraction of surplus value by the capitalist class. Allen Wood interprets Marx as holding that "any 'reforms' of capitalist production which proposed to take surplus value away from capital and put an end to the exploitation of the worker would themselves be injustices of a most straightforward and unambiguous kind. They would violate in the most obvious way the fundamental property rights derived from the capitalist mode of production and constitute the imposition on it of a system of distribution essentially incompatible with it" ("Marxian Critique of Justice," pp. 268-269).

Marx never paid a farthing for these rights. It is in virtue of capitalist property rights that the workers are exploited or treated unjust-

---

tious splits in the International," in *The General Council of the First International: Minutes (1871-1872)* (Moscow: Progress Publishers, n.d.), pp. 356 ff., esp. p. 388.

ly. Marx was not a spokesman for capitalist property, but for the working class. Here are some measures he recommended, for instance, to the German workers who could not begin by proposing "directly communistic measures" since Germany was still undergoing a bourgeois-democratic revolution.

> They [the workers] must drive the proposals of the democrats, who in any case will not act in a revolutionary but in a merely reformist manner, to the extreme and transform them into direct attacks upon private property; thus, for example, if the petty bourgeois propose purchase of the railways and factories, the workers must demand that these railways and factories be confiscated by the state without compensation as being the property of reactionaries. If the democrats propose proportional taxes, the workers must demand progressive taxes; if the democrats themselves put forward a moderately progressive tax, the workers must insist on a tax with rates that rise so steeply that big capital will be ruined by it. . . . [*Address . . . to the Communist League*, SW, 1:116]

These measures were to be imposed politically on the capitalist economic system and illustrate how politics reacts upon the substructure; that is, they are an instance of *Wechselwirkung*. Marx was not a voluntarist; he insisted that an ensemble of objective and subjective conditions is necessary to bring about the demise of capitalism. "Bold leaps" and "legal enactments" (such as the redistributive measures), in themselves, will not overthrow capitalism, but they "can shorten and lessen the birth pangs" (*Capital*, 1:10). Tucker's assertion that, for Marx, the concern with distributive questions was dangerous because "it ultimately pointed the way to abandonment of the revolutionary goal" is as profoundly mistaken as Wood's contention that, for Marx, distributive justice cannot be a revolutionary concept (Tucker, p. 51, Wood, p. 30). The critique of the distribution of income, for Marx, is a critique of the distribution of productive wealth since the two distributions mutually determine one another, and no concern or concept could be more revolutionary than the concern with criticizing and undermining the property relations of a mode of production. Marx always reminded the workers to be concerned not only with real wages (real purchasing power) as opposed to nominal wages but also with "real, relative wages"; that is with their income relative to the income of the propertied classes. To increase their relative share in the net annual income of society is simply to appropriate what is their own since "wages and profit" are "shares in the product of the worker" (*Wage, Labor and Capital, SW, 1*:95-98).

The Moral Evaluation of Capitalism

In *Marginal Notes on Wagner's Textbook on Political Economy*, one of his last works, Marx replied to a comment that he, like other socialists, showed the appropriation of surplus value to be a robbery of the workers.[23] He points out that in addition to doing so, he *explained* this appropriation on the basis of capitalist property relations and the juridical relations expressive of them. Marx is saying that he did not merely *evaluate* capitalism. He also *explained* capitalist practices on the basis of capitalist institutions. This, indeed, summarizes the two-tiered nature of his theoretical project. He thought that, although other socialists evaluated capitalism similarly or dissimilarly, they failed where he succeeded: in giving a scientifically founded theory of capitalism, its functioning, and its development. Such a theory, he held, like other scientific theories is a search for the truth. But Marx again distinguishes himself from other scientific economists not only by his own theoretical contributions to such areas as the theory of capital but also by his doctrine of the unity of theory and praxis. Whereas the young Marx, before formulating historical materialism and developing his own political economy, spoke of philosophy as the intellectual weapon of the proletariat, the mature Marx considered social science in alliance with philosophy as such a weapon. They were to inform the revolutionary politics of the working class.

The two-tiered nature of Marx's project is little understood. Wood and Tucker, in dealing with the theme of capitalist justice, focus on the explanatory aspect of his undertaking and mistake it for the evaluative aspect. When Marx explains how it is that surplus value is appropriated in accordance with capitalist juridical relations, they

23. Marx, "Randglossen zu Adolph Wagners 'Lehrbuch der Politischen Ökonomie,'" in *Werke*, vol. 19 (Berlin: Dietz Verlag, 1962), pp. 355-383, esp. 359 ff.

take him to be giving his own evaluation of this appropriation. That is why they insist, quite mistakenly, that capitalism for Marx was not fraudulent. Marx grants, for the purpose of simplification, that this appropriation is not a violation of the economic law of exchange or of the juridical relations of capitalism and proceeds to show that it results in a non-equivalent transaction. Measured by his socialist principle of justice, this transaction is unjust. Partly in the light of this principle Marx deplores capitalism because it defrauds the workers. To be sure, Marx could not have passed such a judgment by evaluating capitalism from its own juridical standpoint since, on his own simplifying supposition, capitalist practice does not violate capitalist economic laws or juridical norms. The judgment is made from the Marxian ethical standpoint which, Marx held, was a proletarian standpoint. It bears repeating that the explanation of the functioning of capitalism is made on the basis of capitalist institutions, as it must be, but the evaluation is made on the basis of Marx's ethics. Wood's crucial claim that, for Marx, "justice is the rational measure of social acts and institutions from the juridical point of view" and that this point of view is "the point of view of one of the dependent moments of a mode of production, the sphere of political authority of *Staatsrecht*" is a basic fault of his interpretation (Wood, pp. 5, 32, 13). It leads Wood into ascribing to Marx the standpoint of the ruling class and its spokesmen because Wood fails to realize that elements of the superstructure, such as juridical norms, have two levels of determination and that the legal system of a mode of production, according to Marx, expresses the interests of the ruling class.

To begin with, Marx would tell Wood that the so-called juridical point of view is a pernicious abstraction: whose juridical point of view? Surely, the spokesmen of the capitalist class would want to evaluate capitalist practices from the standpoint of capitalist juridical relations because these relations are expressive of a system of private property which is in the interest of the capitalist class. And when they do, as in the labor contract, they regard wages as the price of labor (not of labor power—that is a Marxian distinction not found in capitalist laws); that is, they consider the worker compensated for the whole working day. Marx says that capitalist juridical relations mask the exploitation of the workers. Hence he did not base his evaluation of capitalism on these juridical relations in any fundamental sense. Were Marx to base his evaluation of capitalism on these relations *per se*, he would have viewed capitalism from the standpoint of the ruling class and said that capitalism is just, or he would, at most, have given an internal critique of capitalism by showing that its practice is at variance with its laws. Marx makes this last charge, but his critique of capitalism is far more fundamental than that: it rejects capitalist property together with its legal expression. And, indeed, it is no accident that Wood, in claiming that Marx considered capitalism just, had to foist on Marx the evaluative standard of just exchange which, according to Marx, is the standard used by the vulgar economists in evaluating capitalism, the standard of the apologetic defenders of capitalism. This standard of just exchange is not a legal standard and Wood's repeated assertion that, for Marx, justice "is a juridical or legal concept" is without foundation (Wood, p. 5). The vulgar standard of just exchange, contrary to Wood's implied claim, is an *economic* law, not a *legal* standard. It is the economic law of exchange which states that commodities, under idealized conditions, exchange at their full value and, as a corollary, that labor power is exchanged at its full value. But there is no capitalist legal standard which requires, for example, that the owner of a table should in exchanging it receive its full value. Nor do capitalist legal standards, or the labor contract, require that the worker receive the full value of his labor power. If the worker contracted for starvation wages, and received them, then from the standpoint of capitalist juridical relations justice was done even if these wages were significantly below the value of the worker's labor power. The capitalist legal system can hardly be considered the point of view from which Marx evaluates capitalism. The ruling class establishes the sphere of *Staatsrecht* to express and protect its interests and, says Marx, in so doing misleads itself by reducing justice "to the actual laws" (*German Ideology*, p. 78). Marx's evaluation of capitalist distributive arrangements is overwhelmingly *moral*, not legal. He regarded capitalism as unjust primarily because, as an exploitative system, it does not proportion reward to labor contribution, and because it is not oriented to satisfy human needs, least of all the needs of the producers, within its own productive possibilities. Capitalist distributive arrangements issue in a morally objectionable comparative treatment of individuals belonging to the different social classes, or in an objectionable allotment of benefits and burdens. The non-owning class, the most numerous class, bears most of the burdens of society and enjoys few of its advantages. The owning class, the least numerous class, bears few of the social burdens and enjoys most of the social advantages. The owning class takes advantage of, or uses, the non-owning class. The injustice of capitalist property and income distribution is associated with inequality: the inequality of class power and of life opportunities. Capitalist injustice is also associated with unfreedom: the worker is forced to sell his labor power and to contribute surplus labor; and members of society do not collectively and rationally control the affairs of the common life and especially the system of production.

I wish to thank Gregory Vlastos and Dennis Thompson for their comments on an earlier draft of this paper.

GEORGE G. BRENKERT   Freedom and Private Property
                       in Marx

I

Marx's opposition to private property is well known.[1] He was, after all, quite explicit: "the theory of the Communists may be summed up in the single sentence: Abolition of private property."[2] However, the nature of this opposition is rather controversial.

Some maintain that Marx's opposition is limited to a number of technical and sociohistorical analyses of the nature and fate of private property: for example, the declining rate of profit, the changing organic composition of capital, the concentration of capital, and the increasing size and immiseration of the proletariat.[3] Such analyses, it is said, account for the whole of Marx's opposition to private property, since his views on ideology prohibit a more basic moral criticism of private property. If all moral principles are immanent in the material situation, then to the extent that the capitalist follows the moral and legal rules of bourgeois society, it is mistaken to think that Marx did or could condemn capitalist private property for being unjust or immoral.

This view, however, is at odds with the view others draw from

1. In this essay I discuss only Marx's views on private property. There has been considerable controversy recently about the nature, extent, and insight of Engels' contribution to Marxism. To avoid this problem, I shall look only to Marx's writings or to those writings jointly written by Marx and Engels in which the result was due to Marx's efforts.

2. Karl Marx and Friedrich Engels, "Manifesto of the Communist Party," in *Karl Marx and Friedrich Engels: Collected Works*, vol. 6 (New York: International Publishers, 1976), p. 498.

3. See Allen W. Wood, "The Marxian Critique of Justice," above, pp. 3-41.

Freedom and Private Property
                                          in Marx

Marx's analysis of the exploitative nature of modern private property.[4]
Modern (capitalist) private property is the power possessed by private
individuals in the means of production which allows them to dispose
as they will of the workers' labor-power (that is, the ability of the
worker to labor for certain periods). Though the worker is paid the
full value of his labor-power—that is, the amount it costs to produce
the labor-power—this amount is less than the value such labor-power
is able to create when put to work for a normal working day. This difference Marx calls "surplus value"; he also calls it "unpaid labor." Its
maximization is the sole aim of the capitalist in production. Thus, the
accumulation of surplus value requires that the worker receive *less*
than he produces; part of his labor is unpaid. This situation constitutes the *exploitation* of the worker. Consequently, many have claimed
that Marx condemned the social relations basic to capitalist private
property because he considered such relations unjust. Capitalist private property must be abolished in order to insure an equitable and
just system of production.

It seems to me, however, that both views are mistaken, though for
different reasons. Accordingly, I shall argue, on the one hand, that
Marx does indeed have an underlying moral reason for opposing
private property and that it is expressed in both his early and later
writings. On the other hand, it is implausible that this underlying opposition is based on a principle of justice because Marx's views on ideology do seem to prohibit such a stance. Instead, I shall argue that
Marx's criticism of private property is based on a principle of freedom
and on the effects of private property on individuality and personality.

II

It is important initially to see that Marx's criticism is *at least* based
on the value of freedom. I shall not immediately try to show whether
or not this critique is also founded on justice, or how, given his views
on ideology, it is a possible or consistent criticism for Marx to make
of private property.

In a society founded on private property, Marx contends, individu-

4. See Donald VanDeVeer, "Marx's View of Justice," *Philosophy and Phe-
nomenological Research* 33 (1972-1973): 366-386.

als increasingly and openly view others as separated and antithetical, rather than joined or united, by their interests. People see in others potential limitations on themselves rather than possible aids to the realization of their interests. The nature of this separation and opposition of interests, and hence of Marx's opposition to private property, can be explicated by looking to Marx's views on freedom.

There are at least three dimensions to the freedom Marx advocates. First, one is truly free when free from fortuity and chance in the conditions of one's life, and when able to participate in the control and direction of one's affairs. Clearly part of this aspect of freedom is a knowledge and rational understanding of the nature of one's life conditions, how they arose, and how they operate. Marx does not identify freedom with the cessation of activity as Adam Smith tended to do. Instead, overcoming obstacles and external conditions, gaining control over them, constitutes an exercise in liberty when they ". . . lose their character of mere natural necessities and are established as purposes which the individual himself fixes." "The result," Marx goes on to note, "is self-realisation and objectification of the subject, therefore real freedom, whose activity is precisely labor."[5] That is, obtaining control over the conditions of one's life and subjecting them to a conscious, rational plan is not simply a development of one's freedom but also part of the full—and not merely one-sided—development of one's particular capacities and gifts. Thus, freedom exists when, through the rational control and direction of the conditions of his existence, one develops his capacities and talents so that he may do as he pleases. Private property, in contrast, divides one's life activities, not "*voluntarily*, but naturally" (emphasis added).[6] Far from the current popular use of "natural" which has positive connotations, Marx's use is usually negative. It connotes an unconscious, involuntary—or at least not a rationally planned—occurrence. According to Marx, however, only insofar as there is a general, rational plan agreed on by the members of society will there be a harmony of interests. Since the interests of the propertied and the propertyless are not united by a

5. Karl Marx, *The Grundrisse*, ed. and trans. David McLellan (New York: Harper & Row, 1971), p. 124.
6. Karl Marx and Friedrich Engels, "The German Ideology," *Collected Works*, vol. 5 (New York: International Publishers, 1976), pp. 47-48.

general, rational plan, the relations in which they stand are instances
of the limited or restricted relations prevailing among individuals of
all pre-communist societies. As such, these relations aggravate rather
than harmonize the divergent interests of owners and non-owners so
that each views the other (and nature) as alien and hostile. Consequently, Marx condemns private property as an obstacle to flourishing and harmonious society. The invisible hand and the impersonal
forces of the market are affronts to one's freedom. The social relations constituting private property are historical, human constructions that relate to forces which are amenable to change and control.

Secondly, freedom requires the objectification of man through
his activities, products, and relations. This objectification, however,
must take a particular form. That is, freedom obtains only in those
interactions between people and things which take place in terms of
their own concrete qualities—not those of abstract, symbolic forms
such as exchange-value and money. Freedom, Marx claims, obtains
when "everyone of your relations to men and to nature . . . [is] *a
specific expression*, corresponding to the object of your will, of your
real individual life."[7] Freedom does not and cannot obtain when the
real nature of one's qualities and relations is obscured or disguised.
Marx accepts the traditional close connection of freedom, truth, and
knowledge. One does not know, nor can one deal with, the "truth" of
another being or thing (freedom is not present) unless and until
one's relation to it is based on the specific, concrete qualities of both
oneself and the "object." Insofar as this does not happen man is "lost
in his object"; "his" objects do not confirm and realize his individuality.

Private property, however, culminates in a set of relationships
which concern not the concrete qualities, the use-values, but the
amount of human labor in the abstract (the exchange-value) embodied in whatever is produced or owned. Furthermore, under private
property people "carry on their work independently of each other . . .
and do not come into social contact with each other until they exchange their products. . . ." Thus, "the relations connecting the labor

7. Karl Marx, "The Power of Money," in *Karl Marx and Friedrich Engels:
Collected Works*, vol. 3 (New York: International Publishers, 1975), p. 326.

of one individual with that of the rest appear, not as direct social relations between individuals at work, but as what they really are, material relations between persons and social relations between things."[8] That is, the social relations between individuals in the performance of their labor do not appear as their own mutual personal relations but are separated and disguised from them under the shape of the social relations between the products of labor. Consequently, people come to consider the conditions and forces which determine their lives to be simply natural aspects of their environment, to be manifestations of fate and chance rather than objects of possible rational direction. Individuals find themselves forced into various activities and roles which they often cannot understand, control, or escape from. They become locked into activities and roles which institutionalize divergent interests. Accordingly, the combination of individuals in bourgeois society is but "an agreement about these conditions, within which the individuals were free to enjoy the freaks of fortune."[9] Because private property promotes only the abstract and disguised objectification of oneself in one's objects and relations, private property is a denial of freedom.

Thirdly, freedom is something which can only be achieved in and through the community—in cooperation and association with others. That is, Marx opposes not only the disregard of the interests of others to pursue one's own interests (though surely he is opposed to this too) but also the division and separation of these interests in the first place. In a society based on private property, privacy is raised to an ultimate social principle and given the categorical form: "Mind your own business." Instead, Marx counters, freedom is realized through other people as well. "Personal freedom becomes possible only within the community."[10] The notion of community here is much stronger than the utilitarian view of community in which the separate interests of individuals are made compatible by finding ends which maximally fulfill those interests. Within such a "community," the division of man's life into public and private spheres is simply continued. The

8. Karl Marx, *Capital*, vol. 1: *A Critical Analysis of Capitalist Production* (New York: International Publishers, 1967), p. 73.
9. Marx and Engels, "The German Ideology," *Collected Works*, 5: 80.
10. Ibid., p. 73.

state mediates individual interests through various general ends, but
does not in this way secure freedom for individuals or constitute itself as a community. Rather, a community exists to the extent that
the separateness of individual interests is overcome in the self-conscious realization by individuals that their lives as particular beings
reflect a larger social and rational order. "Only when the real, individual man re-absorbs in himself the abstract citizen, and as an individual human being has become a *species-being* in his everyday life,
in his particular work, and in his particular situation, only when man
has *recognised* and *organised* his '*forces propres*' as *social* forces . . .
only then will human emancipation have been accomplished"[11]—only
then does a community, a harmony of interests, exist.

Private property, however, is inherently opposed to this form of
community. Through its power of disposing of the labor-power of
others, private property seeks to increase the product of their labor.
That is, at the heart of bourgeois society lies the antithesis of private
property to labor. Each has its own separate and opposed interests.
One is in control, the other is under control. The owner seeks to encourage the productivity of the laborer. The benefits of increased production redound primarily to him. The product is his. The laborer, on
the contrary, seeks to husband his labor. Any benefits of increased
productivity return only secondarily to him. He exercises little or no
control over the directions and ends his labor is to follow. The development of such relations manifests itself not simply in the conflict
between the private property owner and the propertyless, but also in
the separation and conflict of interests between town and country,
material labor and mental labor, personal and class individualities,
particular and common interests. Different activities and goods—production and consumption, property and the lack of property—devolve
on different individuals. Consequently, society is divided into diverse
classes, each with its own interests to protect against the hostile and
antagonistic interests of others. Accordingly, only an illusory freedom
obtains in such a society. People are genuinely free, on the contrary,
only in cooperative, harmonious relations with others in which ra-

11. Karl Marx, "On the Jewish Question," in *Karl Marx and Friedrich Engels:
Collected Works*, 3: 168. Emphasis added on *recognised* and *organised*.

tional and voluntary control is exercised over their life-activities. It
is this, once again, that capitalist private property fails to provide.

III

I have argued so far that Marx's analysis of capitalist private property
is (at least) a critique on behalf of freedom. However, it might be
objected, on the one hand, that the references to slavery and exploitation indicate that it is also a critique on behalf of justice. Slavery is
surely an instance of injustice; "exploitation" is often taken as syn-
onymous with "injustice." On the other hand, it might be objected
that Marx's views on ideology preclude *any* such moral condemnation
of private property—whether stated in terms of freedom *or* justice. I
shall consider both these objections.

There are two main reasons why many have claimed Marx's critique was based on considerations of justice.[12] First, Marx's analysis of
the nature of capitalist private property—an analysis formulated in
terms of "exploitation"—identifies the source of the capitalist's profit
as the unpaid labor of the worker. This the capitalist appropriates. As
one commentator expresses it, ". . . if there is no injustice what was
the Marxist fuss about? Why regard the process as one of exploitation?"[13] Secondly, in the "Critique of the Gotha Program," Marx is
supposed to have made statements that show his underlying concern
about justice. For example, Marx speaks of the bourgeois limitations
to the principle of equal right (proposed in the Gotha program) according to which the worker should receive back the undiminished
proceeds of his labor. Such a principle is an inadequate principle of
justice. Indeed, it is a principle of inequality, since "it ignores differences in *need* of each worker and bases its distribution solely on
the contribution of labor power by each worker."[14] Marx goes on to
claim that under communism the narrow banner of bourgeois right

12. See Donald VanDeVeer, "Marx's View of Justice," *Philosophy and Phe-
nomenological Research* 33 (1972-1973): 366-386; Ernest Mandel, *The Formation of the Economic Thought of Karl Marx* (New York: Monthly Review Press,
1971), pp. 14, 16; A. D. Lindsay, *Karl Marx's Capital: An Introductory Essay*
(London: Geoffery Cumberlege, 1947), chap. 5; Derek Allen, "Is Marxism a
Philosophy?" *The Journal of Philosophy* 71 (October 1974): 601-613.
13. VanDeVeer, p. 370.   14. Ibid., p. 372.

will be crossed in its entirety and society will inscribe on its banner: "From each according to his abilities, to each according to his needs." This suggests to some that Marx had a principle of justice in mind. "Thus, for Marx there was a standard of justice superior to that involved in the Gotha program, one taking into account relevant differences in the needs of workers but one incapable of implementation in the first phase of communist society. Only in the higher phase of communist development can this optimal standard of equitable distribution be realised."[15]

We must consider, in assessing these claims, why Marx's critique cannot be one of justice but can be and is one of freedom. In defending this view, we need not deny the claim that slavery and exploitation have been considered instances of injustice in order to maintain that Marx did not so understand the situation. We must first look (briefly) to Marx's views on ideology.

The bases of all human society are to be found in the productive activities through which the needs and wants of people are fulfilled. It is by such activities that man is distinguished in a real and significant way from animals. However, this productive activity not merely satisfies the physical needs and wants of people (as well as creates new needs and wants), it also determines the kind of consciousness people have of themselves, others, and their times. As Marx says in his oft quoted comment: "It is not consciousness that determines life, but life that determines consciousness."[16] Now such consciousness takes various forms—religion, the state, law, morality, science, art, and so on. However, these forms of consciousness are not simply the effects of the mode of production out of which they arise. They are not simply epiphenomena. Marx explicitly allows that they may in turn influence the mode of production. Indeed, he even seems to allow that such forms of consciousness may be in part constitutive of modes of production in a society. He does say, for example, that such forms of consciousness are themselves *particular* modes of production, and fall under its general law."[17] But most crucial for present purposes is

15. Ibid., p. 373.
16. Marx and Engels, "The German Ideology," *Collected Works*, 5: 37.
17. Marx and Engels, "Private Property and Communism," *Collected Works*, 3: 297.

his view that these forms of consciousness may also be said to be "reflections," "expressions," or "manifestations" of the underlying material conditions. He holds this for metaphysical as well as practical reasons. On the one hand, the ideology of a society might be expected to reflect or manifest its practical activities since Marx holds that cause and effect are related in such a way that the effect is "merely the openly manifested cause." "But if the effect is different from the cause," Marx says, "must not the nature of the effect be contained already in the cause? The cause must already carry with it the determining feature that is manifested later in the effect."[18] Marx's view is clearly more Hegelian and Aristotelian than it is Humean. On the other hand, that the dominant material relations give rise to a particular set of ideas, to an ideology, is also due to the fact that "the class which has the means of material production at its disposal, consequently also controls the means of mental production, so that the ideas of those who lack the means of mental production are on the whole subject to it. The ruling ideas are nothing more than the ideal expression of the dominant material relations, the dominant material relations grasped as ideas."[19]

There is one final step Marx takes. Moral principles do not merely reflect or manifest the material conditions out of which they arise, they are also applicable only to or valid for the material conditions of which they are the reflection. Marx admits that most, if not all, pre-communist societies have shared certain commonalities, for example, exploitation. Consequently, he concedes that "the social consciousness of past ages, despite all the multiplicity and variety it displays, moves within certain common forms, or general ideas."[20] Nevertheless, those elements of their ideologies, those moral principles shared by various societies have been shared only abstractly. The principles involved are not to be treated as identical. On the contrary, such principles "retain their full validity only for and within the

18. Karl Marx, "On Friedrich List's Book *Das Nationale System der Politischen Oekonomie*," in *Karl Marx and Friedrich Engels: Collected Works*, vol. 4 (New York: International Publishers, 1975), p. 285.

19. Marx and Engels, "The German Ideology," *Collected Works*, 5: 59.

20. Marx and Engels, "Manifesto of the Communist Party," *Collected Works*, 6: 504.

framework of [the] conditions" out of which they arise.[21] That is, the
validity of the categories and principles of any social formation is
linked to the concrete totality of which they are a part. As abstractions,
divorced from real history, they have no value whatsoever.[22] It is for
these reasons that Marx claims that "right can never be higher than
the economic structure of society and its cultural development conditioned thereby."[23] This statement, then, is to be interpreted to mean
that the only principles of right according to which one can validly
assess the social principles of a given society are those immanent in
that society; it is not, as some have argued, to be read as claiming
that "the highest *attainment* of what is right is strictly limited by the
economic structure of a society at a given stage of development."[24]

Further support for the relativist interpretation of Marx's statement
can be adduced from various other comments of Marx on the nature
of principles of distributive justice. For example, in the "Critique of
the Gotha Program," when Marx asks, "What is a 'fair distribution'?"
he answers himself with the following rhetorical questions: "Is it [the
present-day distribution] not, in fact, the only 'fair' distribution on the
basis of the present-day mode of production? Are economic relations
regulated by legal conceptions or do not, on the contrary, legal relations arise from economic ones?"[25] Or, again, in *Capital* Marx claims
that

> to speak . . . of natural justice . . . is nonsense. The justice of trans-
> actions between agents of production rests on the fact that these
> arise as natural consequences out of the production relationships.
> The juristic forms in which these economic transactions appear as
> wilful acts of the parties concerned, as expressions of their common
> will and as contracts that may be enforced by law against some
> individual party, cannot, being mere forms determine this content.

21. Karl Marx, "Introduction [to the Grundrisse]," in *A Contribution to the
Critique of Political Economy*, ed. Maurice Dobb (New York: International
Publishers, 1970), p. 210.

22. Marx and Engels, "The German Ideology," *Collected Works*, 5: 37.

23. Karl Marx, "Critique of the Gotha Program," in *The Marx-Engels Reader*,
ed. Robert C. Tucker (New York: W. W. Norton & Company, 1972), p. 388.

24. VanDeVeer, "Marx's View of Justice," p. 371.

25. Marx, "Critique of the Gotha Program," p. 385.

They merely express it. This content is just whenever it corresponds, is appropriate, to the mode of production. It is unjust
whenever it contradicts that mode. Slavery on the basis of capitalist
production is unjust; likewise fraud in the quality of commodities.[26]

Now Marx is not simply saying, in such passages, that principles of
justice have a certain basis or origin—but that this is a matter of
indifference with regard to the validity of those principles, or the systems to which they may be applied. Instead, he claims, the validity of
principles of distributive justice is linked to the particular modes of
production out of which they arise. Hence, given the capitalist mode
of production, one gets the system of bourgeois distributive justice.

Accordingly, the view that Marx has an absolute concept of justice
can be maintained only by denying—or avoiding—Marx's views on
ideology.[27] Moral ideas, such as the conception of justice, arise in
certain epochs under particular modes of production and are intelligible only in relation to those conditions. Capitalist private property
depends, for example, on the meaningfulness of distinguishing between various individual proceeds of labor, that is, between the values
which each individual laborer adds to the value of the product. These
individual proceeds of labor are appropriated by the capitalist. When
this is done in such a way that the worker receives full payment for
his labor-power, and the capitalist receives the full use-value of the
worker's labor-power, then justice obtains. But "within the cooperative
society [that is, communism] based on common ownership of the
means of production, the producers do not exchange their products.
. . . The phrase 'proceeds of labor' . . . loses all meaning."[28] Thus,
one of the bases of justice in the transactions of capitalist private
property is undercut, not in the sense that it is shown to be unjust,
but in the more radical sense that it becomes meaningless. Once

26. Karl Marx, *Capital*, vol. 3: *The Process of Capitalist Production as a
Whole* (New York: International Publishers, 1967), pp. 339-340.
27. VanDeVeer acknowledges that Marx was "tempted" towards a relativist
view by his views on ideologies; but this is all that he says. How Marx's position
on justice (as interpreted by VanDeVeer) and Marx's views on ideologies can
be made compatible, VanDeVeer does not say. For the most part, VanDeVeer
simply avoids Marx's views on ideology.
28. Marx, "Critique of the Gotha Program," p. 386.

again, then, principles of justice appear to be relative to the particular
modes of production.

   Finally, it is easy, too easy perhaps, to make a great deal of Marx's
use of the phrase, "From each according to his abilities, to each according to his needs," as constituting not simply Marx's views of
justice under communism but as a principle that would apply to all
societies. The phrase is, according to Tucker, used only once by Marx
—and that in the "Critique of the Gotha Program."[29] Marx himself did
not place a great deal of emphasis on it. However, it is not just for
this reason that it is a mistake to assume the phrase characterizes
Marx's views. Shortly before introducing this notorious phrase, Marx
comments that "right by its very nature can consist only in the application of an equal standard." Under capitalism the equal standard is that
of "labor, human labor in the abstract." In the face of the inequalities
which arise under a bourgeois principle of justice in the first phase of
communism, Marx then claims that to avoid all these defects right,
instead of being equal, will have to be unequal. He is in fact saying
that it is impossible to draw up a principle of right or justice that will
take into account the inequalities of individuals. "Unequal individuals
. . . are measurable only by an equal standard in so far as they are
brought under an equal point of view, are taken from one *definite*
side only, for instance, . . . are regarded *only as workers* and nothing
more is seen in them, everything else being ignored."[30] But this is to
view people within "a narrow horizon," or under "a bourgeois limitation." Accordingly, principles of justice cannot, by their nature, treat
people with regard to their individual complexities, capacities, and
needs. They are by their nature incapable of treating people concretely. When Marx then says that only in communism can the narrow horizon of bourgeois right be crossed in its entirety, he means
quite literally that principles of justice will be left behind. And if this
be indeed correct, then Marx does not and cannot have a universal or
absolute principle of justice that applies to all societies and by which
he can criticize capitalist private property.

   I conclude, therefore, that Marx cannot have a universal, let alone

29. Tucker, *The Marxian Revolutionary Idea*, p. 48.
30. Marx, "Critique of the Gotha Program," p. 387.

absolute, principle of justice. Accordingly, when he speaks of the exploitation of the worker, he cannot be using "exploit" to connote an instance of injustice.[31] To this extent, then, his condemnation of capitalist private property is not and cannot be a condemnation of it for its injustice—at least insofar as its holders follow the standards of bourgeois justice. However, to the extent that they do not follow these standards—for example, the capitalist tries to lengthen the working day beyond its normal limits—the owners of capitalist private property can be condemned as unjust. Marx's views on justice, then, do seem to be what might be called relativistic. As such, the principles of justice relevant to one social or historical setting cannot be applied to or used to criticize another social or historical setting. Still, it should be noted that his views are relativistic in a Pickwickian sense. Marx does not hold that different societies and cultures may have different valid principles of justice, even if their situations are the same. Indeed, it is fairly clear that he holds that when the situations are the same, or relevantly similar, the same principles of justice (or the lack thereof—under communism) obtain. Furthermore, since all pre-communist societies have been subjected (at least) to scarcity as well as to the exploitation of one part of society by another, we may well expect that there have been some moral principles which have held cross-culturally and cross-historically. Nevertheless, Marx maintains that the situations between different cultures have not been wholly similar in relevant ways—they have differed in their productive forces and production relations—and for this reason we cannot apply the same principle of justice to each of them. This is not relativistic in the traditional and strong sense of the term. In this sense, moral principles are relativistic only when those applicable to one society cannot be applied to another society even though the situations in both societies are relevantly similar. However, by claiming that different historical situations cannot be relevantly the same—a claim traditional

31. If "exploitation" does not connote injustice, then what does it connote? What was all the Marxist fuss about? Insofar as the word "exploitation" carries a negative moral connotation, I suggest that it relates to the lack of freedom the worker experiences. He is forced to work in situations and in various ways which are not of his choosing, which do not promote his development. He is not free, in the Marxist sense.

ethicists have implicitly or explicitly denied—the effect of Marx's view is all but the same as relativism: we cannot apply our moral principles of justice to other historical epochs. And, for our present purposes, Marx cannot be viewed as having made a critique of capitalist private property on the grounds of justice.

IV

If Marx's criticism of private property cannot be one of justice—private property meets the principles of bourgeois justice—then do not the preceding arguments also show that his critique cannot be one of freedom? Can Marx have any transcultural, transhistorical moral principles by which he can morally criticize any society or social institution?

The likelihood that there is some sort of contrast in Marx's thought between justice and freedom should be noted. Marx rarely uses the word "justice" in his discussion of private property. When he does speak of "justice" in connection with capitalism he says, more often than not, that capitalism is not unjust. More open and more frequent is his use of the word "freedom" in discussions (and condemnations) of private property. In a typical instance Marx says, "This kind of individual liberty [under capitalist private property] is thus at the same time the most complete suppression of all individual liberty and total subjugation of individuality to social conditions which take the form of material forces—and even of all-powerful objects that are independent of the individuals relating to them."[32] Marx never says —and given his views as explicated above it would be inconceivable that he would say—such things about capitalist private property or bourgeois society using the word "justice." He never claims that individuals under the bourgeoisie are subjected to a complete suppression of justice.

What is the reason for this contrast and for Marx's accusation that capitalist private property creates conditions deficient in freedom? There is an underlying asymmetry between freedom and justice in Marx's views. They are similar, of course, in the following way. Principles of justice relate to the distribution of various goods, honors,

32. Marx, *The Grundrisse*, p. 131.

conditions of production (for example, property). These (ideal) patterns of distribution vary from society to society and are themselves bound up with the modes of production in each society. Similarly, the principles of freedom also correspond to the modes of production. There is, accordingly, a particular view of freedom which is characteristic of bourgeois society. It is held as an ideal principle in this epoch. With this in mind, Marx claims that "the idea of freedom itself is only the product of a social condition based upon Free Competition," and then goes on to say that "by freedom is meant, under the present bourgeois conditions of production, free trade, free selling, and buying."[33] He continues, "this talk of free selling and buying, and all the other 'brave words' of our bourgeoisie about freedom in general have a meaning, if any, only in contrast with restricted selling and buying, with the fettered traders of the Middle Ages but have no meaning when opposed to the communistic abolition of buying and selling, of the bourgeois conditions of production, and of the bourgeoisie itself."[34]

The significant difference between justice and freedom has to do with a difference in their relation to the mode of production. In the case of justice (as noted above), a particular mode of production gives rise to and involves a particular (principle of) distribution. The two are tied more or less closely together. In the case of freedom, there is an intervening factor: the effect of the mode of production on the individuals and society in which it is found. The issue here relates to Marx's views on praxis. Specifically, the way in which people fulfill their needs and wants (that is, by their mode of production) creates not only the means and mode of distribution of their livelihood but also the kind of people they are. Marx was explicit:

> The way in which men produce their means of subsistence depends first of all on the nature of the actual means of subsistence they find in existence and have to reproduce. This mode of production must not be considered simply as being the reproduction of the

33. Karl Marx, "Speech on the Question of Free Trade," *Karl Marx and Friedrich Engels: Collected Works*, vol. 6 (New York: International Publishers, 1976), p. 464.

34. Karl Marx and Friedrich Engels, "Manifesto of the Communist Party," *Collected Works*, 6: 499-500.

physical existence of the individuals. Rather it is a definite form of activity of these individuals, a definite form of expressing their life, a definite *mode of life* on their part. As individuals express their life, so they are.[35]

Part and parcel of this objectification of man through his daily praxis is his attempt to come to conscious control over his environment, to make it more amenable to his rational direction. Man is characterized by his purposiveness, his ability to raise structures in his mind before he erects them in the world, by the control and conscious, rational direction he seeks over the reality about him. Accordingly, the development of the modes of production through various historical epochs is itself the development of the potential and actual powers of individuals and society. As Marx comments, "The history of industry and the established objective existence of industry are the open book of man's essential powers."[36] For Marx there is more than a causal or casual relation between the modes of production and man's powers. The development of the one is the development of the other. We may distinguish two aspects of the mode of production: the forces of production and the relations of production. The forces of production are seen as part of the development of man. To affirm this, is not, as some have portrayed it, to attribute to Marx a simple technological determinism. Marx is not simply claiming that there are technological and productive forces which are distinct and separate factors in society and which, in turn, produce certain effects on people. He is claiming that these productive forces are themselves developments in human powers and abilities. The two are bound up together. Furthermore, such modes of production include both the forces of production and the relations in which they operate. This is important since the relations and connections between individuals are also central to the characterization of the development of individuals. Marx claims that "the universality of the individual is not thought or imagined, but is the universality of his real and ideal relationships."[37]

35. Marx and Engels, "The German Ideology," *Collected Works*, 5: 31.
36. Marx, "Private Property and Communism," *Collected Works*, 3: 302 (emphases omitted).
37. Marx, *The Grundrisse*, p. 121.

What does this have to do with freedom? The connection is quite
direct. It is the development of man, his capacities and abilities,
through his productive forces and relations towards a conscious
mastery and control over these forces and relations (particularly
those of his own creation) which constitutes freedom. Freedom is
linked to the development of the productive forces and relations
through the mediation of the development of the powers and abilities
of individuals. As Marx notes, "for the communists ['free activity' is]
the creative manifestation of life arising from the free development
of all abilities of the 'whole fellow.'" Or, again, freedom is the cultivation of one's gifts in all directions.[38] The centerpiece of this view is
man's self-determination, his ability and desire to control his own
actions and affairs, and not to be susceptible to external, irrational,
and nonrational forces. It is this that serves as the basis of Marx's
critique of capitalist private property on behalf of freedom. Private
property in its developed, capitalist form renders such freedom impossible. It does this through fostering a separation and conflict
of interests among the individuals of a society. There is, however, no
comparable basis for justice. Justice concerns either the pattern of
distribution of goods or some set of rules for distributing goods regardless of the resulting pattern. In either case, justice concerns the
ordering imposed on social goods, *not* the state of development of the
means for producing those goods. Further, this ordering is "only a
consequence of the distribution of the conditions of production themselves. . . . [This distribution is in turn] a feature of the mode of
production itself."[39] But, again, a society is not more just because it
possesses a more highly developed mode of production. There is, then,
given Marx's views on ideology, no basis for transcultural appraisals
of justice. Freedom, however, is different. There is a basis for appraising freedom, as opposed to appraising justice, in the ontological dimension that freedom possesses. Freedom, like justice, is not an
autonomous principle, not an ideal which Marx imposes on society.
Unlike justice, freedom should be appraised, not simply as an outgrowth of, but as an integral part of the development of the forces

38. Marx and Engels, "The German Ideology," *Collected Works*, 5: 225.
39. Marx, "Critique of the Gotha Program," p. 388.

and relations of production upon which all societies are based. The
basic criterion of freedom is the self-development of man and society
through the development of the productive forces of society.

However, Marx's views on freedom are more complicated than the
preceding suggests. It is not simply that increased productive powers
create increased powers of individual self-realization and hence increased freedom. This is part of it, of course. " 'Liberation' is a historical act, not a mental act, and it is brought about by historical conditions, the level of industry, commerce, agriculture, etc." But freedom
cannot be equated simply with an increase in productive powers,
inasmuch as the powers and abilities of the great number of individuals surely have not in fact actually developed. Marx holds that
people have not been getting freer—and this is due to the system of
private property in its extension to the world-market: "In history it is
an empirical fact that separate individuals have, with the broadening
of their activity into world-historical activity, become more and more
enslaved under a power alien to them . . . a power which has become
more and more enormous and turns out to be the world market."[40]
To understand Marx's views on freedom we must also look to the
relations of production and the contradictions between them and the
forces of production.

Hitherto the relations of production, the relations in which individuals stand to one another in their operation of the forces of production, have been characterized by a division and separation of individual and class interests. This has occurred through the institution
of private property and the division of labor. Consequently, increased
productive forces have always been appropriated by a particular class:
"In previous substitutes for the community, etc. personal freedom has
existed only for the individuals who developed under the conditions
of the ruling class, and only insofar as they were individuals of this
class."[41] But this meant that one class dominated others and that the
freedom enjoyed in such a society was an illusory freedom because
not all members of society enjoyed the benefits of that society's mode
of production and, primarily, because it was predicated upon the sep-

40. Marx and Engels, "The German Ideology," *Collected Works*, 5: 38, 51.
41. Ibid., p. 78.

aration of man from man, instead of upon a harmony of interests. Even the dominant classes in past societies have themselves been dominated by man-made and natural forces.

Thus freedom, in addition to being that state of affairs brought about by productive forces, is a dialectical result of the interaction between productive forces and relations of production. The nature of and relation between these two considerations allows Marx a twofold view of freedom—first, a view of freedom as it is manifested in any particular epoch and second, a view of freedom of universal importance and the view that will supposedly be manifested under communism. In the former case, in a particular epoch, given a harmony between the forces of production and the relations of production, freedom is supposed to exist (at least in a derivative and secondary sense). Marx claims that

> the conditions under which individuals have intercourse with each other, so long as the above mentioned contradiction [between the productive forces and the relations of production] is absent, are conditions appertaining to their individuality, in no way external to them; conditions under which these definite individuals, living under it, are thus the conditions of their self-activity and are produced by this self-activity. The definite condition under which they produce, thus corresponds, as long as the contradiction has not appeared, to the reality of their conditioned nature, their one-sided existence, the one-sidedness of which only becomes evident when the contradiction enters on the scene and thus exists for the later individuals. Then this condition appears as an accidental fetter, and the consciousness that it is a fetter is imputed to the earlier age as well.[42]

That is, within a particular epoch, so long as the forces of production and the relations of production do not conflict, so long as the latter does not act as a fetter upon the former, individuals (though living a one-sided and narrow existence) believe themselves to be living under conditions compatible with the development of individuality. They take themselves, or the ideal representatives of their period, to be free.

42. Ibid., p. 82.

However, Marx's views about the development of the production
forces and the relations of production that might be instituted allow
him a much stronger view of freedom on the basis of which he may
condemn capitalism and also criticize past societies. The harmony of
productive forces and relations of production (in the above sense) is
only a necessary condition—not a sufficient condition—of genuine
freedom. What is also required for genuine freedom is an end to the
separation and conflict of interests which have characterized pre-communist societies. This harmony of interests is required since freedom
is not, for Marx, simply an individual and negative affair—not the
absence of coercion of one's actions. Rather, one can be free only in
and through the community, through one's rational, cooperative associations with others. To the extent this does not obtain, the interests of
individuals are separated and in conflict. To that extent, "the social
character of activity, and the social form of the product, as well as
the share of the individual in production, are opposed to individuals
as something alien and material; this does not consist in the behavior
of some to others, but in their subordination to relations that exist
independently of them and arise from the collision of indifferent individuals with one another." This, however, is a denial of freedom in
that "free individuality . . . is founded on the universal development
of individuals and the domination of their communal and social productivity, which has become their social power. . . ."[43] Accordingly,
freedom requires the overcoming of the separation and conflict of interests. This involves a radical adjustment of the relations of production and is itself possible only with the development of the forces of
production which come to fruition under capitalism. Thus, by looking
to the degree of development of the forces of production, to the
separation or harmony of interests that characterize the relations of
production, and to the relation of both these factors, Marx can appraise the development of freedom of present as well as of past societies.

Capitalism and capitalist private property are, then, condemned
for limiting freedom. True, it is only through capitalism that the conditions (the forces of production) for a totally free and unrestricted

43. Marx, *The Grundrisse*, pp. 76, 67.

self-development, for freedom, will be produced. Nevertheless, capitalism is also characterized by an extreme separation and conflict of interests among the various individuals and classes of society. This is evident, for example, in the contradiction between the forces of production and the relations within which people exist—which operate as fetters on them. It is in light of this contradiction and of the conflict of interests, that Marx criticizes capitalist private property on the basis of freedom. He says that

> the accidental nature of the conditions of life for the individual . . . appears only with the emergence of the class, which is itself a product of the bourgeoisie. This accidental character is only engendered and developed by competition and the struggle of individuals among themselves. Thus, in imagination, individuals seem freer under the dominance of the bourgeoisie than before, because their conditions of life seem accidental; in reality, of course, they are less free, because they are more subjected to the violence of things.[44]

In the same way, Marx approaches the problem of India and the destructive effects the British imposed upon traditional society. He notes the misery and the devastating effects that English industry brought to India. Nevertheless, "whatever bitterness the spectacle of the crumbling of an ancient world may have for our personal feelings," Marx approves what the British were doing. His reasons are instructive: "The bourgeois period of history has to create the material basis of the new world—on the one hand the universal intercourse founded upon the mutual dependence of mankind, and the means of that intercourse; on the other hand the development of the productive powers of man and the transformation of material production into a scientific domination of natural agencies."[45] Because the British are

44. Marx and Engels, "The German Ideology," *Collected Works*, 5: 70-79. I have, however, modified the last part of this passage in accord with the earlier translation of S. Ryazanskaya, which was published by the Foreign Languages Publishing House, Moscow, in 1964. The German in question is: "in der Wirklichkeit sind sie natürlich unfreier, weil mehr unter sachliche Gewalt subsumiert."

45. Karl Marx, "The Future Results of British Rule in India," in *The Marx-*

laying the foundations for a genuine freedom in India, their actions
are to be approved even though the process may involve particulars
personally distasteful to us. Accordingly, both traditional Indian society and modern capitalism (and capitalist private property) are
found wanting in the freedom they engender.

Thus, Marx does indeed seem to have a transcultural and transhistorical principle of freedom by which he not only can—but does—
judge various societies and times. I have argued that this principle
has a foundation which coheres with his other views and makes sense
of his various claims. This notion of freedom is universally applicable
and not simply ideological in the way that other, weaker notions of
freedom are and in the way that the notion of justice is. It is true that
from the mode of production follows the dominant conception of both
justice and freedom in a society. Again, it is true that from the mode
of production follows a certain distribution of goods for consumption
and that the degree of freedom men can achieve is limited. Finally,
it is true that any interesting critical notion of freedom or justice must
be related to the mode of production. However, what has been shown
above is that such critical notions address themselves in significantly
different ways to the mode of production. It does not follow from the
three preceding truths that Marx can evaluate modes of production
on the basis of a concept of justice as he can with his concept of freedom.

Principles of justice derive from or reflect the mode of production—
just as other principles of morality do (such as principles relating to
responsibility and beneficence). But none of these principles is linked
to the mode of production in such a way that a more developed mode
of production (one with greater productive forces and a greater integration of interests) can also be said to produce a more developed,
or "higher," principle of justice, responsibility, or beneficence. We do
not necessarily have greater justice in a society with a more developed
mode of production, nor can people be said to judge themselves by a
higher principle of moral responsibility simply because they live under

Engels Reader, ed. Robert C. Tucker (New York: W. W. Norton & Company,
1972), pp. 587-588.

a more, rather than under a less, developed mode of production. Since these principles are not defined in terms of the development of the mode of production, any increase in the development of the latter cannot be read off onto the former. Further, since there is no other basis against which these principles can be defined, they remain relative to, but not measurable by, the particular mode of production which gives rise to them.

The situation is different with principles of freedom. Freedom *is* defined in terms of the development of the mode of production—both in terms of the greater development of the forces of production and in terms of the lessening of the separation of interests within the relations of production. True, there is no basis outside of the mode of production to define the principle of freedom, but this is not necessary since freedom is linked to the mode of production. Only through the mode of production, and the principle of freedom which is defined in relation to it, can we compare and appraise different modes of production. Hence, freedom can be used, whereas justice cannot be used, for transcultural appraisals. For both conceptions we must address ourselves to the mode of production, but the dissimilar ways in which we must do this makes all the difference. Accordingly, Marx's criticism of private property is at least a critique in behalf of freedom; and when one considers his views on justice and ideology, it is at most a critique in behalf of freedom.

V

In conclusion, let us consider two related questions on the nature of freedom. (1) Is freedom a moral or non-moral notion? (2) Does Marx have a moral theory at all? Marx is sometimes thought to have a non-moral notion of freedom because he is supposed to have a utilitarian view of morality. Freedom, then, is one of the non-moral goods to be maximized. But, fairly clearly, Marx is not a utilitarian. His notion of freedom is also said to be non-moral inasmuch as he is thought not to have held a moral theory at all. This is a more complicated issue which I shall discuss only briefly.

Many discussions of this problem have confused two questions.[46]

46. Cf. Robert Tucker, *Philosophy and Myth in Karl Marx* (Cambridge: Cam-

On the one hand, there is the question whether Marx can be said *to have formulated* a moral theory. This is to ask whether Marx was an ethicist or a moral philosopher. There is, on the other hand, the question whether Marx can be said *to have* a moral theory. This question is not whether he is a moral philosopher, but whether—however one might identify Marx's endeavors—he can be said to have presupposed or used a moral theory in these endeavors. Since these two questions are confused, it is supposed that the answer to the former is the answer to the latter. Thus, it is assumed that to formulate a moral theory one must suspend one's commitments so that one may seek about in some neutral way for the correct theory. However, since Marx is supposed not to have suspended his commitments, it is concluded not only that he could not be an ethical thinker but also that he does not have a moral theory. This view is mistaken. First, Marx himself quite explicitly says that he did withhold judgment before declaring himself to be a communist.

> . . . At that time when the good will "to go further" greatly outweighed knowledge of the subject, a philosophically weakly tinged echo of French socialism and communism made itself audible in the *Rheinische Zeitung*. I declared myself against this amateurism, but frankly confessed at the same time in a controversy with the *Allgemeine Augsburger Zeitung* that my previous studies did not permit me even to venture any judgment on the content of the French tendencies. Instead, I eagerly seized on [an opportunity] . . . to withdraw from the public stage into the study.[47]

Accordingly, even if we accept the criterion of those who deny Marx to be an ethical thinker, it would seem that he was one.

Secondly, however, it is not obvious that to formulate a moral theory one must suspend one's commitments. I will not, however, try to defend this counter-claim here since the point that most needs to be made against the first question is simply its irrelevance to the issue of

---

bridge University Press, 1961), pp. 13-21; and Bertell Ollman, *Alienation* (Cambridge: Cambridge University Press, 1971), pp. 43-46.

47. Karl Marx, *A Contribution to the Critique of Political Economy*, ed. Maurice Dobb (New York: International Publishers, 1970), p. 20.

whether Marx's criticism of capitalist private property on the basis of freedom is a moral criticism. The answer to the question of whether Marx can be said to have formulated a moral theory, or to be an ethical thinker, says nothing about whether or not Marx might have presupposed or used a moral theory. A person may be said to subscribe to a moral theory, even though he never doubted it, or scrutinized it with the calm, neutral eye of reason.

The important question is, then, Did Marx have a moral theory? Clearly he did not write volumes formulating one. Now if one begins by assuming that morality is a set of "constraints," absolute and invariant, applying to us without regard to our desires and interests, then surely Marx has no moral theory. But to assume this would be simply to presuppose some kind of Kantianism. On the other hand, if by "moral theory" one will allow that we refer to a view which relates to some fundamental good for all humans and which is also of overriding importance, then there is no difficulty in saying that Marx had a moral theory and that freedom played a crucial role in it. Charles Taylor has put the point nicely:

> Thus, if "morality" means the Kantian morality, whose foundation is the moral quality of the will, and which issues in injunctions binding without regard to time or circumstance, then clearly Marx is bound to reject "morality." But if we use the term in a less restricted way, if we mean by "morality" a doctrine touching the fundamental human good and the way to realize it, where "fundamental" good is taken to mean a good which is inescapably and universally the good of man, then there can be no objection to speaking of a Marxist morality.[48]

To opt for the former of these two alternative views of morality would not only eliminate talk of Marx as having a moral theory, but also talk of the moral theory of J. S. Mill. Furthermore, it would proscribe characterizing as moral, interpersonal relations which are rational, cooperative, and viewed not as constraints upon oneself but the very

48. Charles Taylor, "Marxism and Empiricism," in *British Analytical Philosophy*, ed. B. Williams and A. Montefiore (New York: Humanities Press, 1966), pp. 244-245.

development and expression of oneself. That is, it would prevent characterizing as moral not only the harmonious ways of acting that constitute Marx's notion of freedom but also the states of character which Aristotle describes as morally virtuous. The consequences, then, of restricting the notion of morality in such a way that Marx could not be said to have a moral theory are undesirable. Morality ranges more widely. It includes Marx's critique of private property from the point of view of freedom.

   I have benefited from the helpful comments of Loyd D. Easton, William McBride, and Allen W. Wood on an earlier version of this paper. I am also indebted to the Editors of *Philosophy & Public Affairs* for help in improving the present paper.

ALLEN W. WOOD Marx on Right and Justice:
A Reply to Husami

From one point of view, Marx's writings make it quite plain why he favors the overthrow of capitalism. Capitalism is an irrational and inhuman system, a system which exploits and dehumanizes the productive majority of society, and which is becoming increasingly unable even to maintain the slaves of capital in their condition of servitude. Whether we agree or disagree with these claims, it is at least fairly clear what they mean, and it is difficult for anyone to deny that if they are correct, then Marx has powerful reasons for attacking capitalism and advocating its revolutionary overthrow.

But from another point of view, Marx has dissatisfyingly little to say about his reasons for denouncing capitalist society. He does not ask the sorts of questions philosophers are fond of asking about the assessment of social institutions. He takes no pains to specify the norms, standards, or values he employs in deciding that capitalism is an intolerable system. Marx may show his acceptance of certain values in the course of attacking capitalism, but he seldom reflects on what these values are, or on how they might be justified philosophically. Whether or not this silence constitutes a serious lacuna in Marx's thought, it has certainly given rise to puzzlement on the part of his readers, and it has sometimes led to disputes even between those who are in general agreement about the merits of his critique of capitalism.

Ziyad I. Husami's recent article, "Marx on Distributive Justice," contains in my judgment the best case which has yet been made for the thesis that Marx condemns capitalism at least in part because he thinks it involves distributive injustice.[1] That even Husami's case is as weak as it is strikes me as good evidence that the thesis is untenable.

I

In an earlier article of mine, which Husami subjects to extensive and vigorous criticism, I argued that for Marx the justice or injustice of an economic transaction or social institution depends on its relationship to the prevailing mode of production. A transaction is just if it harmonizes with the productive mode, unjust if it contradicts the productive mode.[2] Marx holds this view, I think, because he sees right (*Recht*) and justice (*Gerechtigkeit*) as juridical concepts (*Rechtsbegriffe*), concepts whose proper function is in the moral or legal institutions of sociey, what Marx calls its "juridical relations" (*Rechtsverhältnisse*). Such institutions and relations, however, according to Marx's materialist conception of history, are part of the social "superstructure," they are the juridical (*rechtlich*) expression of society's "production relations" (*Produktionsverhältnisse*). In any given society, the actual content of juridical relations, and hence of the juridical norms which regulate them, is determined by the society's production relations, which in turn correspond to the stage of development of its "productive powers" (*Produktivkräfte*).

Otherwise put, the standards of right and justice appropriate to a given society are those which in fact fulfill a function in social production. Applying this account to capitalism, the rights people may claim and the standards of justice they may use to decide the justice or injustice of transactions between them are those which correspond to the capitalist mode of production, which harmonize with this mode, and which fulfill an actual function relative to it. But if Marx does think (as he obviously does) that the exploitation of wage labor by capital is essential to the capitalist mode of production, then we

---

1. See above, pp. 42-89, hereafter cited as Husami.
2. Allen W. Wood, "The Marxian Critique of Justice," above, pp. 3-41, hereafter cited as Wood.

should not be surprised to find him saying (as he also does) that there is nothing unjust about the transactions through which capital exploits labor, and that the workers' rights are not violated by capital's appropriation of their surplus value or by the capitalist system of distribution generally.

Of course, the fact that capitalist exploitation is just (given the way Marx understands that fact) is no defense of capitalism, and worthless to its apologists. For as Marx interprets it, the justice of capitalist transactions consists merely in their being essentially capitalist, in the correspondence of capitalist appropriation and distribution to those standards of justice which serve the system itself. Marx's attacks on capitalism are attacks on the system as a whole, not merely on its system of distribution. And since their import is not that the system violates its own juridical standards, these attacks are not conceived of in terms of rights or of justice.

Husami notes that there is a distinction to be drawn between *explaining* the fact that certain rights or standards of justice prevail in a society or are recognized in it, and *agreeing* that practices conforming to these standards are really right or just (or as he misleadingly puts it, "evaluating them as just," p. 76). I call this misleading because it implies the mistaken idea that if we are to use a term such as "just" and formulate theories about its proper extension, we must subscribe to the preferences and evaluations which it is commonly used to express. For Marx, justice is the property a transaction possesses when it stands in a certain functional relationship to the mode of production in which it takes place. It is a separate question whether, when, and from whose point of view just transactions are something valuable.

From the fact that Marx explains the prevalence under capitalism of standards according to which the transactions between capital and labor are just, it does not follow that he accepts those standards, even for capitalism. But it does follow if Marx believes that the only rational basis for applying any standard of justice to a transaction or institution is the conformity of this standard to the mode of production within which the transaction or institution is to be found. As I see it, this is Marx's belief.

Marx says:

The justice of transactions which go on between agents of production rests on the fact that these transactions arise as natural consequences from the relations of production. The juridical [*rechtlich*] forms in which these economic transactions appear as voluntary actions of the participants, as expressions of their common will and as contracts that may be enforced by the state against a single party, cannot, being mere forms, determine this content. They only express it. This content is just whenever it corresponds to the mode of production, is adequate to it. It is unjust whenever it contradicts that mode.[3]

Husami must read this passage as meaning something different from what it says: "Marx is explaining how it is that certain transactions come to be considered just, how certain conceptions of justice become dominant" (Husami, p. 52n.). This reading of the passage is tortured. In context, Marx is taking Gilbart to task for trying to explain why interest on borrowed capital is due to the lender by claiming that it is due "by natural justice." Marx's point is that there is no such thing as "natural justice": that the justice of economic transactions is only a matter of their correspondence to the prevailing productive mode.[4] The explanation of the fact that interest is justly due to a lender of capital depends not on nature but on the way this payment fits into the capitalist mode of production. And Marx goes on to show how it does so. There is no indication, however, here or elsewhere, that Marx regards the payment of interest on borrowed money as an injustice to the borrower. Husami attempts to controvert this by pointing to Marx's citation of Luther's "savage" condemnations of usury. But the

3. Marx-Engels *Werke* (Berlin, 1959), 25: 351 (hereafter cited as *MEW*): Cf. *Capital*, trans. S. Moore and E. Aveling (New York, 1968), 3: 339-340. All translations are my own. Standard English translations are also cited for the reader's convenience.

4. As Marx puts it: "To speak here, with Gilbart, of natural justice is nonsense" (*MEW* 25: 351; *Capital* 3: 339).

question is not whether Marx is enamored of the institution of paying interest on borrowed money, but whether he thinks the collection of interest is unjust. In the passage Husami cites from *Capital*, Marx makes quite explicit what he infers from Luther: "Luther makes it very graphic how the love of dominion [*Herrschsucht*] is an element in the impulse to get rich [*Bereicherungstriebs*]" (*MEW* 23: 619; *Capital* 1: 592).

Marx has no motive here for being concerned only with "what is considered just" or with "dominant conceptions of justice" as opposed to what is really just. For Gilbart is not trying to explain the payment of interest on the basis of dominant conceptions, but on the basis of what really is just in the nature of things. If Marx were concerned only with "dominant conceptions" of justice, as Husami claims, then he would have misunderstood the intent of Gilbart's explanation, and his criticism of the explanation would not be to the point. Only if we take Marx at his word are his remarks relevant to the context.

II

One important test of any interpretation of Marx's views about right and justice is its explanation of the things he actually says about the justice or injustice of capitalism. We shall be considering some more of these things in a moment. But another crucial test of any such interpretation is its ability to explain the fact that Marx says so little about the justice or injustice of capitalism. (As Husami puts it: "His *direct* and *explicit* statements on this subject are few and far between," p. 43.) On my reading of Marx, the explanation for this fact is that the justice or injustice of capitalist institutions has little or no significance for Marx, explanatory or evaluative. Unjust institutions or practices (such as consumer fraud or stock-market swindling) are only abuses of the system, and not fundamental defects of it. At most, they are symptoms of such defects.[5] And the justice of capitalist institutions, as Marx understands it, amounts to little more than their being essentially capitalist.

5. On this point see Engels, *Selected Correspondence* (Moscow, 1955), pp. 454-455.

But if one holds (as Husami does) that Marx's condemnation of capitalism rests in large part on the thesis that capitalism is unjust, then it ought to be very puzzling that he never "directly and explicitly" states this thesis. It ought to be even more puzzling that he scorns the preoccupation of other socialists with questions of right and distributive justice as "ideological shuffles" (*ideologische Flausen*).[6] I find nothing in Husami's paper by way of explanation for Marx's habit of contemptuous silence on the subject of capitalism's alleged injustices.

According to Husami, my reading of Marx is "based largely on the strength of a single passage in which Marx seems to be saying that the appropriation of surplus labor—that is, the exploitation of labor power—is 'a piece of good luck for the buyer [of labor power, the capitalist], but by no means an injustice (*Unrecht*) to the seller [the worker]' " (Husami, p. 44; *MEW* 23: 208; *Capital* 1: 194). Husami's remark here is inaccurate in at least two respects. First, my use of the passage he quotes was only to show that Marx refuses to endorse the argument of certain Ricardian socialists that the exchanges between capitalists and workers are unjust exchanges because they are exchanges of nonequivalent values. Since Marx's theory of surplus value *postulates* that all exchanges between capitalists and workers are exchanges of equivalent values, and even prides itself on its ability to explain the origin of surplus value without violating this postulate, I find it difficult to see how Husami could disagree with this point.

I see no ground at all for saying that this postulate represents only "the standard [of exchange] with which vulgar political economy evaluates capitalism" (Husami, p. 69). Marx obviously believes that there is good economic method in the postulate that only equivalent values are exchanged, since he makes its satisfaction a condition of any acceptable solution to the riddle of surplus value. Husami is of course correct in saying that the postulate involves a conscious simplification on Marx's part. Marx knows that all commodities (including labor power) quite often sell at prices above or below their values as measured by socially necessary labor time. But the postulate was in no sense for Marx a "standard" for "evaluating" capitalist exchanges.

6. *MEW* 19: 23; *Selected Works in One Volume* (New York, 1968), p. 325 (hereafter cited as *SW*). See also *Selected Correspondence*, p. 148.

The socially necessary labor time embodied in a commodity is nothing like an (Aristotelian) "just price" for Marx. If an oversupply of my commodity (whether it is gold, beans, or labor power) lowers its price below its value, Marx does not think that I have a right to demand that consumers pay a higher price and that they are doing me an injustice if they refuse to pay an equivalent value for it. So the fact that reality sometimes violates Marx's postulate and capitalists sometimes succeed in driving the price of labor power down below its value does not in the least show that capital does labor an injustice. Of course, the worker is exploited to a greater extent (all other things being equal) when his labor power is bought below its value than he would be if it were bought at its value or above. But this does not tend to show that any injustice is done him unless we already assume that all exploitation for Marx is unjust, which is precisely the point at issue.

Another fact to which Husami appeals is that capital regularly pays for labor power out of the surplus value it has previously squeezed from the workers. This, however, implies nothing at all about whether the exchanges between capital and labor themselves are exchanges of equivalents. I think Marx believes it does imply that the exchange involves exploitation, or at least it brings out one respect in which these exchanges are systematically exploitative of the workers. But once again this does nothing to show there is injustice in the exchanges unless we already assume that all exploitation for Marx is unjust.

Second, there are (and I quoted) other texts in which Marx makes it at least as explicit that he does not regard capitalism as distributively unjust or as violating the rights of the workers. We shall be looking at two such texts shortly.

Husami claims that in the passage where Marx says that the purchase of labor power by capital involves no wrong or injustice (*Unrecht*) to the worker he is speaking, "ironically"; he is "satirizing capitalism," describing from the standpoint of "vulgar economy" the "trick" by which capital appropriates the surplus product of the worker. Now I agree that Marx finds it ironic that capital's appropriation of surplus value is just, since this fact (as he interprets it) is apologetically worthless. It shows how both the critics and the defenders of capitalism have been hoodwinked by ideological nonsense about right and justice. But I do not agree that when Marx says that capital's appropriation of surplus value is "by no means an injustice" to the worker, he is not speaking in his own person or does not mean what he is saying. It is true that in this section Marx has been carrying on an imaginary dialogue with the capitalist, who has been presenting the justifications of the vulgar economists for the fact that the capitalist earns profit on his investments. But this dialogue has come to an end in the paragraph previous to the one from which the quoted passage is taken. In this passage, Marx is at last giving his *own* theory of the origin of surplus value, his *own* account of why the capitalist's "trick" succeeds. Apparently Husami thinks Marx does not mean what he is saying because he represents the capitalist (who in reality "would not give a brass farthing for the creed of the economists he has been chanting") as agreeing with Marx's account of surplus value. But Marx tells us why he represents the capitalist as agreeing with him: "He is a practical man, who may not always consider what he is saying outside of business, but in his business always knows what he is doing" (*MEW* 23: 207; *Capital* 1: 193). It is clearly the practical, businesslike side of the capitalist and not his extracurricular economic theory which is represented as agreeing with the account of surplus value Marx presents. Besides, if Marx does not endorse the explanation of surplus value presented in this passage, it is hard to see what his own theory of surplus value could be.

III

But since there are other passages, let us not haggle any further over this one. For brevity's sake, I will discuss only two more texts where Marx makes it very "direct and explicit" that he does not regard capitalist distribution or the transactions between labor and capital as unjust. In the *Critique of the Gotha Program* (which Husami describes on p. 46 as "the *locus classicus* of Marx's treatment of distributive justice") Marx replies to the Gotha Program's demand for "a just distribution of the proceeds of labor" with a series of rhetorical questions:

What is a "just distribution"?

Do not the bourgeois assert that the present distribution is just? And isn't it in fact the only just distribution on the basis of the present mode of production? Are economic relations [*ökonomische Verhältnisse*] ruled by juridical concepts [*Rechtsbegriffe*], or do not, on the contrary, juridical relations [*Rechtsverhältnisse*] arise out of economic ones? [*MEW* 19: 18; *SW* 321-322.]

I take it that the second and third questions are to be answered affirmatively. The bourgeois *do* assert that the present distribution is just, and it *is* in fact the only just distribution on the basis of the present mode of production. Lest we think that the justice or injustice of a system of distribution might be judged on some other basis, the implied answer to the fourth rhetorical question reminds us that juridical concepts *do not* rule economic relations but, on the contrary, juridical relations (the actual justice or injustice of transactions between agents of production) *do* arise out of economic ones. All this accords perfectly with Marx's account of the justice of transactions as presented in *Capital*.

Although I quoted this passage in my earlier article, Husami never mentions it. Perhaps he would say that here too Marx is not talking about what is really just or unjust, but about what is "considered just" on the basis of the present mode of production or about the "dominant conceptions" of justice. Here again this reading would turn Marx's trenchant criticism into an irrelevancy. For the Lassalleans who drew up the Gotha Program's demand were presumably not denying that the present distribution is commonly considered just or that it might be just according to (false) dominant conceptions. Their demand is that distribution should be *really* just, just according to a correct conception of justice. Unless Marx is talking about what he himself considers to be really just when he expresses his agreement with what the bourgeois assert, he is not saying anything which is relevant to the Gotha Program's demand for a "just distribution." Besides, if Husami's interpretation of Marx is correct, it is hard to see what Marx could possibly have against the simple demand for a "just distribution." For as Husami reads him, this is precisely Marx's own demand.

The other text I shall discuss is drawn from Marx's critical notes to Adolph Wagner's textbook on political economy. I shall quote two passages:

> This obscurantist foists on me the view that "surplus value, which is produced by the workers alone, remains with the capitalist entrepreneurs in a *wrongful* manner" [*ungebührlicher Weise*]. But I say the direct opposite: namely, that at a certain point, the production of commodities necessarily becomes "capitalistic" production of commodities, and that according to the *law of value* which rules that production, "surplus value" is due [*gebührt*] to the capitalist and not to the worker.

> In my presentation, the earnings on capital are not in fact [as Wagner alleges] "only a deduction or 'robbery' of the worker." On the contrary, I present the capitalist as a necessary functionary of capitalist production, and show at length that he does not only "deduct" or "rob" but forces the production of surplus value, and thus helps create what is to be deducted; further I show in detail that even if in commodity exchange *only equivalents* are exchanged, the capitalist—as soon as he pays the worker the actual value of his labor power—earns *surplus value* with full right, i.e. the right corresponding to this mode of production. [*MEW* 19: 382, 359.]

In these passages, there is absolutely no reason to think that Marx is speaking disingenuously when he postulates that the capitalist and the worker exchange equivalents, and says that the capitalist "earns surplus value with full right." Perhaps Husami would argue that Marx is implicitly contrasting the "right corresponding to this mode of production" with some other (better or truer) standard of right according to which Marx (again implicitly) condemns capitalism as unjust. But this strains credibility to the breaking point. Wagner reads Marx as holding that capitalism is unjust to the worker, that surplus value is not due (*gebührt*) to the capitalist, but is appropriated by him with no right, by a simple act of "deduction" or "robbery." Wagner surely must think that Marx makes such judgments relative, not merely to some commonly accepted standards of right or justice, but relative to standards which Marx himself accepts. If Marx's repudiation of the view Wagner "foists" on him referred only to standards of right which Marx does not accept, then it would not after all be a repudiation of Wagner's interpretation. I submit that the only natural reading of these passages is one which sees them as directly and explicitly (not to say indignantly) repudiating the very interpretation of Marx which Husami himself holds.

IV

Husami appears to concede (what I think is true) that Marx never explicitly says that capitalism is unjust or violates the workers' rights. Husami does not, however, concede this about Engels. To the contrary, his text says that Marx's explanation of surplus value "removed the last justification for all the hypocritical phrases of the possessing classes to the effect that in the present social order right and justice, equality of rights and duties and a general harmony of interests prevail" (Husami, p. 68). But this passage, as I read it, does not say directly that capitalism is unjust. Rather, it says that Marx's theory succeeds in refuting the apologetic phrases of those who defend capitalism by claiming (among other things) that it is just. Marx's theory does this in two ways: First, bourgeois moralists believe (as does Husami) that if capitalism exploits the workers, then it is unjust. Marx's theory thus brings their own moral beliefs into conflict with their apologetic claims, whether or not Marx agrees with those beliefs. Second, although Marx in a sense agrees with the apologists' claims that capitalism is just, it is clear, when we understand what his agreement comes to, that it constitutes no real defense of capitalist society.

But let us suppose that Engels *is* saying in this passage that capitalism is unjust. He nevertheless makes it quite explicit that he does not regard this as having any relevance to Marx's critique of capitalism: "According to the laws of political economy, the greatest part of the product does not belong to the workers who have produced it. Now if we say: that is unjust, that ought not to be, then this has nothing to do with economics. We are saying merely that this economic fact contradicts our moral feelings. Hence Marx never based his communist demands on this" (*MEW* 21: 178; *Poverty of Philosophy*, New

York, 1963, p. 11). This passage even gives us some reason to think
that Engels does not believe capitalism is unjust. For elsewhere he
insists that objective social justice or injustice is not a matter of the
relation of social relations to our moral feelings, but is "decided by
the science which deals with the material facts of production and
exchange, the science of political economy" (*Kleine ökonomische
Schriften*, Berlin, 1955, p. 412). This remark, of course, sounds very
similar to Marx's account of justice in *Capital*. Engels also has similar
disparaging things to say about people who condemn slavery in the
ancient world as an unjust institution (*MEW* 20: 169; *Anti-Dühring*,
Moscow, 1962, p. 250).

Of course, Marx does say in many places that capital exploits the
worker, and Husami claims that Marx believes all exploitation is unjust (p. 73). He cites no passages, however—and I know of none he
could cite—where Marx says anything of the kind. Admittedly it sounds
paradoxical to say that Marx believes exploitation can be just. But it
was precisely to help explain this apparent paradox that I wrote my
earlier essay. Husami, however, cites other passages which must
sound even more paradoxical to anyone tempted by my interpretation
of Marx. He cites passages where Marx calls the appropriation of
surplus value not only "exploitation" of the worker, but even "theft"
and "robbery." In effect, Husami uses these passages as decisive proof
in favor of his claim that Marx criticizes capitalism for its injustice
to the workers. But to do so, he must ascribe the following argument
to Marx: "If the capitalist *robs* the worker, then he appropriates what
is not rightfully his own or he appropriates what rightfully belongs to
the worker. Thus there is no meaningful sense in which the capitalist
can simultaneously rob the worker and treat him justly" (Husami,
p. 45).

Whatever the intrinsic merits of this argument, however, it is quite
evident that Marx does not accept it. For in the notes on Wagner, Marx
agrees that he says the capitalist "robs" the worker, but nevertheless
insists (in the same sentence) that on his theory the capitalist "earns
surplus value with full right." Plainly the sort of "robbery" or "theft"
involved in capital's exploitation of labor is not one which Marx sees

as constituting an injustice to those who are robbed or a violation of their rights.

What sort of "robbery" does Marx have in mind when he describes capitalist exploitation using this term? I suggest that he is not thinking of the practices of thieves, burglars, or holdup men who might steal your car, break into your house, or take your purse on a dark street. The capitalist class for Marx stands to the proletariat in a relation somewhat analogous to that of a conquering people to a less organized and less well-armed (but more productive) population which it regularly plunders, or from which—in lieu of this—it exacts tribute.[7] If this is the analogy, then it is not so clear that "robbery" has to be unjust, given Marx's conception of justice. For (as Marx and Engels observe) the relationship between plunderers or conquerors and their victims or tributaries is not something economically accidental, but—insofar as it constitutes part of a regular way of life for the two groups—must constitute a regular production relation and be determined by the existing stage of development of the victims' productive powers.[8] Hence there is good reason to think that the regular transactions (ranging from military incursions to the collection of taxes) between plunderers and plundered do correspond, in Marx's view, to the prevailing mode of production and are therefore just according to Marx's conception of justice. Likewise, if this is the analogy, there is good reason to think that Marx regarded capitalist "robbery" of the worker as right and just, as the passage from the Wagner notes says it is. In the case of capitalism, moreover, the robbers even play a positive role in production on Marx's theory, "helping to create" what they steal.

Along with Husami, I believe that one essential feature of all economic exploitation for Marx is coercion. The conqueror coerces by the sword; the capitalist, more subtle and civilized, coerces through his control over the means of production. That is, he coerces through the constant threat of depriving the worker of his means of livelihood

---

7. As Husami notes (p. 68), Marx explicitly uses this analogy. See *Capital* 1: 162, 582.

8. *MEW* 3: 64; *Collected Works* (New York, 1976), 5: 84–85 (hereafter cited as *CW*).

unless he continues to produce surplus value for capital. Marx's frequent insinuations that capital not only robs but also cheats or defrauds the worker are due to Marx's belief that capital's coercion is disguised by the *fictio juris* of the voluntary contract between individual capitalists and workers. But very few people would hold that all coercion as such is unjust, and there is no reason to ascribe any such view to Marx. No doubt the coercion involved in capital's exploitation of labor strikes many of us as unjust (it "contradicts our moral feelings," as Engels would put it). But whether Marx shares the opinions represented by these feelings is precisely the point at issue. Some moral theorists hold that all talk about coercion depends on assumptions (implicit or explicit) about people's rights. As I read Marx, he is committed to rejecting any such account of the nature of coercion.

V

Husami complains that my interpretation of Marx "makes it impossible for the oppressed to criticize the injustice of their life situations" (p. 52). But in Marx's view, this involves only the abandonment of "ideological shuffles" and does not affect any of the real grounds the workers have for overthrowing capitalism. Similarly, the fact that the capitalist has a "full right" to his surplus value does not in the least imply that the workers should not do everything in their power to deprive him of it.

Husami (pp. 73-74) appears to believe that my interpretation of Marx commits Marx to "the all-or-none principle": to the view that workers should try to overthrow capitalism, but should not put forth any effort to raise their wages or improve their lot within capitalism. But all it really commits Marx to is refusing to regard such efforts (which of course he strongly supports) as rectifying injustices. In my earlier article I said that "any 'reforms' of capitalist production which proposed to take surplus value away from capital . . . would be injustices" (Wood, p. 27). But I never meant to imply that Marx sees this as any argument against taking surplus value away from capital. On the contrary, Marx is an outspoken advocate of what he calls

"despotic encroachments on property rights" in the interest of eman-
cipating the oppressed (*MEW* 4: 481; *CW* 6: 504).

What *are* the workers' real grounds for abolishing capitalism? My
earlier essay did not convey my real views if it created the impression
that "Marx's opposition [to capitalism] is limited to a number of technical and sociohistorical analyses of the nature and fate of private
property."[9] I agree with Husami that Marx's reasons for condemning
capitalism rest on the fact that (according to Marx) the capitalist
system deprives people of such essential human goods as freedom,
community, and self-actualization. But Husami wonders whether I
can agree with him here without attributing an inconsistency to Marx:

> . . . Tucker and Wood state that Marx criticizes capitalism, at least
> in part, for its inequality and unfreedom. But if the *only* applicable
> norm of justice is the one that accords with the capitalist mode of
> production then, similarly, the only applicable norms of equality
> and freedom must be the ones that accord with this mode of produc-
> tion. Consequently, the position taken by Tucker and Wood implies
> that Marx could not have validly criticized capitalist freedom as
> unfreedom and capitalist equality as inequality. For him to have
> done so presupposes the use of standards of freedom and equality
> that are incongruent with the capitalist mode of production. But
> neither Wood nor Tucker detect any inconsistency in Marx on this
> score. [Husami, pp. 52-53.]

I agree with Husami that Marx's condemnations of capitalism are
based on appeals to values such as self-actualization, community, and
freedom. About "equality" I am less certain. The *Critique of the Gotha
Program* (*MEW* 19: 20-21; *SW* 324) makes it quite clear that Marx
is no friend to the idea that "equality" is something good in itself. But
Marx also clearly believes that the systematic disparities between
wealth and social power of different social groups (what Marx would
prefer to call "class oppression") have pernicious consequences for
such things as freedom, community, and self-actualization. In this
sense, it seems to be true that he condemns capitalism because of its

9. See George G. Brenkert, "Freedom and Private Property in Marx," above,
pp. 80-105, hereafter cited as Brenkert.

"inequality." Both Marx's endorsement of the demand for equality, when and only when it is understood in this sense, and his suspicions about equality as an ideological notion are confirmed by Engels. After pointing to the bourgeois origins of the ideal of equality, the latter continues: "The demand for equality in the mouth of the proletariat has a double significance. Either it is . . . a natural reaction against crying social inequalities, against the contrast between . . . those who surfeit and those who starve: . . . simply an expression of the revolutionary instinct . . . ; or else it has arisen in reaction against the bourgeois demand for equality, . . . serving as a means of agitation in order to stir the workers up against the capitalists using the capitalists' own assertions, and in this case it stands or falls with bourgeois equality itself. In both cases the actual content of the proletarian demand for equality is the demand for the *abolition of classes*" (*MEW* 20: 99; *Anti-Dühring*, pp. 147-148).

Of course Marx never describes freedom or self-actualization (as he does describe right and justice) as the correspondence of anything to prevailing production relations. But this does not imply that he is inconsistent. All it implies is that his conceptions of right and justice differ in this respect from his conceptions of freedom and self-actualization. The only question provoked by Husami's remarks is, What is this difference? This question raises some deep issues, which I did not address in my earlier essay. The main reason I did not do so is that the Marxian texts are almost totally silent about these issues, and so any attempt to say what Marx thought about them must be rather speculative. Here I shall present only a sketch of my own speculations. The most I claim for what I am about to say is that it seems to me the best explanation for the things Marx actually says, and it is not explicitly contradicted by anything in the texts. (This is more than can be said for Husami's interpretation of Marx on distributive justice.) Even if I am completely wrong in ascribing the following views to Marx, there is still no reason to think that Marx (as I interpret him) is inconsistent until it is shown that he must view such values as freedom, community, and self-actualization in the same way as he views right and justice.

My suggestion, then, is this: right and justice are juridical or moral notions. As such, they must be distinguished from non-moral goods such as self-actualization, community, and freedom. Juridical and moral facts, in Marx's view, are facts about the relation of an act, transaction, or institution to the prevailing mode of production. The fact that people are free or unfree, self-actualized or alienated depends on the degree to which they understand and control the conditions of their existence, and the degree to which these conditions enable them to develop and exercise what Marx calls their "human essential powers" (*menschliche Wesenskräfte*). Here I agree with Brenkert, when he insists that there is a "contrast in Marx's thought between justice and freedom" (Brenkert, p. 93). Social relations may promote or inhibit freedom, community, or self-actualization, but the content of these three is not determined by the correspondence to prevailing social relations of what people are or do. Justice, right, and other moral standards, however, have no meaning or content apart from that which is given them by their function as norms within a given mode of production.

Marx never draws a distinction between moral and non-moral goods. But the distinction is a familiar one (both in philosophy and in everyday life) and it is not implausible to suppose that Marx observes it, even if he never consciously attends to it.

Surely we all know the difference between valuing or doing something because conscience or the "moral law" tells us we "ought" to, and valuing or doing something because it satisfies our needs, our wants, or our conception of what is good for us (or for someone else whose welfare we want to promote—desires for non-moral goods are not necessarily selfish desires). This difference roughly marks off "moral" goods from "nonmoral" goods as I mean to use those terms here. Non-moral goods include such things as pleasure and happiness, things which we would regard as desirable and good for people to have even if no moral credit accrued from pursuing or attaining them. Freedom, community, and self-actualization are pretty clearly goods of which this is true. Moral goods, on the other hand, include such things as virtue, right, justice, the fulfillment of duty, and the possession or cultivation of morally meritorious qualities of character. The two kinds of goods, though different, may not be unrelated.

It is arguable that qualities we esteem as morally good (such as benevolence, courage, and self-control) are also non-morally good for us to have. On the other hand, some moral theorists (such as utilitarians) believe that what is morally good is determined by what is conducive to the greatest non-moral good. (The fact that Marx sees no fundamental moral defects in capitalism while insisting that it produces misery and unfulfillment for the vast majority is strong evidence that he has no great sympathy with theories of this kind.) Moralists typically hold that people have rights to non-moral goods (such as freedom or economic opportunity) and that justice requires a certain distribution of non-moral goods (such as wealth or social power). But the various interrelations (real or imagined) between moral and non-moral theory at all" (Brenkert, p. 102). Brenkert insists, however, that

VI

Brenkert does not admit that freedom for Marx is a non-moral good. But the issue between him and myself may be in part only verbal. He says: "Marx is sometimes thought to have a non-moral notion of freedom because he is supposed to have a utilitarian view of morality. Freedom, then, is one of the non-moral goods to be maximized. But, fairly clearly, Marx is not a utilitarian. His notion of freedom is also said to be non-moral inasmuch as he is thought not to have held a moral theory at all" (Brenkert, p. 144). Brenkert insists, however, that Marx does hold such a theory.

Now I agree with Brenkert that Marx is not a utilitarian. I do, however, think that Marx regards freedom and other non-moral goods as something to be pursued and even to be maximized, to the extent that one can make sense of this phrase in the case of such heterogeneous and nonquantifiable goods as freedom, community, and self-actualization. Marx is not a utilitarian because (among other things) he regards moral standards as determined by the requirements of the prevailing mode of production and not by the pursuit of the greatest non-moral good.

I think I am even forced to agree that Marx "holds a moral theory," when I realize that by a "moral theory" Brenkert means "a view which relates to some fundamental good for all humans which is of over-riding importance" (Brenkert, p. 104). But I would question whether Marx believes there is only one such good, as this formula implies. Perhaps Brenkert means to use the term "fundamental" in such a way that there can be only one "fundamental" good. In that case, I would deny that freedom (or anything else) is a fundamental good for Marx, and say instead that such things as freedom, security, comfort, community and self-actualization are in his view all highly important human goods, which he believes capitalism frustrates.

Given Brenkert's sense of "moral theory," and assuming that a "moral good" is any good which figures fundamentally in a "moral theory," no one who agrees that freedom for Marx is a "fundamental human good" can consistently deny that freedom for Marx is a "moral good." But Brenkert's understanding of the terms "moral theory" and "moral good" comes close to trivializing the claims that Marx holds a "moral theory" and that freedom is for him a "moral good." In so doing, it muddles the issues raised by these claims.

Consider the case of Friedrich Nietzsche. I think it is a fair representation of his views to say that he condemns all morality, all moral principles, values, and goals, because he thinks they are detrimental to (even hostile to) certain goods (such as strength, creativity, and abundant life) which he thinks are fundamentally important to human beings, and preferable to what people esteem on moral grounds. But if (following Brenkert) we say that any view at all about what is fundamentally good for human beings is a "moral theory" and any good which figures in such a view is a "moral good," then Nietzsche's own view that strength, creativity, and abundant life are fundamental goods must count as a moral theory, and these goods must count among the moral values Nietzsche himself is attacking. But Nietzsche's attack on morality surely does not involve a trivial incoherence of this kind, even if it is incoherent in other ways. The natural thing to say is that not everything someone regards as fundamentally good for human beings counts as a "moral good," and in Nietzsche's case the fundamental goods are conceived by him as non-moral (even anti-moral). The conclusion to be drawn is that Brenkert's sense of "moral" is too inclusive to be useful in describing views like Nietzsche's.

As I read him, Marx is, like Nietzsche, a critic of morality. Like Nietzsche, he seeks to understand the actual function in human life of moral values and standards, and to make an assessment of them on the basis of non-moral goods. (Marx's assessment, though, seems to me less wholeheartedly negative than Nietzsche's.) Perhaps this reading of Marx is altogether mistaken. But we cannot consider it seriously at all until we cease to understand "moral good" in the extremely inclusive sense Brenkert does. I suggest that right and justice are moral goods while freedom, community, and self-actualization are non-moral goods. This is intended to explain the "contrast" Brenkert notes between Marx's views about moral and non-moral goods. We pursue the first solely or chiefly on account of the moral merit attaching to them; the second we would find desirable, even abstracted from considerations of moral praiseworthiness and blameworthiness.

This distinction between moral and non-moral goods is certainly one moral philosophers have been aware of. Kant is clearly cognizant of it when he distinguishes the "moral" good from the "natural" (or "physical") good, or the "good" (*Gut*) from "well-being" (*Wohl*).[10] Mill acknowledges it when he distinguishes the "utilitarian theory of life" (a hedonistic theory about the non-moral good) from the "utilitarian theory of morality" (which holds that the moral good consists in what is conducive to the greatest non-moral good). The distinction even makes possible two of the basic issues on which Kant and Mill disagree:

A. Does the pursuit of moral good ultimately diverge from the pursuit of non-moral good?
B. Which good is the more fundamental and (if the two ultimately diverge) the overriding human good?

On issue *A*, Kant returns an affirmative answer, while Mill gives a negative one. Kant of course does not think the two kinds of good are

10. See Kant, *Gesammelte Schriften*, Berlin Academy Edition, 5: 59-60; *Critique of Practical Reason* tr. L. W. Beck (New York, 1956), pp. 61-62. See also John Stuart Mill, *Utilitarianism* (Indianapolis, 1957), p. 10.

incompatible or diametrically opposed, only that what morality demands is sometimes in conflict with the greatest non-moral good (which he sees as the welfare only of the sensuous part of our nature). Mill recognizes that the moral good may conflict with particular lots of non-moral good (a particular pleasure, or the happiness of a particular person or group). But since what is morally good is determined by what is conducive to the greatest total non-moral good, there can be no ultimate divergence.

On issue *B*, Kant holds that the moral good is the unconditioned good, which must take precedence whenever the two goods conflict. Mill, since he sees morality merely as a device for maximizing the nonmoral good, holds the latter to be fundamental.

As I read him, Marx agrees with Kant on issue *A* and with Mill on issue *B*. But this means that unlike either of them, he can hold that the non-moral good systematically overrides the moral good in certain situations. I think this is, in effect, what he is doing when he advocates the overthrow of capitalism while agreeing that it is just. (But perhaps this is a misleading way to put it. For I do not think Marx regards the justice of obsolete social institutions as any defense at all of them; in urging the overthrow of capitalism's inhuman exploitation, Marx does not have to contend with any regrets springing from the fact that it is just.) Another way in which I think Marx differs from both Kant and Mill is that their theories of the non-moral good are hedonistic, whereas I see no reason to ascribe any such view to Marx.

VII

Marx often bases his condemnation of capitalism explicitly on its failure to provide people with non-moral goods (freedom, community, self-actualization, security) which the existing powers of social production might yield if society were organized more rationally. But unless we use "moral theory" as Brenkert does, it is a mistake to jump to the conclusion that Marx holds some moral theory according to which we have a duty to provide people with the non-moral goods to which he alludes. Marx never claims that these goods ought to be provided to people because they have a right to them or because justice (or some other moral norm) demands it.

Remarks made in a well-known early essay (1843), seem to me too slight to support the thesis that Marx's critique of capitalism throughout his career is morally based.[11] In general, I see no ground for postulating a fundamental discontinuity or "break" between Marx's early writings and his mature theory. But in a few cases (this is one of them) there does seem to be a definite shift of attitude. If the passages from the 1843 essay are expressions of a morally based criticism of capitalism, then the absence of any similar passages from his later writings and the consistent disparagement of morally based social criticism certainly provides strong evidence that Marx changed his views on this point as he developed his materialist conception of history, and his interpretation of morality as a social phenomenon.

There is evidence that Marx's concern with the working class movement may be prompted in part by moral considerations (or at least by a distaste for the sort of person he would be if he were indifferent to human suffering).[12] But Marx never appeals to such considerations in urging others to support the movement. Evidently he is persuaded that the obvious non-moral value of these goods is sufficient, quite apart from appeals to our love of virtue or sense of guilt, to convince any reasonable person to favor the overthrow of a social order which unnecessarily frustrates them, and to advocate its replacement by a social order which realizes them.

On the other hand, Marx consistently avoids social criticism based on moral goods or norms, and consistently exhibits an attitude of suspicion and hostility toward those who do engage in such criticism. Likewise, he is angered by those who, like Wagner, interpret Marx

11. Marx does say that "the essential sentiment [of criticism] is indignation," and that "the critique of religion ends with the doctrine that man is the highest being for man, and thus with the categorical imperative to overthrow all relations in which man is a debased, enslaved, forsaken and despicable being" (MEW 1: 380, 385; CW 3: 177, 182). Compare Engels' early essay, Outlines of a Critique of Political Economy (CW 3: 418-443), where both the capitalist economic system and Malthus' theory of population are repeatedly condemned as "immoral."

12. See Selected Correspondence, p. 185.

himself as putting forward a critique of capitalism which is morally based. The reason for this, I think, is that whereas Marx views non-moral goods as founded on the actual (though historically conditioned and variable) potentialities, needs, and interests of human beings, he sees moral norms as having no better rational foundation than their serviceability to transient forms of human social intercourse, and most fundamentally to the needs of a given mode of production.

This rather skeptical attitude toward the rational foundation of morality is made explicit at several places. The *German Ideology* claims that historical materialism has "broken the staff of all morality" by exhibiting the connection between morality and the conditions of life out of which it arises. When an imaginary bourgeois critic charges that "communism does away with religion and morality instead of forming them anew," the *Communist Manifesto* replies, not by denying that the charge is true, but by observing that "the communist revolution is the most radical break with traditional property relations; no wonder that in the course of its development there is the most radical break with traditional ideas" (*MEW* 3: 404; *CW* 5: 419; *MEW* 4: 480-481; *CW* 6: 504).

Such flashy, iconoclastic passages as these probably give us an exaggerated picture of the extent to which Marx regards historical materialism as undermining morality. I believe Marx does unqualifiedly reject moral standards as acceptable vehicles of social criticism or apologetics (at least in situations of fundamental social revolution, where the entire framework of a given mode of production is to be challenged or defended). But I very much doubt that he rejects morality as a legitimate ground for approving or disapproving of the conduct of individuals, or for judging the attitudes people take toward social institutions. Certainly Marx's own writings (throughout his career) seethe with moral indignation against the callousness, complacency, and hypocrisy of people who can tolerate (and even have the gall to defend) a social system which needlessly condemns the vast majority to lives of unfreedom, alienation, and misery. Marx's moralistic self-indulgence here contrasts strikingly with his abstemious and even contemptuous attitude toward the use of moral norms and values (such as right and justice) in the criticism or defense of basic social

arrangements themselves. I believe this contrast has a credible explanation, though I shall not attempt to give it here. At least there is no
obvious inconsistency between morally condemning people's complacency in the face of massive and remediable, non-moral evil, and
refusing to condemn morally the non-moral evil itself. But on the
question of whether communist society will really "do away with all
morality instead of forming it anew," it is difficult to reconcile the
Manifesto with Engels' prospect of an "actual human morality," which
lies beyond class society (*MEW* 20: 88; *Anti-Dühring*, 132). This
difficulty remains, whatever interpretation of Marx's views on morality we adopt, and probably represents a genuine tension between the
Communist Manifesto and *Anti-Dühring*.

Husami points out that Marx does not confuse the "social origin
of ideas with their truth" (p. 40). Marx never argues that an idea is
true merely because it is a proletarian idea, or false merely because
it is a bourgeois idea. But I think he does believe that in the case of
moral ideas, as in the case of religious ones, a materialist explanation
of ideas with their truth" (p. 55). Marx never argues that an idea is
is to support a particular social order and to serve as a mask for class
interests. The fact that moral standards and ideas serve such functions does not by itself show that they have no other rational foundation than this; but I think Marx's view is that once we come to see what
the appeal of moral and religious ideas really rests on, we will no
longer be in thrall to them, and we will at last be in a position to
recognize (what is evident on other grounds) that they have no firmer
foundation than the one Marx's theory gives them.

VIII

The moral standards which serve a given social order simultaneously
promote the interests of the oppressing classes within that social order.
The oppressed, however, have interests too, and these interests may
also be represented by moral ideologies (see Husami, p. 47). Why
doesn't Marx condemn capitalism morally by appealing to standards
drawn from proletarian ideology? The answer, I believe, is this. The
fact that capitalism is just (by the standards appropriate to capitalist

production) provides no rational defense of capitalist society. Likewise, the fact that it could be condemned as unjust by applying some
foreign standard constitutes no valid criticism of capitalist relations.
The rational content of proletarian moral ideologies consists in the
real proletarian interests represented by these ideologies, and the
(non-moral) goods which will come about as a result of the victory
of these interests in the historical struggle. Marx prefers to criticize
capitalism directly in terms of this rational content, and sees no point
in presenting his criticisms in the mystified form they would assume
in a moral ideology.

Engels of course does speak of the "proletarian morality of the
future" in contrast to the "Christian-feudal morality" and the "modern
bourgeois morality." But neither Marx nor Engels ever employs the
standards of this future morality to condemn the present social order.
In fact, Engels explicitly denies that the "proletarian morality of the
future" is "true" as contrasted with its predecessors. In its behalf he
claims only that it represents a higher type of society (as measured,
presumably, by the non-moral goods people will enjoy in this society),
and that it promises greater permanence and applicability to the
future than the Christian or bourgeois moralities (*MEW* 20: 87; *Anti-
Dühring*, 130).

Husami provides a long discussion of the principles "to each according to his labor-time" and "from each according to his ability, to each
according to his needs." He evidently believes that in the context of
the *Critique of the Gotha Program* these principles are intended as
"proletarian" principles of justice against which Marx is measuring
capitalist distribution and (implicitly) declaring it to be unjust. But
this seems to me a mistake. I agree with Husami that Marx "indicates
these principles will be realized in post-capitalist society," since his
point in introducing them is to predict what distribution will probably
be like once the workers have taken control. But I can see no foundation at all for Husami's view that these principles "are presented as
suitable for adoption by a proletarian party" (Husami, p. 46). Marx
nowhere suggests that the Gotha Program is defective because it failed
to include these or any other principles of distributive justice. On the
contrary, as his caustic remarks about the demand for "a just distribu-

tion" indicate, Marx's *basic* criticism of section 3 of the Gotha Program
is that demands phrased in terms of right and justice should not be
included in a working class program at all.[13] Marx sketches the pro-
spective mode of distribution in post-capitalist society merely in order
to make the additional (and subsidiary) point that the demands made
by the Gotha Program are particularly vague, crude, and naive. He
then goes on to criticize the idea that "equal right" (however we conceive it) is an end in itself by showing how it necessarily leads to a
defective mode of distribution even in its socialist form. To do away
with these defects, he says, one must "wholly transcend the narrow
horizon of bourgeois right" represented by all principles of equality.
Marx alludes to Louis Blanc's slogan "from each according to his
abilities, to each according to his needs" precisely because this is not
in any sense a principle of "equality"; it does not treat people alike or
equally from any point of view but considers them simply as individuals with their own special needs and faculties. Marx emphasizes
that there will be different (progressively higher) systems of distribution in post-capitalist society in order to drive home the point
that no demands based on specific principles of distribution can really
represent the long-term goals of the working class. Finally, he condemns the distributive orientation as a whole, and with it the "crime"
of "forcing on our party again, as dogmas, ideas which had meaning
for a certain time but now have become obsolete trash phrases, while
again perverting the realistic viewpoint (brought into the party with
so much trouble) with ideological shuffles about right and other
things" (*MEW* 19: 21-22; *SW* 325). Husami seems to me to have
seriously misread the entire section of the *Critique of the Gotha Program* from which he draws his cherished proletarian principles of
justice.

Marx does not hold that an idea is true merely because it is a proletarian idea. If Marx had condemned capitalism by measuring it
against Husami's "proletarian norms of justice," then it would still
be quite pertinent to inquire after the rational foundation of these
norms, and the grounds for regarding them as applicable to capital-

---

13. For Marx's reluctance to include any talk about "duty, right, truth, morality or justice" in such documents, see *Selected Correspondence*, p. 148.

ism. These questions are not settled (and Marx does not think they can be settled) merely by calling these norms "proletarian" or even by showing that their popularization or satisfaction would serve proletarian interests. For Marx, as I read him, standards of justice based on correspondence to the existing mode of production can be given some sort of rational foundation (albeit one which makes them worthless both critically and apologetically). Alternative "proletarian" standards, however, cannot be given even that much foundation.

The only thing which might be said for alternative standards is that people whose heads are stuffed with this ideological fluff would be easier converts to the proletarian cause. But one of the chief aims of that cause, as Marx pictures it, is to enable people to disenthrall themselves of all ideology, to cast off the need for it. To create a "proletarian morality" or "proletarian concept of justice" by disseminating a set of ideas which working-class agitators find politically advantageous would strike Marx as a shortsighted and self-defeating course for the movement to adopt. It is far safer and more efficacious in the long run to rely simply on the genuine (non-moral) reasons people have for wanting an obsolete and inhuman social system to be overthrown and replaced by a higher form of society.

Utilitarians will probably say here that (given Marx's other beliefs) "proletarian" standards of right and justice might be grounded on the fact that their adoption would have (non-morally) good consequences. This, however, does not show that these standards are actually valid for existing society, but only that it would be nice if there existed a social order in which they were valid. (It does not show, in other words, that the exploitative transactions between capital and labor are actually unjust; it shows only that it would be nice if there existed a social order to which exploitative transactions would not correspond, and in which, therefore, such transactions would all be unjust.) To think that a moral standard is actually valid wherever its adoption would promote the greatest non-moral good is (on Marx's social theory) to entertain a false and fantastic conception of the actual role morality plays in human society (a conception which has proven its "utility" for the classes whose interests are served by the moral standards which do correspond to the prevailing mode of production).

Some utilitarians, however, might agree with Marx that the moral standards which have prevailed in society up to now have not been conducive to the greatest non-moral good. But they will reply that the real force of their utilitarianism is only that moral standards conducive to the greatest non-moral good *should* prevail. The "should" here must not be construed morally; for if it were, our utilitarians would be appealing to some as yet unjustified moral standard to ground the moral standards they claim to be giving a non-moral foundation. But in that case, why don't they say directly (without the mystification of moral talk) that social production "should" be organized in such a way as to maximize the non-moral good? The main reason, I think, is that these utilitarians still believe quite uncritically that "economic relations are ruled by juridical conceptions," that the right way to bring about economic changes is to reform the moral ideas people carry around in their heads. Marx, on the contrary, holds that both the prevailing moral ideologies and the moral or juridical relations which are valid for a given society arise out of the economic relations belonging to its mode of production. Changes in the prevailing standards of right and justice do not cause social revolutions but only accompany them. This, of course, is not to deny that bringing about changes in the moral, legal, and political superstructure of society is for Marx an important subordinate moment of revolutionary practice. But on Marx's theory, new standards of right come to be valid *because* revolutionary changes occur in economic relations; it is *not* the case that revolutions do occur or should occur because postrevolutionary standards of right are *already* valid for pre-revolutionary society. (See Wood, pp. 26-31.)

Perhaps there is excessive harshness in Marx's skeptical attitude toward the rational basis of morality and toward the worth of moral standards for social criticism. Marx may owe an argument (which he never really provides) to the many who believe that standards of right and justice can be given stronger foundations and a wider range of applicability than the Marxian theory accords them. Certainly anyone who wishes to defend Marx's view owes some reply to the moral theorists who claim to have put justice on a firmer basis. If Marx is mistaken here, then it may prove advisable (or even imperative) for Marxists to see how far his critique of capitalism can be used to support the claim that capitalism is unjust as measured by whatever standards of justice can be given this stronger rational foundation. To those who wish to undertake this task Husami's paper may prove helpful, by identifying some relevant Marxian doctrines and texts. But I continue to believe that Marx's actual views about right and justice are sufficiently unconventional, interesting, and plausible to be worth considering for their own sake.

G. A. COHEN

The Labor Theory of Value and the Concept of Exploitation

> It is we who ploughed the prairies, built the cities where they trade,
> Dug the mines and built the workshops, endless miles of railroad laid,
> Now we stand outcast and starving, 'mid the wonders we have made. . . .
>
> "Solidarity," by Ralph Chaplin (to the tune of "Battle Hymn of the Republic")

This essay shows that the relationship between the labor theory of value and the concept of exploitation is one of mutual irrelevance. The labor theory of value is not a suitable basis for the charge of exploitation laid against capitalism by Marxists, and the real foundation of that charge is something much simpler which, for reasons to be stated, is widely confused with the labor theory of value.

I

I begin with a short exposition of the labor theory of value as we find it in Volume 1 of *Capital*. (Differences between Volume 1 and later parts of *Capital* will be adverted to later.) I shall first define the term "value," and then state what the labor theory says about what it denotes. What follows is one way of presenting the first few pages of Volume 1 of *Capital*. Having completed the presentation, I shall describe a different way, which I do not think is right.

It is convenient to define value by reference to exchange-value, with which we therefore begin.

Exchange-value is a property of things which are desired; in Marxian language, then, it is a property of use-values.[1] It is, however, a property, not of all use-values, but of those use-values which are bought and sold, which undergo market transactions. Such use-values Marxism calls "commodities." Exchange-value, then, is a property of commodities.

What property is it? The exchange-value of a commodity is its power of exchanging against quantities of other commodities. It is measured by the number of commodities of any other kind for which it will exchange under equilibrium conditions. Thus the exchange-value of a coat might be eight shirts, and also three hats, and also ten pounds sterling.

Exchange-value is a relative magnitude. Underlying the exchange-value of a commodity is its value, an absolute magnitude. A commodity a has n units of commodity b as its exchange-value just in case the ratio between the values of a and b is $n : 1$. The exchange-values relative to one another of two commodities will remain the same when each changes in value if the changes are identical in direction and proportion.

The central claim of the labor theory of value is that magnitude of value is determined by socially necessary labor time. To be more precise: the exchange-value of a commodity varies directly and uniformly with the quantity of labor time required to produce it under standard conditions of productivity, and inversely and uniformly with the quantity of labor time standardly required to produce other commodities, and with no further circumstance. The first condition alone states the mode of determination of value *tout court*.

The labor theory of value is not true by the very definition of value, as we defined it. In alternative presentations of the opening pages of Volume 1, value is *defined* as socially necessary labor time. But a stipulative definition of a technical term is not a theory, and when value is defined as socially necessary labor time, it cannot also be a central theoretical claim of the labor theory that socially necessary labor time determines value. Still, those who favor the alternative definition

1. Fuller definitions of the technical terms used here will be found in my *Karl Marx's Theory of History* (Oxford and Princeton, 1978), Appendix II.

sometimes do advance to a theoretical thesis, namely that value determines (long-run) equilibrium price: in equilibrium, price equals value, the latter being defined in terms of socially necessary labor time.

The size of this dispute can be exaggerated. We have two propositions:

(1) Socially necessary labor time determines value.

(2) Value determines equilibrium price.

We say that (2) is true by definition. Others say that (1) is.[2] But whoever is right, the conjunction of (1) and (2) entails that

(3) Socially necessary labor time determines equilibrium price,

and (3) is not true by definition, on any reckoning. As long as it is agreed that the labor theory of value, Volume 1 version, says (3), and that (3) is not true by definition, I do not wish to insist on my view that the definitional truth is (2) rather than (1). Almost all of what follows could be restated so as to accommodate the other definition. (One bad reason why the other definition finds favor will be presented later.)

We now turn to a supposed[3] corollary of the labor theory of value, the labor theory of surplus value.

The labor theory of surplus value is intended to explain the origin of non-wage income under capitalism. Call the energies and faculties the worker uses when laboring his *labor power*. Now note that under capitalism labor power is a commodity. It is sold in temporal packets by the worker to the capitalist. Being a commodity, it has a value, and like any commodity its value is, according to (1), determined by the amount of time required to produce it. But the amount of time required to produce it is identical with the amount of time required to produce the means of subsistence of the worker, since a man's labor power is produced if and only if he is produced. Thus "the value

3. The labor theory of surplus value is not, as I shall show elsewhere, validly derived from the labor theory of value.

2. For example, Ronald Meek, in *Smith, Ricardo and Marx* (London, 1977), p. 95. Meek treats (1) as true by definition and (2) as the substantive thesis. He acknowledges on p. 127 that the issue is contestable.

of labour power is the value of the means of subsistence necessary for
the maintenance of the labourer."[4] The origin of non-wage income is,
then, the difference between the value of labor power and the value
produced by him in whom it inheres. It is the difference between the
amount of time it takes to produce what is needed to keep a producer
in being for a certain period and the amount of time he spends producing during that period.

The capital paid out as wages is equal to the value of the producer's
labor power. It is known as *variable capital*. The value produced by
the worker over and above that represented by variable capital is
called *surplus value*. The ratio of surplus value to variable capital is
called *the rate of exploitation*:

$$\begin{aligned} \text{The rate} \\ \text{of exploitation} \end{aligned} = \frac{\text{surplus value}}{\text{variable capital}}$$

$$= \frac{\text{surplus value}}{\text{value of labor power}}$$

$$= \frac{\text{time worked} - \text{time required to produce the worker}}{\text{time required to produce the worker}}$$

II

Why is the term "exploitation" used for what the rate of exploitation
is a rate of? Is it because the term, as used in that phrase, denotes a
kind of injustice? It is hard to think of any other good reason for using
such a term.

Yet many Marxists say that the Marxian concept of exploitation is
a *purely* scientific one, with no moral content. They say that to assert,
in the language of Marxism, that *a* exploits *b*, is to offer no condemnation or criticism of *a*, or of the arrangements under which *a* operates.
For them, (4) is false:

4. Karl Marx, *Capital*, vol. 1 (Moscow, 1961), p. 171. Strictly speaking, the
value of labor power is, according to Marx, the value of the means of subsistence
needed to reproduce the labor supply, and therefore includes the value of the
means of raising children. This complication, which does not benefit the theory,
will be ignored here.

(4) One reason for overthrowing capitalism is that it is a regime of exploitation (and exploitation is unjust).

Two kinds of Marxist deny (4). The first kind does so because he denies that there is *any* reason for overthrowing capitalism. One just does it, as it were. Or one does it because of one's class situation, or one's morally ungrounded identification with the class situation of other people.

The second kind believes that there are good reasons for overthrowing capitalism, but that injustice is not one of them, since justice, he says, is not a Marxian value. What is wrong with capitalism is not that it is unjust, but that it crushes human potential, destroys fraternity, encourages the inhumane treatment of man by man, and has other grave defects generically different from injustice.

Now I am certain that many Marxists have held (4), among them Karl Marx. But I shall not defend the last sentence. Marxists who deny it will find this essay less challenging, but I hope they will read it anyway. For while my main topic is the relationship between (4) and the labor theory of value, in pursuing it I uncover deep and neglected ambiguities in the labor theory of value itself, and no Marxist will deny that many Marxists do affirm the theory of value.

III

I begin with an argument which is based on the labor theory of value, and whose conclusion is that the worker is exploited, where that is taken to entail an injustice. We can call it the Traditional Marxian Argument. It may be attributed to those believers in (4) who hold that the labor theory of value supports (4):

      (5) Labor and labor alone creates value.
      (6) The laborer receives the value of his labor power.
      (7) The value of the product is greater than the value of his labor power.
∴   (8) The laborer receives less value than he creates.
      (9) The capitalist receives the remaining value.
∴ (10) The laborer is exploited by the capitalist.

Premise (5) comes from the labor theory of value, and the labor theory of surplus value supplies premises (6), (7), and (9).

This statement of the Traditional Marxian Argument is incomplete in two respects. First, an essential normative premise is not stated. Its content, in very general terms, is that, under certain conditions, it is (unjust) exploitation to obtain something from someone without giving him anything in return. To specify the conditions, and thereby make the premise more precise, is beyond the concern of this essay. A rough idea of exploitation, as a certain kind of lack of reciprocity, is all that we require.

The other incompleteness, also not to be rectified here, is the argument's failure, as stated, to characterize pertinent features of the relationship between capital and labor, such as the fact that the laborer is *forced*, by his propertylessness, to work for the capitalist. This disputed truth will not here receive the refined statement it deserves.[5]

Note, finally, that the Traditional Argument, like the rest of this essay, speaks of "*the* laborer" and "*the* capitalist," thereby individualizing the class relationship, in imitation of *Capital*'s practice. This sidesteps the problem of identifying the working and capitalist classes, which is greater now than it was in Marx's time. I am certain that the problem has a solution which preserves the application of arguments like the Traditional one, but it, too, is not provided in this paper.

IV

The Traditional Argument employs the labor theory of surplus value, which yields premises (6), (7), and (9). But they can be replaced by a truism, which will contribute no less well than they to the conclusion that the laborer is exploited. The result is this simpler Marxian argument (statement (11) is the truism):

5. One who disputes this truth is Robert Nozick, in *Anarchy, State, and Utopia* (New York, 1974), pp. 262-264. The truth is defended against Nozick in my "Robert Nozick and Wilt Chamberlain," in J. Arthur and W. H. Shaw, eds., *Justice and Economic Distribution* (Englewood Cliffs, 1978), pp. 257-259. Some refinements are attempted in my "Capitalism, Freedom and the Proletariat," in a *Festschrift* for Isaiah Berlin to appear in 1979.

(5) Labor and labor alone creates value.

(11) The capitalist receives some of the value of the product.

∴   (8) The laborer receives less value than he creates, and

(12) The capitalist receives some of the value the laborer creates.

∴   (10) The laborer is exploited by the capitalist.

The labor theory of *surplus* value is, then, unnecessary to the moral claim Marxists make when they say that capitalism is exploitative. It does not matter what *explains* the difference between the value the worker produces and the value he receives.[6] What matters is just that there is that difference. (Note that although the Simpler Marxian Argument drops the labor theory of surplus value, there is still *a* recognizable concept of surplus value in it, namely the difference between the value the worker produces and the value he receives; and the value he receives can still be called variable capital.)[7]

V

We began with the labor theory of value, the thesis that the value of a commodity is determined by the socially necessary labor time required to produce it. We have arrived at an argument whose conclusion is that the laborer is exploited by the capitalist, and which supposedly draws one of its controversial premises from the labor theory of value. That is premise (5), that labor and labor alone creates value. But we shall now show that the labor theory does not entail (5). It entails, moreover, that (5) is false.[8]

6. It does not matter to the moral claim about exploitation, even if it is interesting from other points of view.

7. It is the concept of variable capital, not that of the value of labor power, which is crucial in the key theoretical applications of the labor theory of value, for example, in the reproduction schemas, in the transformation of values into prices, in the doctrine of the tendency of the rate of profit to fall. *Capital* allows at least short-term divergences between the value of labor power and variable capital per laborer; and wherever there is such a divergence, it is the second, not the first, which must be inscribed in the relevant equations.

8. In the traditional sense of (5), according to which part of what is claimed in saying that labor creates value is that quantity of value is a function of quantity of labor. Other possible senses, such as that dealt with in section X below, are irrelevant here.

Suppose a commodity has a certain value at a time t. Then that value, says the labor theory, is determined by the socially necessary labor time required to produce a commodity of that kind. Let us now ask: required to produce it *when*? The answer is: at t, the time when it has the value to be explained. The amount of time required to produce it in the past, and, *a fortiori*, the amount of time actually spent producing it are magnitudes strictly irrelevant to its value, if the labor theory is true.

Extreme cases make the point clear. (a) Suppose there is a use-value a, which was produced in the past, when things such as a could come into being only through labor, but that labor is no longer required for things such as a to appear (perhaps a is a quantity of manna, produced by men at a time before God started what we imagine is His now usual practice of dropping it). Then according to the labor theory of value, a is valueless, despite the labor "embodied" in it. (b) Contrariwise, suppose there is a commodity b now on the market, and that b was not produced by labor, but that a great deal of labor is now required for b-like things to appear. (B might be a quantity of clean air bottled before it became necessary to manufacture clean air.) Then b has a value, even though no labor is "embodied" in it.[9]

These statements follow from the labor theory of value. The theory entails that past labor is irrelevant to how much value a commodity now has.[10] But past labor would not be irrelevant if it created the value

9. It might be objected that b cannot have a value for Marx, since he defines value for products of labor only. The textual point is probably correct (see *Capital*, vol. 1, p. 38, for support), but no wise defender of Marx will want to urge in his defense the unfortunate lack of generality of the labor theory. Still, if anyone is impressed by the objection, let him imagine that *very little* labor went into b. The crucial point, which the extreme examples are only meant to dramatize, is that there is, according to the labor theory, "continuous change of value-relations," since the amount of labor required to produce something of a certain kind is subject to variation. See *Capital*, vol. 2 (Moscow, 1957), p. 72.

10. Despite the misleading terminology in which it is cast, this is true even of Sraffa's "dated quantities of labour" analysis. See P. Sraffa, *Production of Commodities by Means of Commodities* (Cambridge, 1960), chap. 6; and I. Steedman, *Marx After Sraffa* (London, 1977), p. 70, fn. 3.

of the commodity. It follows that *labor does not create value, if the labor theory of value is true*.

Let us call the thesis that value is determined by socially necessary labor time—that is, the labor theory of value—*the strict doctrine*, and let us say that such sentences as (5), or ones which speak of value as embodied or congealed labor, belong to *the popular doctrine*. Strict and popular doctrine are commonly confused with one another, for several reasons. The least interesting reason—more interesting ones will be mentioned later—is that Marx often set formulations from the two doctrines side by side. Examples:

> The value of one commodity is to the value of any other, as the labour-time necessary for the production of the one is to the labour-time necessary for the production of the other. "As values, all commodities are only definite masses of congealed labour time."

> . . . so far as the *quantity of value* of a commodity is determined, according to my account, through the *quantity of labour-time contained in it* etc., then [it is determined] through the normal amount of labour which the production of an object costs etc. . . .[11]

I am not saying that Marx never showed any awareness of the difference between the strict and the popular doctrine. This sentence proves otherwise:

> What determines value is not the amount of labour time incorporated in products, but rather the amount of labour time currently necessary.[12]

"Currently necessary": at the time, that is, when the commodity has the given value. The relevant socially necessary labor time is that required now, not that required when it was produced:

11. For the first example, see *Capital*, vol. 1, pp. 39-40. (Marx is quoting from his earlier work, *A Contribution to the Critique of Political Economy*.) For the second, see "Notes on Adolph Wagner," in T. Carver, ed., *Karl Marx: Texts on Method* (Oxford, 1975), p. 184.

12. Karl Marx, *Grundrisse*, trans. M. Nicolaus (Harmondsworth, 1973), p. 135. I have replaced Nicolaus's "at a given moment" by "currently," which gives a more literal translation.

The value of every commodity . . . is determined not by the necessary labour-time contained in it, but by the social labour-time required for its reproduction.[13]

So I do not say that Marx was ignorant of the difference between
the two doctrines. But I do say that the difference is damaging to
key Marxian theses. It has grave implications, which are widely unnoticed and which were not noticed by Marx. Our chief concern is
with implications for the idea of exploitation. There are also implications for pure economic theory, some of which will occupy us in a
subsequent digression. But first let us look more carefully at the differences between the two formulations.

There are two reasons why the amount of labor which was actually
spent on a particular product might differ from the amount now
standardly required to produce that kind of product. The first is a
non-standard level of efficiency in the actual labor process, which can
be more or less efficient than the social norm. The second is technological change, which alters that norm.

Consider the case of inefficient labor. Marxists have always regarded it as a particularly inept criticism of the labor theory of value
to object that it entails that an inefficiently produced lamp has more
value than one produced efficiently and therefore in less time. And the
asserted consequence does indeed fail to follow from the strict doctrine. But why should it not follow from the popular doctrine? If
labor creates value by, as it were, congealing in the product, then if
more labor is spent, must not more labor congeal, and will there not
then be more value in the product?

The case of inefficient labor shows the incompatibility between the
strict and the popular doctrines. Marxists know about that case, but
they are nevertheless reluctant to reject the popular doctrine. After
all, the reason why both doctrines exist in Marxist culture, why neither one is enough, is that each has intellectual or political functions
(or both) of its own to fulfill. Accordingly, faced with problems such
as that of inefficient labor, many Marxists propose a mixed formula-

13. *Capital*, vol. 3 (Moscow, 1966), p. 141. (To reproduce a commodity is to
produce another just like it.)

tion, the purpose of which is so to modify the popular doctrine as to bring it into line with the strict doctrine. And so it is said, in response to the case of inefficient labor, that

> (13) The worker creates value *if, and only in so far as*, his labor is socially necessary.

To the extent that actual labor time exceeds what is standardly required, labor is not value-creating. The formulation is obviously intended to preserve the popular idea of creation, without contradicting the strict doctrine. But we shall show that this cannot be done. The strict doctrine allows no such mixed formulations.

The strict doctrine certainly rules out (13), since (13) cites the wrong amount of socially necessary labor time, namely that which is required when the commodity is being created,[14] rather than that which is required when the commodity is on the market. To have any prospect of being faithful to the strict doctrine, a mixed formulation must say not (13) but some such thing as this:

> (14) The worker creates value *if, and only in so far as*, the amount of labor he performs *will be* socially necessary when the product is marketed.

Marxists think (14) follows from the strict doctrine because they mistakenly suppose that (14) follows from something the strict doctrine does entail, but which is of no relevant interest, namely,

> (15) Value is determined by (that is, *inferable from*) expended labor time when the amount expended is what will be socially necessary when the product is marketed.

Statement (15) does follow from the strict doctrine, just as (16) follows from the true doctrine about barometers:

> (16) The height of a mercury column on day 2 is determined by (that is, *inferable from*) the atmospheric pressure on day 1 when day 1's atmospheric pressure is what day 2's atmospheric pressure will be.

14. There may, of course, be no such unique quantity: so much the worse for (13).

Statement (16) is entailed by the truth that day 2's atmospheric pressure makes the height of the mercury column on day 2 what it is. But (16) does not entail that day 1's atmospheric pressure makes the height of the mercury column on day 2 what it is. And (15), similarly, gives no support to (14).

The general point is that if a magnitude m causally depends upon a magnitude m', and it is given that a magnitude m'' is equal to m', then whatever m'' is a magnitude of, magnitude m will be inferable from magnitude m''. There could then be an illusion that magnitude m'' *explains* magnitude m. Just that illusion, I claim, seizes anyone who supposes that (14) is consistent with the strict doctrine.

An additional problem for the mixed formulation is the case of abnormally efficient labor, or of labor which used means of production superior to those now available, where in each instance *less* labor than is now socially necessary was expended. One cannot begin to claim in such a case that value is created by labor subject to the constraint that the amount expended will be socially necessary, since here not enough labor is expended. When there is *inefficiency*, there is a chance of pretending that some of the labor which occurred did not create value. Where there is special *efficiency*, there can be no similar pretense that labor which did not occur did create value.

We conclude that attempts to salvage the popular idea of creation by recourse to mixed formulations will not succeed.

VI

What was required in the past, and still more what happened in the past—these facts are in principle irrelevant to how much value a commodity has, if the labor theory of value is true. But they are not epistemically irrelevant. For since technical conditions change relatively slowly, socially necessary labor time in the recent past is usually a good guide to socially necessary labor time now. Typical past actual labor time is, moreover, the best guide to how much labor time was necessary in the past. Thereby what did occur becomes a good index of what is now required. It does not follow that it creates the value of the commodity.

Our argument shows that if the labor theory of value is true, labor does not create value. But it would be quixotic to seek a basis *other than* the labor theory of value for the proposition that labor creates value.[15] We may therefore take it that labor does not create value, whether or not the labor theory of value is true.

Some will ask, If labor does not create value, what does? But it is a prejudice to suppose that value must be *created*. Something must, of course, explain value and its magnitudes, but not all explainers are creators. One putative explanation of value magnitudes is the labor theory of value, the strict doctrine. But it identifies no creator of value, unless we suppose that explaining is creating. *What would now be needed to produce a commodity of a certain kind*—that is not a creator in any literal sense.

Why is the popular doctrine popular? One reason is that it appears more appropriate than the strict doctrine as a basis for a charge of exploitation. We shall see (sections VIII and IX) that neither doctrine supports such a charge, but it is clear that the popular doctrine *seems* better suited to do so, just because it alone says that labor *creates* value. But a partly distinct reason for the popularity of the popular doctrine is that certain arguments against the strict doctrine tend to be met by an illicit shift to popular formulations. This will be explained in the next section, where the theme of exploitation is in abeyance, and where I argue that the strict doctrine is false. The discussion of exploitation is completed in sections VIII, IX, and X, which do not presuppose the next one.

VII

An obvious argument against the labor theory of value is that magnitude of value is affected by things other than socially necessary labor time. One such different thing is the pattern of ownership of means of production, which can affect values, through the distribution of bargaining power which reflects it. Products of means of production on which there is some degree of monopoly are likely for that reason

15. In, that is, the traditional sense of "labor creates value," which is the relevant sense here: see fn. 8.

to command a higher price in equilibrium than they otherwise would, and therefore to have a higher value, under the definition of value we have given.

But if value is something the explanation of which must literally create it, then since ownership of means of production literally creates nothing, it would follow that, despite appearances, the pattern of that ownership cannot affect value formation. And that is what a Marxist says. He says that labor alone creates *value*: the pattern of ownership can affect price, and hence how much value various owners *get*. But no part of what they get is created by ownership.

But this line of defense depends essentially on the idea that labor *creates* value. If we stay with the strict doctrine, which rightly does not require that anything *creates* value, it has no motivation whatsoever.

To make this more clear, we return to the three propositions in our initial presentation of the labor theory of value:

(1) Socially necessary labor time determines value.
(2) Value determines equilibrium price.
(3) Socially necessary labor time determines equilibrium price.

Recall our view that the definitional statement is (2), and that (1) is the substantive theory. (1) and (2) entail (3). We said we would say why some prefer to see (1) as true by definition. Here is one reason why.

Counterexamples to (3) abound, such as the one we noted about pattern of ownership of means of production, or the cases of divergences in period of production and organic composition of capital. Statement (3) is false, and much of Volumes 2 and 3 of *Capital* is devoted to this fact.

Now if (3) is false, one *at least* of (1) and (2) must be false. If (2) is true by definition, then (1) is false, and the labor theory of value is sunk. What Marxists therefore do is to treat (1) as true by definition—so that counterexamples to (3) cannot touch it—and then simply drop (2). But this deprives the labor theory of all substance. That consequence, is, however, concealed by construing (1) in a popular fashion, by thinking of it as saying something like: labor *creates*

value, for that does not look like a definition. It is then said that whatever determines market ratios, and thereby who gets what amounts
of value, labor alone creates the value there is to get. The popular doctrine supplies an appearance of substance when, under pressure of
counterexample, (1) is treated as true by definition, (2) is dropped,
and the theory is, in reality, drained of all substance. Volume 1 of
Capital, because of its simplifying assumptions, can proceed under
definition (2) of value. When the assumptions are relaxed, (1) and
(2) cannot both be true. Hence, in Volumes 2 and 3, statement (2)
is abandoned.

At this point it is instructive to look at a central part of Marx's
critique of Ricardo. If I am right, it depends on popular formulations.

Ricardo defined value as at (2) above, and provisionally asserted
something like (1), and therefore, too, (3). He then acknowledged
that variations in period of production falsify (3), and therefore falsify (1) (since (2) is true by definition). So he allowed deviation of
value (that is, equilibrium price) from socially necessary labor time.[16]

According to Marx, Ricardo was here misled by appearances. The
true deviation is not of value from socially necessary labor time, but
of equilibrium price from value (that is, socially necessary labor
time).[17]

Now both Ricardo and Marx say that equilibrium price deviates
from socially necessary labor time. What then is the theoretical difference between them? I believe that it can be stated only in popular
discourse, to which Marx therefore resorts here. For he says that variations in period of production and organic composition do not affect
how much value is *created*, but only how much is *appropriated* at the
various sites of its creation. But if one asked, Exactly what is it that
labor is here said to create? then, I contend, there would be no answer,
once value is no longer, as now it cannot be, defined as at (2).[18]

16. See chap. 1 of any edition of Ricardo's *Principles of Political Economy*;
and see Mark Blaug, *Economic Theory in Retrospect* (London, 1968), pp. 96 ff.
for a brief accessible exposition.

17. See *Theories of Surplus Value*, vol. 2 (Moscow, 1968), pp. 106, 174-180,
and *Grundrisse*, pp. 562-563.

18. Hence, if I am right, the transformation problem is a strictly incoherent
problem, whether or not it has a mathematical "solution."

The labor theory of value comes in two versions, strict and popular. The two contradict one another. But the labor theorist cannot, by way of remedy, simply drop the popular version. For despite their mutual inconsistency, each version can appear true only when it is thought to receive support from the other: "Labor creates value" seems (but is not) a simple consequence of the thesis that value is determined by socially necessary labor time, and that thesis appears to survive refutation only when it is treated as interchangeable with the idea that labor creates value.

VIII

In this section I shall identify the real basis of the Marxian imputation of exploitation to the capitalist production process, the proposition which really animates Marxists, whatever they may think and say. The real basis is not the commonly stated one, sentence (5), but a fairly obvious truth which owes nothing to the labor theory of value, and which is widely confused with (5). And since (5) is itself confused with the labor theory of value, the latter is confused with the fairly obvious truth to be stated.[19]

A byproduct of our discussion, then, will be an explanation why the labor theory of value, which ought to be controversial, is considered even by very intelligent Marxists to be a fairly obvious truth. When Marxists think obviously true what others think not obvious at all, one side at least is very wrong, and an explanation of the error in terms of class position or ideological standpoint is not enough, because it does not show how the error is possible, by what intellectual mechanism it can occur. What follows will help to explain how it is possible for very intelligent Marxists to be mistaken.

Recall what has been shown. We have seen that if the labor theory of value is true, then labor does not create value. For if labor creates value, past labor creates value; and if past labor creates value, then past labor determines the value of the product. But the labor theory of value says that value magnitudes are determined by currently nec-

---

19. "Is confused with" is not a transitive relation, but the above statement is nonetheless true.

essary labor time. It follows that past labor does not create value, if the labor theory of value is true. There is, moreover, no plausible alternative basis on which to assert that labor creates value. Hence it is false that labor creates value. And we shall show in section IX, that even if it were true, it would not be a sound basis for a charge of exploitation.

Nor does the labor theory of value itself, strictly formulated, form such a basis. Any such impression disappears once we see that it does not entail that the workers create value. In fact, the labor theory of value does not entail that the workers create anything.

Yet the workers manifestly do create something. They create the product. They do not create *value*, but they create *what has value*. The small difference of phrasing covers an enormous difference of conception. What raises a charge of exploitation is not that the capitalist gets some of the value the worker produces, but that he gets some of the value *of what* the worker produces. Whether or not workers produce value, they produce the product, that which has value.

And no one else does. Or, to speak with greater care, producers are the only persons who produce what has value: it is true by definition that no human activity other than production produces what has value. This does not answer the difficult question, Who is a producer? But whatever the answer may be, only those whom it identifies can be said to produce what has value. And we know before we have the full answer that owners of capital, considered as such, cannot be said to do so.

Note that I am not saying that whatever has value was produced by labor, for I have not said that whatever has value was produced. I also do not deny that tools and raw materials are usually needed to produce what has value. The assertion is that laborers, in the broadest possible sense, are the only persons who produce anything which has value, and that capitalists are not laborers in that sense. If they were, capital and labor would not be distinct "factors of production": [20] the

20. I use scare-quotes because there are good Marxian objections to the classification of capital and labor as distinct but comparable factors of production: note that in a sense all that is required for production is capital, since capital buys not only means of production but also labor. That only hints at the objec-

capitalist supplies capital, which is not a kind of labor.

Some will question the claim that owners of capital, considered as such, do not produce anything. An owner of capital can, of course, *also* do some producing, for example, by carrying out a task which would otherwise fall to someone in his hire. Then he is a producer, but not *as* an owner of capital. More pertinent is the objection that owners of capital, in their very capacity as such, fulfill significant productive functions, in risking capital, making investment decisions, and so forth. But whether or not that is true, it does not entail that they produce anything in the importantly distinct sense in issue here. It does not entail, to put it one way, that they engage in the activity of producing.

To act productively it is enough that one does something which helps to bring it about that a thing is produced, and that does not entail participating in producing it. You cannot cut without a knife, but it does not follow that, if you lack one and I lend you one, thereby making cutting possible, then I am a cutter, or any other sort of producer. The distinction is between productive activities and producing activities. Capitalists arguably engage in the former, but once the distinction is clear, it is evident that they do not (unless they are not only capitalists) engage in the latter.

To be sure, *if*—what I here neither assert nor deny—the capitalist is a *productive* nonproducer, that will have a bearing on the thesis that he is an exploiter. It will be a challenge to a charge of exploitation whose premise is that he produces nothing. But it would be wrong to direct the challenge against the *premise* of that charge, that he produces nothing. As this is generally intended, it cannot be denied.

And it is this fairly obvious truth which, I contend, lies at the heart of the Marxist charge of exploitation. The real basis of that charge is not that the workers produce value, but that they produce what has it. The real Marxian argument for (10) is not the Simpler Marxian Argument (see section IV), but this different one (the Plain Argument):

---

tions, which are given in chap. 48 of vol. 3 of *Capital*, and which do not affect the point made in the text above.

    (17) The laborer is the only person who creates the product, that which has value.

    (11) The capitalist receives some of the value of the product.

∴ (18) The laborer receives less value than the value of what he creates, and

    (19) The capitalist receives some of the value of what the laborer creates.

∴ (10) The laborer is exploited by the capitalist.

The Plain Argument is constructed in analogy with the Simpler Marxian Argument, under the constraint that premise (17) replaces premise (5). The arguments are totally different, but very easy to confuse with one another.

IX

I have said that it is labor's creation of what has value, not its (supposed) creation of value, which founds the charge that capitalism is a system of exploitation. I must now defend this position.

We have seen that labor does not create value. I now argue that even if it did, that would have no bearing on the question of exploitation.

The proposition that labor creates value is, to begin with, unnecessary to the thesis that labor is exploited. For if we suppose that something else creates value, the impression that labor is exploited, if it was there before, persists. Thus imagine that the magnitude of value of a commodity is wholly determined by the extent and intensity of desire for it, and that we can therefore say that value is created by desire and not by labor. If it remains true that labor creates all that has value, and that the capitalist appropriates some of the value, does the charge of exploitation lose force? Surely not. Then the assertion that the workers create value cannot be necessary to that charge, since here we suppose that something else creates value, and the charge persists.

But the claim that labor creates value is not only unnecessary to the charge of exploitation. It is no reason whatever for laying such a charge. Once again, we make the point by imagining that desire creates value. If labor's creation of value would give the laborer a claim to value *because* he had created it, then so would the desirer's creation of value give him a claim on that basis. Yet would we say that desirers are exploited because they create the value of the product, and the capitalist receives part of that value? The suggestion is absurd.[21] It must then be equally absurd to think that laborers are exploited *because* they create value which others receive.

It is absurd, but it does not seem absurd, and the explanation of the discrepancy is that it is impossible to forget that labor creates what has value. Creating value, when we suppose that workers do that, seems to count, because we naturally think that they could create value only by creating what has it, and the relevance of the latter is mistakenly transmitted to the former. Part of the case for saying that (17) is the real basis of the charge of exploitation is that (5) cannot be yet seems to be, and the relationship between (17) and (5) explains the illusion.

But there is also more direct reason for thinking that the essential thing is labor's creation of what has value. Look at the lines from "Solidarity," with which this article began. They say nothing about value, and the labor theory is not required to appreciate their point, which is that "we" are exploited. They do say that "we" have made all these valuable things.

It is, then, neither the labor theory of value (that socially necessary labor time determines value), nor its popular surrogate (that labor

21. Note that I am not saying that a person's desire for something is no reason why he should receive it. Of course it is a reason, albeit one singularly capable of being overridden. But a man's desire for something cannot be a reason for his receiving it *on the ground* that his desire for it enhances its value, even if his desire for it does enhance its value. That ground is surely unintelligible.

One more caveat. I do not suppose in the above paragraphs or anywhere else that the correct principle of reward is according to productive contribution. One can hold that the capitalist exploits the worker by appropriating part of the value of what the worker produces without holding that all of that value should go to the worker. One can affirm a principle of distribution according to need, and add that the capitalist exploits the worker because need is not the basis on which he receives part of the value of what the worker produces.

creates value), but the fairly obvious truth (that labor creates what has value) rehearsed in the song, which is the real basis of the Marxian imputation of exploitation.

We have been discussing the exploitation of the propertyless wage worker under capitalism. But if anything is the *paridigm* of exploitation in Marxism, it is the exploitation of the feudal serf, who does not, according to Marx, produce value. His exploitation is the most manifest. The proletarian's is more covert, and it is by arguing that his position may in fact be assimilated to the serf's that Marx seeks to show that he too is exploited.

The exploitation of the serf is manifest, because nothing is more clear than that part of what he produces redounds not to him but to his feudal superior. This is not so in the same plain sense under capitalism, where the product itself is not divided between capitalist and worker, but marketed.[22]

Now Marxists allege that the labor theory of value is required to uncover the exploitation of the wage worker, but I disagree. What is needed is not the false and irrelevant labor theory, but the mere concept of value, as defined, independently of the labor theory, in our sentence (2). It enables us to say that, whatever may be responsible for magnitudes of value, the worker does not receive all of the value of his product.

Marxists say that

(20) The serf produces the whole product, but the feudal lord appropriates part of the product; and
(21) The proletarian produces all of the value of the product, but the capitalist appropriates part of the value of the product.

I accept (20), but modify the first part of (21) so that it resembles the first part of (20), with this result:

(22) The proletarian produces the whole product, but the capitalist appropriates part of the value of the product.

22. Fur further discussion and textual references, see my *Karl Marx's Theory of History*, pp. 333-334.

The exploitation of the proletarian is, on my account, more similar to
the exploitation of the serf than traditional Marxism says.

X

In the last two sections I have insisted that labor creates what has
value, and I have continued to deny that labor creates value itself. Yet
it might be objected that the insistence contradicts the denial, that, in
short, (23) is true:

   (23) Since labor creates what has value, labor creates value.

But the objection is misguided. For *if* there is a sense of "labor creates value" in which (23) is true, it is not the relevant traditional
sense, that intended by Marxists when they assert (5). "Labor creates what has value" could not entail "labor creates value" where the
latter is a contribution to explaining the magnitude of the value of
commodities, as (5) is supposed to be. How could it follow from the
fact that labor creates what has value that the *amount* of value in
what it creates varies directly and uniformly with the amount of labor
expended?[23]

Is there a sense, distinct from that of (5), in which "labor creates
value" does follow from "labor creates what has value"? Probably
there is. If an artist creates a beautiful object out of something which
was less beautiful, then we find it natural to say that he creates beauty.
And it would be similarly natural to say of a worker who creates a
valuable object out of something less valuable that he creates value.
But that would not support the popular version of the labor theory of
value, though it would help to explain why so many Marxists mistakenly adhere to it.

I have argued that if anything justifies the Marxian charge that the
capitalist exploits the worker it is the true proposition (17), that
workers alone create the product. It does not follow that (17) is a

23. And if it did follow, then the labor theory of value, the strict doctrine,
would be false.

sound justification, and that the Plain Argument, suitably expanded,[24] is a good argument. Having disposed of the distracting labor theory of value, I hope to provide an evaluation of the Plain Argument elsewhere.

24. By addition of refined versions of the premises adverted to in section III above.

I am most grateful to Alison Assiter, Chris Arthur, David Braybrooke, Daniel Goldstick, Keith Graham, Edward Hyland, David Lloyd-Thomas, Colin McGinn, John McMurtry, Jan Narveson, Edward Nell, Christopher Provis, Stein Rafoss, William Shaw and Arnold Zuboff, all of whom wrote critical comments on an earlier version of this paper.

I thank the Editors of *Philosophy & Public Affairs* for an excellent set of suggestions, and for tolerating my unwillingness to accept some of them.

JEFFRIE G. MURPHY   Marxism and Retribution

Punishment in general has been defended as a means either of amel-
iorating or of intimidating. Now what right have you to punish me for
the amelioration or intimidation of others? And besides there is his-
tory—there is such a thing as statistics—which prove with the most
complete evidence that since Cain the world has been neither intimi-
dated nor ameliorated by punishment. Quite the contrary. From the
point of view of abstract right, there is only one theory of punishment
which recognizes human dignity in the abstract, and that is the theory
of Kant, especially in the more rigid formula given to it by Hegel.
Hegel says: "Punishment is the right *of the criminal. It is an act of his*
own will. The violation of right has been proclaimed by the criminal
as his own right. His crime is the negation of right. Punishment is the
negation of this negation, and consequently an affirmation of right,
solicited and forced upon the criminal by himself."

There is no doubt something specious in this formula, inasmuch as
Hegel, instead of looking upon the criminal as the mere object, the
slave of justice, elevates him to the position of a free and self-deter-

An earlier version of this essay was delivered to the Third Annual Colloquium
in Philosophy ("The Philosophy of Punishment") at the University of Dayton
in October, 1972. I am grateful to the Department of Philosophy at the University of Dayton for inviting me to participate and to a number of persons at the
Colloquium for the useful discussion on my paper at the time. I am also grateful
to Anthony D. Woozley of the University of Virginia and to two of my colleagues,
Robert M. Harnish and Francis V. Raab, for helping me to clarify the expression
of my views.

mined being. Looking, however, more closely into the matter, we discover that German idealism here, as in most other instances, has but given a transcendental sanction to the rules of existing society. Is it not a delusion to substitute for the individual with his real motives, with multifarious social circumstances pressing upon him, the abstraction of "free will"—one among the many qualities of man for man himself? . . . Is there not a necessity for deeply reflecting upon an alteration of the system that breeds these crimes, instead of glorifying the hangman who executes a lot of criminals to make room only for the supply of new ones?

Karl Marx, "Capital Punishment,"
New York Daily Tribune, *18 February 1853*[1]

Philosophers have written at great length about the moral problems involved in punishing the innocent—particularly as these problems raise obstacles to an acceptance of the moral theory of Utilitarianism. Punishment of an innocent man in order to bring about good social consequences is, at the very least, not always clearly wrong on utilitarian principles. This being so, utilitarian principles are then to be condemned by any morality that may be called Kantian in character. For punishing an innocent man, in Kantian language, involves using that man as a mere means or instrument to some social good and is

1. In a sense, my paper may be viewed as an elaborate commentary on this one passage, excerpted from a discussion generally concerned with the efficacy of capital punishment in eliminating crime. For in this passage, Marx (to the surprise of many I should think) expresses a certain admiration for the classical retributive theory of punishment. Also (again surprisingly) he expresses this admiration in a kind of language he normally avoids—i.e., the moral language of rights and justice. He then, of course, goes on to reject the applicability of that theory. But the question that initially perplexed me is the following: what is the explanation of Marx's ambivalence concerning the retributive theory; why is he both attracted and repelled by it? (This ambivalence is not shared, for example, by utilitarians—who feel nothing but repulsion when the retributive theory is even mentioned.) Now except for some very brief passages in *The Holy Family*, Marx himself has nothing more to say on the topic of punishment beyond what is contained in this brief *Daily Tribune* article. Thus my essay is in no sense an exercise in textual scholarship (there are not enough texts) but is rather an attempt to construct an assessment of punishment, Marxist at least in spirit, that might account for the ambivalence found in the quoted passage. My main outside help comes, not from Marx himself, but from the writings of the Marxist criminologist Willem Bonger.

thus not to treat him as an end in himself, in accord with his dignity or worth as a person.

The Kantian position on the issue of punishing the innocent, and the many ways in which the utilitarian might try to accommodate that position, constitute extremely well-worn ground in contemporary moral and legal philosophy.[2] I do not propose to wear the ground further by adding additional comments on the issue here. What I do want to point out, however, is something which seems to me quite obvious but which philosophical commentators on punishment have almost universally failed to see—namely, that problems of the very same kind and seriousness arise for the utilitarian theory with respect to the punishment of the guilty. For a utilitarian theory of punishment (Bentham's is a paradigm) must involve justifying punishment in terms of its social results—e.g., deterrence, incapacitation, and rehabilitation. And thus even a guilty man is, on this theory, being punished because of the instrumental value the action of punishment will have in the future. He is being used as a means to some future good—e.g., the deterrence of others. Thus those of a Kantian persuasion, who see the importance of worrying about the treatment of persons as mere means, must, it would seem, object just as strenuously to the punishment of the guilty on utilitarian grounds as to the punishment of the innocent. Indeed the former worry, in some respects, seems more serious. For a utilitarian can perhaps refine his theory in such a way that it does not commit him to the punishment of the innocent. However, if he is to approve of punishment at all, he must approve of punishing the guilty in at least some cases. This makes the worry about punishing the guilty formidable indeed, and it is odd that this has gone generally unnoticed.[3] It has generally been assumed that if the utilitarian theory can just avoid entailing the permissibility of punishing the innocent, then all objections of a Kantian character to the theory will have been met. This seems to me simply not to be the case.

2. Many of the leading articles on this topic have been reprinted in *The Philosophy of Punishment*, ed. H. B. Acton (London, 1969). Those papers not included are cited in Acton's excellent bibliography.

3. One writer who has noticed this is Richard Wasserstrom. See his "Why Punish the Guilty?" *Princeton University Magazine* 20 (1964), pp. 14-19.

What the utilitarian theory really cannot capture, I would suggest, is the notion of persons having rights. And it is just this notion that is central to any Kantian outlook on morality. Any Kantian can certainly agree that punishing persons (guilty or innocent) may have either good or bad or indifferent consequences and that insofar as the consequences (whether in a particular case or for an institution) are good, this is something in favor of punishment. But the Kantian will maintain that this consequential outlook, important as it may be, leaves out of consideration entirely that which is most morally crucial —namely, the question of rights. Even if punishment of a person would have good consequences, what gives us (i.e., society) the moral right to inflict it? If we have such a right, what is its origin or derivation? What social circumstances must be present for it to be applicable? What does this right to punish tell us about the status of the person to be punished—e.g., how are we to analyze his rights, the sense in which he must deserve to be punished, his obligations in the matter? It is this family of questions which any Kantian must regard as morally central and which the utilitarian cannot easily accommodate into his theory. And it is surely this aspect of Kant's and Hegel's retributivism, this seeing of rights as basic, which appeals to Marx in the quoted passage. As Marx himself puts it: "What right have you to punish me for the amelioration or intimidation of others?" And he further praises Hegel for seeing that punishment, if justified, must involve respecting the rights of the person to be punished.[4] Thus Marx, like Kant, seems prepared to draw the important distinction between (a) what it would be good to do on grounds of utility and (b) what we have a right to do. Since we do not always have the right to do what it would be good to do, this distinction is of the greatest moral importance; and missing the distinction is the Achilles heel of all forms of Utilitarianism. For consider the following example: A Jehovah's Witness needs a blood

4. Marx normally avoids the language of rights and justice because he regards such language to be corrupted by bourgeois ideology. However, if we think very broadly of what an appeal to rights involves—namely, a protest against unjustified coercion—there is no reason why Marx may not legitimately avail himself on occasion of this way of speaking. For there is surely at least some moral overlap between Marx's protests against exploitation and the evils of a division of labor, for example, and the claims that people have a right not to be used solely for the benefit of others and a right to self-determination.

transfusion in order to live; but, because of his (we can agree absurd) religious belief that such transfusions are against God's commands, he instructs his doctor not to give him one. Here is a case where it would seem to be good or for the best to give the transfusion and yet, at the very least, it is highly doubtful that the doctor has a right to give it. This kind of distinction is elementary, and any theory which misses it is morally degenerate.[5]

To move specifically to the topic of punishment: How exactly does retributivism (of a Kantian or Hegelian variety) respect the rights of persons? Is Marx really correct on this? I believe that he is. I believe that retributivism can be formulated in such a way that it is the only morally defensible theory of punishment. I also believe that arguments, which may be regarded as Marxist at least in spirit, can be formulated which show that social conditions as they obtain in most societies make this form of retributivism largely inapplicable within those societies. As Marx says, in those societies retributivism functions merely to provide a "transcendental sanction" for the status quo. If this is so, then the only morally defensible theory of punishment is largely inapplicable in modern societies. The consequence: modern societies largely lack the moral right to punish.[6] The upshot is that a Kantian moral theory (which in general seems to me correct) and a Marxist analysis of criminality (which, if properly qualified, also seems to me correct) produce a radical and not merely reformist attack not just on the scope and manner of punishment in our society but on the institution of punishment itself. Institutions of punishment constitute

5. I do not mean to suggest that under no conceivable circumstances would the doctor be justified in giving the transfusion even though, in one clear sense, he had no right to do it. If, for example, the Jehovah's Witness was a key man whose survival was necessary to prevent the outbreak of a destructive war, we might well regard the transfusion as on the whole justified. However, even in such a case, a morally sensitive man would have to regretfully realize that he was sacrificing an important principle. Such a realization would be impossible (because inconsistent) for a utilitarian, for his theory admits only one principle —namely, do that which on the whole maximizes utility. An occupational disease of utilitarians is a blindness to the possibility of genuine moral dilemmas—i.e., a blindness to the possibility that important moral principles can conflict in ways that are not obviously resolvable by a rational decision procedure.

6. I qualify my thesis by the word "largely" to show at this point my realization, explored in more detail later, that no single theory can account for all criminal behavior.

what Bernard Harrison has called structural injustices[7] and are, in the absence of a major social change, to be resisted by all who take human rights to be morally serious—i.e., regard them as genuine action guides and not merely as rhetorical devices which allow people to morally sanctify institutions which in fact can only be defended on grounds of social expediency.

Stating all of this is one thing and proving it, of course, is another. Whether I can ever do this is doubtful. That I cannot do it in one brief article is certain. I cannot, for example, here defend in detail my belief that a generally Kantian outlook on moral matters is correct.[8] Thus I shall content myself for the present with attempting to render at least plausible two major claims involved in the view that I have outlined thus far: (1) that a retributive theory, in spite of the bad press that it has received, is a morally credible theory of punishment—that it can be, H. L. A. Hart to the contrary,[9] a reasonable general justifying aim of punishment; and (2) that a Marxist analysis of a society can undercut the practical applicability of that theory.

THE RIGHT OF THE STATE TO PUNISH

It is strong evidence of the influence of a utilitarian outlook in moral and legal matters that discussions of punishment no longer involve a consideration of the right of anyone to inflict it. Yet in the eighteenth and nineteenth centuries, this tended to be regarded as the central aspect of the problem meriting philosophical consideration. Kant, Hegel, Bosanquet, Green—all tended to entitle their chapters on punishment along the lines explicitly used by Green: "The Right of the State to Punish."[10] This is not just a matter of terminology but reflects, I think, something of deeper philosophical substance. These theorists, unlike the utilitarian, did not view man as primarily a maximizer of personal satisfactions—a maximizer of individual utilities. They were

7. Bernard Harrison, "Violence and the Rule of Law," in *Violence*, ed. Jerome A. Shaffer (New York, 1971), pp. 139-176.

8. I have made a start toward such a defense in my "The Killing of the Innocent," forthcoming in *The Monist* 57, no. 4 (October 1973).

9. H. L. A. Hart, "Prolegomenon to the Principles of Punishment," from *Punishment and Responsibility* (Oxford, 1968), pp. 1-27.

10. Thomas Hill Green, *Lectures on the Principles of Political Obligation* (1885), (Ann Arbor, 1967), pp. 180-205.

inclined, in various ways, to adopt a different model of man—man as a free or spontaneous creator, man as autonomous. (Marx, it may be noted, is much more in line with this tradition than with the utilitarian outlook.)[11] This being so, these theorists were inclined to view punishment (a certain kind of coercion by the state) as not merely a causal contributor to pain and suffering, but rather as presenting at least a prima facie challenge to the values of autonomy and personal dignity and self-realization—the very values which, in their view, the state existed to nurture. The problem as they saw it, therefore, was that of reconciling punishment as state coercion with the value of individual autonomy. (This is an instance of the more general problem which Robert Paul Wolff has called the central problem of political philosophy—namely, how is individual moral autonomy to be reconciled with legitimate political authority?)[12] This kind of problem, which I am inclined to agree is quite basic, cannot even be formulated intelligibly from a utilitarian perspective. Thus the utilitarian cannot even see the relevance of Marx's charge: Even if punishment has wonderful social consequences, what gives anyone the right to inflict it on me?

Now one fairly typical way in which others acquire rights over us is by our own consent. If a neighbor locks up my liquor cabinet to protect me against my tendencies to drink too heavily, I might well regard this as a presumptuous interference with my own freedom, no matter how good the result intended or accomplished. He had no right to do it and indeed violated my rights in doing it. If, on the other hand, I had asked him to do this or had given my free consent to his suggestion that he do it, the same sort of objection on my part would be quite out of order. I had given him the right to do it, and he had the right to do it. In doing it, he violated no rights of mine—even if, at the time of his doing it, I did not desire or want the action to be performed. Here then we seem to have a case where my autonomy may be regarded as intact even though a desire of mine is thwarted. For there is a sense in which the thwarting of the desire can be imputed to me

11. For an elaboration of this point, see Steven Lukes, "Alienation and Anomie," in *Philosophy, Politics and Society* (Third Series), ed. Peter Laslett and W. G. Runciman (Oxford, 1967), pp. 134-156.

12. Robert Paul Wolff, *In Defense of Anarchism* (New York, 1970).

(my choice or decision) and not to the arbitrary intervention of another.

How does this apply to our problem? The answer, I think, is obvious. What is needed, in order to reconcile my undesired suffering of
punishment at the hands of the state with my autonomy (and thus
with the state's right to punish me), is a political theory which makes
the state's decision to punish me in some sense my own decision. If I
have willed my own punishment (consented to it, agreed to it) then—
even if at the time I happen not to desire it—it can be said that my
autonomy and dignity remain intact. Theories of the General Will and
Social Contract theories are two such theories which attempt this
reconciliation of autonomy with legitimate state authority (including
the right or authority of the state to punish). Since Kant's theory
happens to incorporate elements of both, it will be useful to take it
for our sample.

MORAL RIGHTS AND THE RETRIBUTIVE THEORY OF PUNISHMENT

To justify government or the state is necessarily to justify at least
some coercion.[13] This poses a problem for someone, like Kant, who
maintains that human freedom is the ultimate or most sacred moral
value. Kant's own attempt to justify the state, expressed in his doctrine of the *moral title* (*Befugnis*),[14] involves an argument that coercion is justified only in so far as it is used to prevent invasions against
freedom. Freedom itself is the only value which can be used to limit
freedom, for the appeal to any other value (e.g., utility) would under-

13. In this section, I have adapted some of my previously published material:
Kant: The Philosophy of Right (London, 1970), pp. 109-112 and 140-144;
"Three Mistakes About Retributivism," *Analysis* (April 1971): 166-169; and
"Kant's Theory of Criminal Punishment," in *Proceedings of the Third International Kant Congress*, ed. Lewis White Beck (Dordrecht, 1972), pp. 434-441.
I am perfectly aware that Kant's views on the issues to be considered here are
often obscure and inconsistent—e.g., the analysis of "willing one's own punishment" which I shall later quote from Kant occurs in a passage the primary purpose of which is to argue that the idea of "willing one's own punishment" makes
no sense! My present objective, however, is not to attempt accurate Kant scholarship. My goal is rather to build upon some remarks of Kant's which I find
philosophically suggestive.

14. Immanuel Kant, *The Metaphysical Elements of Justice* (1797), trans. John
Ladd (Indianapolis, 1965), pp. 35ff.

mine the ultimate status of the value of freedom. Thus Kant attempts to establish the claim that some forms of coercion (as opposed to violence) are morally permissible because, contrary to appearance, they are really consistent with rational freedom. The argument, in broad outline, goes in the following way. Coercion may keep people from doing what they desire or want to do on a particular occasion and is thus prima facie wrong. However, such coercion can be shown to be morally justified (and thus not absolutely wrong) if it can be established that the coercion is such that it could have been rationally willed even by the person whose desire is interfered with:

> Accordingly, when it is said that a creditor has a right to demand from his debtor the payment of a debt, this does not mean that he can *persuade* the debtor that his own reason itself obligates him to this performance; on the contrary, to say that he has such a right means only that the use of coercion to make anyone do this is entirely compatible with everyone's freedom, *including the freedom of the debtor*, in accordance with universal laws.[15]

Like Rousseau, Kant thinks that it is only in a context governed by social practice (particularly civil government and its Rule of Law) that this can make sense. Laws may require of a person some action that he does not desire to perform. This is not a violent invasion of his freedom, however, if it can be shown that in some antecedent position of choice (what John Rawls calls "the original position"),[16] he would have been rational to adopt a Rule of Law (and thus run the risk of having some of his desires thwarted) rather than some other alternative arrangement like the classical State of Nature. This is, indeed, the only sense that Kant is able to make of classical Social Contract theories. Such theories are to be viewed, not as historical fantasies, but as ideal models of rational decision. For what these theories actually claim is that the only coercive institutions that are morally justified are those which a group of rational beings could agree to adopt in a position of having to pick social institutions to govern their relations:

15. *Ibid.*, p. 37.
16. John Rawls, "Justice as Fairness," *The Philosophical Review* 67 (1958): 164-194; and *A Theory of Justice* (Cambridge, Mass., 1971), especially pp. 17-22.

The contract, which is called *contractus originarius*, or *pactum sociale* . . . need not be assumed to be a fact, indeed it is not [even possible as such. To suppose that would be like insisting] that before anyone would be bound to respect such a civic constitution, it be proved first of all from history that a people, whose rights and obligations we have entered into as their descendants, had *once upon a time* executed such an act and had left a reliable document or instrument, either orally or in writing, concerning this contract. Instead, this contract is a *mere idea* of reason which has undoubted practical reality; namely, to oblige every legislator to give us laws in such a manner that the laws *could* have originated from the united will of the entire people and to regard every subject in so far as he is a citizen as though he had consented to such [an expression of the general] will. This is the testing stone of the rightness of every publicly-known law, for if a law were such that it was impossible for an entire people to give consent to it (as for example a law that a certain class of subjects, by inheritance, should have the privilege of the *status of lords*), then such a law is unjust. On the other hand, if there is a mere *possibility* that a people might consent to a (certain) law, then it is a duty to consider that the law is just even though at the moment the people might be in such a position or have a point of view that would result in their refusing to give their consent to it if asked.[17]

The problem of organizing a state, however hard it may seem, can be solved even for a race of devils, if only they are intelligent. The problem is: "Given a multiple of rational beings requiring universal laws for their preservation, but each of whom is secretly inclined to exempt himself from them, to establish a constitution in such a way that, although their private intentions conflict, they check each other, with the result that their public conduct is the same as if they had no such intentions."[18]

17. Immanuel Kant, "Concerning the Common Saying: This May be True in Theory but Does Not Apply in Practice (1793)," in *The Philosophy of Kant*, ed. and trans. Carl J. Friedrich (New York, 1949), pp. 421-422.
18. Immanuel Kant, *Perpetual Peace* (1795), trans. Lewis White Beck in the Kant anthology *On History* (Indianapolis 1963), p. 112.

Though Kant's doctrine is superficially similar to Mill's later self-protection principle, the substance is really quite different. For though Kant in some general sense argues that coercion is justified only to prevent harm to others, he understands by "harm" only certain invasions of freedom and not simply disutility. Also, his defense of the principle is not grounded, as is Mill's, on its utility. Rather it is to be regarded as a principle of justice, by which Kant means a principle that rational beings could adopt in a situation of mutual choice:

> The concept [of justice] applies only to the relationship of a will to another person's will, not to his wishes or desires (or even just his needs) which are the concern of acts of benevolence and charity. . . . In applying the concept of justice we take into consideration only the form of the relationship between the wills insofar as they are regarded as free, and whether the action of one of them can be conjoined with the freedom of the other in accordance with universal law. Justice is therefore the aggregate of those conditions under which the will of one person can be conjoined with the will of another in accordance with a universal law of freedom.[19]

How does this bear specifically on punishment? Kant, as everyone knows, defends a strong form of a retributive theory of punishment. He holds that guilt merits, and is a sufficient condition for, the infliction of punishment. And this claim has been universally condemned—particularly by utilitarians—as primitive, unenlightened and barbaric.

But why is it so condemned? Typically, the charge is that infliction of punishment on such grounds is nothing but pointless vengeance. But what is meant by the claim that the infliction is "pointless"? If "pointless" is tacitly being analyzed as "disutilitarian," then the whole question is simply being begged. You cannot refute a retributive theory merely by noting that it is a retributive theory and not a utilitarian theory. This is to confuse redescription with refutation and involves an argument whose circularity is not even complicated enough to be interesting.

19. Immanuel Kant, *The Metaphysical Elements of Justice*, p. 34.

Why, then, might someone claim that guilt merits punishment? Such a claim might be made for either of two very different reasons. (1) Someone (e.g., a Moral Sense theorist) might maintain that the claim is a primitive and unanalyzable proposition that is morally ultimate—that we can just intuit the "fittingness" of guilt and punishment. (2) It might be maintained that the retributivist claim is demanded by a general theory of political obligation which is more plausible than any alternative theory. Such a theory will typically provide a technical analysis of such concepts as crime and punishment and will thus not regard the retributivist claim as an indisputable primitive. It will be argued for as a kind of theorem within the system.

Kant's theory is of the second sort. He does not opt for retributivism as a bit of intuitive moral knowledge. Rather he offers a theory of punishment that is based on his general view that political obligation is to be analyzed, quasi-contractually, in terms of reciprocity. If the law is to remain just, it is important to guarantee that those who disobey it will not gain an unfair advantage over those who do obey voluntarily. It is important that no man profit from his own criminal wrongdoing, and a certain kind of "profit" (i.e., not bearing the burden of self-restraint) is intrinsic to criminal wrongdoing. Criminal punishment, then, has as its object the restoration of a proper balance between benefit and obedience. The criminal himself has no complaint, because he has rationally consented to or willed his own punishment. That is, those very rules which he has broken work, when they are obeyed by others, to his own advantage as a citizen. He would have chosen such rules for himself and others in the original position of choice. And, since he derives and voluntarily accepts benefits from their operation, he owes his own obedience as a debt to his fellow-citizens for their sacrifices in maintaining them. If he chooses not to sacrifice by exercising self-restraint and obedience, this is tantamount to his choosing to sacrifice in another way—namely, by paying the prescribed penalty:

> A transgression of the public law that makes him who commits it unfit to be a citizen is called . . . a crime. . . .
>
> What kind and what degree of punishment does public legal justice adopt as its principle and standard? None other than the principle

of equality (illustrated by the pointer of the scales of justice), that
is, the principle of not treating one side more favorably than the
other. Accordingly, any undeserved evil that you inflict on someone else among the people is one you do to yourself. If you vilify
him, you vilify yourself; if you steal from him, you steal from yourself; if you kill him, you kill yourself. . . .

To say, "I will to be punished if I murder someone" can mean nothing more than, "I submit myself along with everyone else to those
laws which, if there are any criminals among the people, will naturally include penal laws."[20]

This analysis of punishment regards it as a debt owed to the law-
abiding members of one's community; and, once paid, it allows re-
entry into the community of good citizens on equal status.

Now some of the foregoing no doubt sounds implausible or even
obscurantist. Since criminals typically desire not to be punished, what
can it really mean to say that they have, as rational men, really willed
their own punishment? Or that, as Hegel says, they have a right to
it? Perhaps a comparison of the traditional retributivist views with
those of a contemporary Kantian—John Rawls—will help to make the
points clearer.[21] Rawls (like Kant) does not regard the idea of the
social contract as an historical fact. It is rather a model of rational
decision. Respecting a man's autonomy, at least on one view, is not
respecting what he now happens, however uncritically, to desire;
rather it is to respect what he desires (or would desire) as a rational
man. (On Rawls's view, for example, rational men are said to be
unmoved by feelings of envy; and thus it is not regarded as unjust
to a person or a violation of his rights, if he is placed in a situation
where he will envy another's advantage or position. A rational man

20. *Ibid.*, pp. 99, 101, and 105, in the order quoted.
21. In addition to the works on justice by Rawls previously cited, the reader
should consult the following for Rawls's application of his general theory to the
problem of political obligation: John Rawls, "Legal Obligation and the Duty of
Fair Play," in *Law and Philosophy*, ed. Sidney Hook (New York, 1964), pp. 3-18.
This has been reprinted in my anthology *Civil Disobedience and Violence* (Belmont, Cal., 1971), pp. 39-52. For a direct application of a similar theory to the
problem of punishment, see Herbert Morris, "Persons and Punishment," *The
Monist* 52, no. 4 (October 1968): 475-501.

would object, and thus would never consent to, a practice where another might derive a benefit from a position at his expense. He would not, however, envy the position *simpliciter*, would not regard the position as itself a benefit.) Now on Kant's (and also, I think, on Rawls's) view, a man is genuinely free or autonomous only in so far as he is rational. Thus it is man's rational will that is to be respected.

Now this idea of treating people, not as they in fact say that they want to be treated, but rather in terms of how you think they would, if rational, will to be treated, has obviously dangerous (indeed Fascistic) implications. Surely we want to avoid cramming indignities down the throats of people with the offhand observation that, no matter how much they scream, they are really rationally willing every bit of it. It would be particularly ironic for such arbitrary repression to come under the mask of respecting autonomy. And yet, most of us would agree, the general principle (though subject to abuse) also has important applications—for example, preventing the suicide of a person who, in a state of psychotic depression, wants to kill himself. What we need, then, to make the general view work, is a check on its arbitrary application; and a start toward providing such a check would be in the formulation of a public, objective theory of rationality and rational willing. It is just this, according to both Kant and Rawls, which the social contract theory can provide. On this theory, a man may be said to rationally will X if, and only if, X is called for by a rule that the man would necessarily have adopted in the original position of choice—i.e., in a position of coming together with others to pick rules for the regulation of their mutual affairs. This avoids arbitrariness because, according to Kant and Rawls at any rate, the question of whether such a rule would be picked in such a position is objectively determinable given certain (in their view) noncontroversial assumptions about human nature and rational calculation. Thus I can be said to will my own punishment if, in an antecedent position of choice, I and my fellows would have chosen institutions of punishment as the most rational means of dealing with those who might break the other generally beneficial social rules that had been adopted.

Let us take an analogous example: I may not, in our actual society, desire to treat a certain person fairly—e.g., I may not desire to honor a contract I have made with him because so doing would adversely affect my own self-interest. However, if I am forced to honor the contract by the state, I cannot charge (1) that the state has no right to do this, or (2) that my rights or dignity are being violated by my being coerced into doing it. Indeed, it can be said that I rationally will it since, in the original position, I would have chosen rules of justice (rather than rules of utility) and the principle, "contracts are to be honored," follows from the rules of justice.

Coercion and autonomy are thus reconciled, at least apparently. To use Marx's language, we may say (as Marx did in the quoted passage) that one virtue of the retributive theory, at least as expounded by Kant and Hegel on lines of the General Will and Social Contract theory, is that it manifests at least a formal or abstract respect for rights, dignity, and autonomy. For it at least recognizes the importance of attempting to construe state coercion in such a way that it is a product of each man's rational will. Utilitarian deterrence theory does not even satisfy this formal demand.

The question of primary interest to Marx, of course, is whether this formal respect also involves a material respect; i.e., does the theory have application in concrete fact in the actual social world in which we live? Marx is confident that it does not, and it is to this sort of consideration that I shall now pass.

ALIENATION AND PUNISHMENT

What can the philosopher learn from Marx? This question is a part of a more general question: What can philosophy learn from social science? Philosophers, it may be thought, are concerned to offer a priori theories, theories about how certain concepts are to be analyzed and their application justified. And what can the mundane facts that are the object of behavioral science have to do with exalted theories of this sort?

The answer, I think, is that philosophical theories, though not themselves empirical, often have such a character that their intelligibility depends upon certain empirical presuppositions. For example, our moral language presupposes, as Hart has argued,[22] that we are vulnerable creatures—creatures who can harm and be harmed by each

22. H. L. A. Hart, *The Concept of Law* (Oxford, 1961), pp. 189-195.

other. Also, as I have argued elsewhere,[23] our moral language presupposes that we all share certain psychological characteristics—e.g., sympathy, a sense of justice, and the capacity to feel guilt, shame, regret, and remorse. If these facts were radically different (if, as Hart imagines for example, we all developed crustaceanlike exoskeletons and thus could not harm each other), the old moral language, and the moral theories which employ it, would lack application to the world in which we live. To use a crude example, moral prohibitions against killing presuppose that it is in fact possible for us to kill each other.

Now one of Marx's most important contributions to social philosophy, in my judgment, is simply his insight that philosophical theories are in peril if they are constructed in disregard of the nature of the empirical world to which they are supposed to apply.[24] A theory may be formally correct (i.e., coherent, or true for some possible world) but materially incorrect (i.e., inapplicable to the actual world in which we live). This insight, then, establishes the relevance of empirical research to philosophical theory and is a part, I think, of what Marx meant by "the union of theory and practice." Specifically relevant to the argument I want to develop are the following two related points:

(1) The theories of moral, social, political and legal philosophy presuppose certain empirical propositions about man and society. If these propositions are false, then the theory (even if coherent or formally correct) is materially defective and practically inapplicable. (For example, if persons tempted to engage in criminal conduct do not in fact tend to calculate carefully the consequences of their actions, this renders much of deterrence theory suspect.)

23. Jeffrie G. Murphy, "Moral Death: A Kantian Essay on Psychopathy," *Ethics* 82, no. 4 (July 1972): 284-298.

24. Banal as this point may seem, it could be persuasively argued that all Enlightenment political theory (e.g., that of Hobbes, Locke and Kant) is built upon ignoring it. For example, once we have substantial empirical evidence concerning how democracies really work in fact, how sympathetic can we really be to classical theories for the justification of democracy? For more on this, see C. B. Macpherson, "The Maximization of Democracy," in *Philosophy, Politics and Society* (Third Series), ed. Peter Laslett and W. G. Runciman (Oxford, 1967), pp. 83-103. This article is also relevant to the point raised in note 11 above.

(2) Philosophical theories may put forth as a necessary truth that which is in fact merely an historically conditioned contingency. (For example, Hobbes argued that all men are necessarily selfish and competitive. It is possible, as many Marxists have argued, that Hobbes was really doing nothing more than elevating to the status of a necessary truth the contingent fact that the people around him in the capitalistic society in which he lived were in fact selfish and competitive.)[25]

In outline, then, I want to argue the following: that when Marx challenges the material adequacy of the retributive theory of punishment, he is suggesting (a) that it presupposes a certain view of man and society that is false and (b) that key concepts involved in the support of the theory (e.g., the concept of "rationality" in Social Contract theory) are given analyses which, though they purport to be necessary truths, are in fact mere reflections of certain historical circumstances.

In trying to develop this case, I shall draw primarily upon Willem Bonger's *Criminality and Economic Conditions* (1916), one of the few sustained Marxist analyses of crime and punishment.[26] Though I shall not have time here to qualify my support of Bonger in certain necessary ways, let me make clear that I am perfectly aware that his analysis is not the whole story. (No monolithic theory of anything so diverse as criminal behavior could be the whole story.) However, I am convinced that he has discovered part of the story. And my point is simply that insofar as Bonger's Marxist analysis is correct, then to that same degree is the retributive theory of punishment inapplicable in modern societies. (Let me emphasize again exactly how this objection

25. This point is well developed in C. B. Macpherson, *The Political Theory of Possessive Individualism* (Oxford, 1962). In a sense, this point affects even the formal correctness of a theory. For it demonstrates an empirical source of corruption in the analyses of the very concepts in the theory.

26. The writings of Willem Adriaan Bonger (1876-1940), a Dutch criminologist, have fallen into totally unjustified neglect in recent years. Anticipating contemporary sociological theories of crime, he was insisting that criminal behavior is in the province of normal psychology (though abnormal society) at a time when most other writers were viewing criminality as a symptom of psychopathology. His major works are: *Criminality and Economic Conditions* (Boston, 1916); *An Introduction to Criminology* (London, 1936); and *Race and Crime* (New York, 1943).

to retributivism differs from those traditionally offered. Traditionally, retributivism has been rejected because it conflicts with the moral theory of its opponent, usually a utilitarian. This is not the kind of objection I want to develop. Indeed, with Marx, I have argued that the retributive theory of punishment grows out of the moral theory—Kantianism—which seems to me generally correct. The objection I want to pursue concerns the empirical falsity of the factual presuppositions of the theory. If the empirical presuppositions of the theory are false, this does indeed render its application immoral. But the immorality consists, not in a conflict with some other moral theory, but immorality in terms of a moral theory that is at least close in spirit to the very moral theory which generates retributivism itself—i.e., a theory of justice.)[27]

To return to Bonger. Put bluntly, his theory is as follows. Criminality has two primary sources: (1) need and deprivation on the part of disadvantaged members of society, and (2) motives of greed and selfishness that are generated and reinforced in competitive capitalistic societies. Thus criminality is economically based—either directly in the case of crimes from need, or indirectly in the case of crimes growing out of motives or psychological states that are encouraged and developed in capitalistic society. In Marx's own language, such an economic system alienates men from themselves and from each other. It alienates men from themselves by creating motives and needs that are not "truly human." It alienates men from their fellows by encouraging a kind of competitiveness that forms an obstacle to the development of genuine communities to replace mere social aggregates.[28] And in Bonger's thought, the concept of community is

27. I say "at least in spirit" to avoid begging the controversial question of whether Marx can be said to embrace a theory of justice. Though (as I suggested in note 4) much of Marx's own evaluative rhetoric seems to overlap more traditional appeals to rights and justice (and a total lack of sympathy with anything like Utilitarianism), it must be admitted that he also frequently ridicules at least the terms "rights" and "justice" because of their apparent entrenchment in bourgeois ethics. For an interesting discussion of this issue, see Allen W. Wood, "The Marxian Critique of Justice," above, pp. 3-41.

28. The importance of community is also, I think, recognized in Gabriel de Tarde's notion of "social similarity" as a condition of criminal responsibility. See his *Penal Philosophy* (Boston, 1912). I have drawn on de Tarde's general account in my "Moral Death: A Kantian Essay on Psychopathy."

central. He argues that moral relations and moral restraint are possible only in genuine communities characterized by bonds of sympathetic identification and mutual aid resting upon a perception of common humanity. All this he includes under the general rubric of reciprocity.[29] In the absence of reciprocity in this rich sense, moral relations among men will break down and criminality will increase.[30] Within bourgeois society, then, crimes are to be regarded as normal, and not psychopathological, acts. That is, they grow out of need, greed, indifference to others, and sometimes even a sense of indignation—all, alas, perfectly typical human motives.

To appreciate the force of Bonger's analysis, it is necessary to read his books and grasp the richness and detail of the evidence he provides for his claims. Here I can but quote a few passages at random to give the reader a tantalizing sample in the hope that he will be encouraged to read further into Bonger's own text:

> The abnormal element in crime is a social, not a biological, element. With the exception of a few special cases, crime lies within the boundaries of normal psychology and physiology. . . .

> We clearly see that [the egoistic tendencies of the present economic system and of its consequences] are very strong. Because of these tendencies the social instinct of man is not greatly developed; they have weakened the moral force in man which combats the inclination towards egoistic acts, and hence toward the crimes which are one form of these acts. . . . Compassion for the misfortunes of

29. By "reciprocity" Bonger intends something which includes, but is much richer than, a notion of "fair trading or bargaining" that might initially be read into the term. He also has in mind such things as sympathetic identification with others and tendencies to provide mutual aid. Thus, for Bonger, reciprocity and egoism have a strong tendency to conflict. I mention this lest Bonger's notion of reciprocity be too quickly identified with the more restricted notion found in, for example, Kant and Rawls.

30. It is interesting how greatly Bonger's analysis differs from classical deterrence theory—e.g., that of Bentham. Bentham, who views men as machines driven by desires to attain pleasure and avoid pain, tends to regard terror as the primary restraint against crime. Bonger believes that, at least in a healthy society, moral motives would function as a major restraint against crime. When an environment that destroys moral motivation is created, even terror (as statistics tend to confirm) will not eradicate crime.

others inevitably becomes blunted, and a great part of morality consequently disappears. . . .

As a consequence of the present environment, man has become very egoistic and hence more *capable of crime*, than if the environment had developed the germs of altruism. . . .

There can be no doubt that one of the factors of criminality among the bourgeoisie is bad [moral] education. . . . The children—speaking of course in a general way—are brought up with the idea that they must succeed, no matter how; the aim of life is presented to them as getting money and shining in the world. . . .

Poverty (taken in the sense of absolute want) kills the social sentiments in man, destroys in fact all relations between men. He who is abandoned by all can no longer have any feeling for those who have left him to his fate. . . .

[Upon perception that the system tends to legalize the egoistic actions of the bourgeoisie and to penalize those of the proletariat], the oppressed resort to means which they would otherwise scorn. As we have seen above, the basis of the social feeling is reciprocity. As soon as this is trodden under foot by the ruling class the social sentiments of the oppressed become weak towards them. . . .[31]

The essence of this theory has been summed up by Austin J. Turk. "Criminal behavior," he says, "is almost entirely attributable to the combination of egoism and an environment in which opportunities are not equitably distributed."[32]

31. *Introduction to Criminology*, pp. 75-76, and *Criminality and Economic Conditions*, pp. 532, 402, 483-484, 436, and 407, in the order quoted. Bonger explicitly attacks Hobbes: "The adherents of [Hobbes's theory] have studied principally men who live under capitalism, or under civilization; their correct conclusion has been that egoism is the predominant characteristic of these men, and they have adopted the simplest explanation of the phenomenon and say that this trait is inborn." If Hobbists can cite Freud for modern support, Bonger can cite Darwin. For, as Darwin had argued in the *Descent of Man*, men would not have survived as a species if they had not initially had considerably greater social sentiments than Hobbes allows them.

32. Austin J. Turk, in the Introduction to his abridged edition of Bonger's *Criminality and Economic Conditions* (Bloomington, 1969), p. 14.

No doubt this claim will strike many as extreme and intemper-
ate—a sample of the old-fashioned Marxist rhetoric that sophisticated intellectuals have outgrown. Those who are inclined to react
in this way might consider just one sobering fact: of the 1.3 million
criminal offenders handled each day by some agency of the United
States correctional system, the vast majority (80 percent on some
estimates) are members of the lowest 15-percent income level—that
percent which is below the "poverty level" as defined by the Social
Security Administration.[33] Unless one wants to embrace the belief
that all these people are poor because they are bad, it might be well
to reconsider Bonger's suggestion that many of them are "bad" because they are poor.[34] At any rate, let us suppose for purposes of discussion that Bonger's picture of the relation between crime and economic conditions is generally accurate. At what points will this
challenge the credentials of the contractarian retributive theory as

33. Statistical data on characteristics of offenders in America are drawn primarily from surveys by the Bureau of Census and the National Council on Crime
and Delinquency. While there is of course wide disagreement on how such data
are to be interpreted, there is no serious disagreement concerning at least the
general accuracy of statistics like the one I have cited. Even government pub-
lications openly acknowledge a high correlation between crime and socio-
economic disadvantages: "From arrest records, probation reports, and prison
statistics a 'portrait' of the offender emerges that progressively highlights the
disadvantaged character of his life. The offender at the end of the road in prison
is likely to be a member of the lowest social and economic groups in the country,
poorly educated and perhaps unemployed. . . . Material failure, then, in a culture firmly oriented toward material success, is the most common denominator
of offenders" (The Challenge of Crime in a Free Society, A Report by the Presi-
dent's Commission on Law Enforcement and Administration of Justice, U. S.
Government Printing Office, Washington, D.C., 1967, pp. 44 and 160). The
Marxist implications of this admission have not gone unnoticed by prisoners.
See Samuel Jorden, "Prison Reform: In Whose Interest?" Criminal Law Bulletin
7, no. 9 (November 1971): 779-787.
    34. There are, of course, other factors which enter into an explanation of this
statistic. One of them is the fact that economically disadvantaged guilty persons
are more likely to wind up arrested or in prison (and thus be reflected in this
statistic) than are economically advantaged guilty persons. Thus economic conditions enter into the explanation, not just of criminal behavior, but of society's
response to criminal behavior. For a general discussion on the many ways in
which crime and poverty are related, see Patricia M. Wald, "Poverty and Criminal Justice," Task Force Report: The Courts, U.S. Government Printing Office,
Washington, D.C., 1967, pp. 139-151.

outlined above? I should like to organize my answer to this question around three basic topics:

1. *Rational Choice.* The model of rational choice found in Social Contract theory is egoistic—rational institutions are those that would be agreed to by calculating egoists ("devils" in Kant's more colorful terminology). The obvious question that would be raised by any Marxist is: Why give egoism this special status such that it is built, a priori, into the analysis of the concept of rationality? Is this not simply to regard as necessary that which may be only contingently found in the society around us? Starting from such an analysis, a certain result is inevitable—namely, a transcendental sanction for the status quo. Start with a bourgeois model of rationality and you will, of course, wind up defending a bourgeois theory of consent, a bourgeois theory of justice, and a bourgeois theory of punishment.

Though I cannot explore the point in detail here, it seems to me that this Marxist claim may cause some serious problems for Rawls's well-known theory of justice, a theory which I have already used to unpack some of the evaluative support for the retributive theory of punishment. One cannot help suspecting that there is a certain sterility in Rawls's entire project of providing a rational proof for the preferability of a certain conception of justice over all possible alternative evaluative principles, for the description which he gives of the rational contractors in the original position is such as to guarantee that they will come up with his two principles. This would be acceptable if the analysis of rationality presupposed were intuitively obvious or argued for on independent grounds. But it is not. Why, to take just one example, is a desire for wealth a rational trait whereas envy is not? One cannot help feeling that the desired result dictates the premises.[35]

35. The idea that the principles of justice could be proved as a kind of theorem (Rawls's claim in "Justice as Fairness") seems to be absent, if I understand the work correctly, in Rawls's recent *A Theory of Justice.* In this book, Rawls seems to be content with something less than a decision procedure. He is no longer trying to pull his theory of justice up by its own bootstraps, but now seems concerned simply to *exhibit* a certain elaborate conception of justice in the belief that it will do a good job of systematizing and ordering most of our considered and reflective intuitions about moral matters. To this, of course, the Marxist will want to say something like the following: "The considered and reflective in-

2. *Justice, Benefits, and Community.* The retributive theory claims to be grounded on justice; but is it just to punish people who act out of those very motives that society encourages and reinforces? If Bonger is correct, much criminality is motivated by greed, selfishness, and indifference to one's fellows; but does not the whole society encourage motives of greed and selfishness ("making it," "getting ahead"), and does not the competitive nature of the society alienate men from each other and thereby encourage indifference—even, perhaps, what psychiatrists call psychopathy? The moral problem here is similar to one that arises with respect to some war crimes. When you have trained a man to believe that the enemy is not a genuine human person (but only a gook, or a chink), it does not seem quite fair to punish the man if, in a war situation, he kills indiscriminately. For the psychological trait you have conditioned him to have, like greed, is not one that invites fine moral and legal distinctions. There is something perverse in applying principles that presuppose a sense of community in a society which is structured to destroy genuine community.[36]

Related to this is the whole allocation of benefits in contemporary

---

tuitions current in our society are a product of bourgeois culture, and thus any theory based upon them begs the question against us and in favor of the status quo." I am not sure that this charge cannot be answered, but I am sure that it deserves an answer. Someday Rawls may be remembered, to paraphrase Georg Lukács's description of Thomas Mann, as the last and greatest philosopher of bourgeois liberalism. The virtue of this description is that it perceives the limitations of his outlook in a way consistent with acknowledging his indisputable genius. (None of my remarks here, I should point out, are to be interpreted as denying that our civilization derived major moral benefits from the tradition of bourgeois liberalism. Just because the freedoms and procedures we associate with bourgeois liberalism—speech, press, assembly, due process of law, etc.—are not the only important freedoms and procedures, we are not to conclude with some witless radicals that these freedoms are not terribly important and that the victories of bourgeois revolutions are not worth preserving. My point is much more modest and noncontroversial—namely, that even bourgeois liberalism requires a critique. It is not self-justifying and, in certain very important respects, is not justified at all.)

36. Kant has some doubts about punishing bastard infanticide and dueling on similar grounds. Given the stigma that Kant's society attached to illegitimacy and the halo that the same society placed around military honor, it did not seem totally fair to punish those whose criminality in part grew out of such approved motives. See *Metaphysical Elements of Justice*, pp. 106-107.

society. The retributive theory really presupposes what might be called a "gentlemen's club" picture of the relation between man and society—i.e., men are viewed as being part of a community of shared values and rules. The rules benefit all concerned and, as a kind of debt for the benefits derived, each man owes obedience to the rules. In the absence of such obedience, he deserves punishment in the sense that he owes payment for the benefits. For, as rational man, he can see that the rules benefit everyone (himself included) and that he would have selected them in the original position of choice.

Now this may not be too far off for certain kinds of criminals—e.g., business executives guilty of tax fraud. (Though even here we might regard their motives of greed to be a function of societal reinforcement.) But to think that it applies to the typical criminal, from the poorer classes, is to live in a world of social and political fantasy. Criminals typically are not members of a shared community of values with their jailers; they suffer from what Marx calls alienation. And they certainly would be hard-pressed to name the benefits for which they are supposed to owe obedience. If justice, as both Kant and Rawls suggest, is based on reciprocity, it is hard to see what these persons are supposed to reciprocate for. Bonger addresses this point in a passage quoted earlier (p. 236): "The oppressed resort to means which they would otherwise scorn. . . . The basis of social feelings is reciprocity. As soon as this is trodden under foot by the ruling class, the social sentiments of the oppressed become weak towards them."

3. *Voluntary Acceptance*. Central to the Social Contract idea is the claim that we owe allegiance to the law because the benefits we have derived have been voluntarily accepted. This is one place where our autonomy is supposed to come in. That is, having benefited from the Rule of Law when it was possible to leave, I have in a sense consented to it and to its consequences—even my own punishment if I violate the rules. To see how silly the factual presuppositions of this account are, we can do no better than quote a famous passage from David Hume's essay "Of the Original Contract":

Can we seriously say that a poor peasant or artisan has a free choice to leave his country—when he knows no foreign language or manners, and lives from day to day by the small wages which he acquires? We may as well assert that a man, by remaining in a vessel, freely consents to the dominion of the master, though he was carried on board while asleep, and must leap into the ocean and perish the moment he leaves her.

A banal empirical observation, one may say. But it is through ignoring such banalities that philosophers generate theories which allow them to spread iniquity in the ignorant belief that they are spreading righteousness.

It does, then, seem as if there may be some truth in Marx's claim that the retributive theory, though formally correct, is materially inadequate. At root, the retributive theory fails to acknowledge that criminality is, to a large extent, a phenomenon of economic class. To acknowledge this is to challenge the empirical presupposition of the retributive theory—the presupposition that all men, including criminals, are voluntary participants in a reciprocal system of benefits and that the justice of this arrangement can be derived from some eternal and ahistorical concept of rationality.

THE upshot of all this seems rather upsetting, as indeed it is. How can it be the case that everything we are ordinarily inclined to say about punishment (in terms of utility and retribution) can be quite beside the point? To anyone with ordinary language sympathies (one who is inclined to maintain that what is correct to say is a function of what we do say), this will seem madness. Marx will agree that there is madness, all right, but in his view the madness will lie in what we do say—what we say only because of our massive (and often self-deceiving and self-serving) factual ignorance or indifference to the circumstances of the social world in which we live. Just as our whole way of talking about mental phenomena hardened before we knew any neurophysiology—and this leads us astray, so Marx would argue that our whole way of talking about moral and political phenomena hardened before we knew any of the relevant empirical facts about man and society—and this, too, leads us astray. We all suffer from what might be called the *embourgeoisment* of language, and thus part of any revolution will be a linguistic or conceptual revolution. We have grown accustomed to modifying our language or conceptual structures under the impact of empirical discoveries in physics. There is no reason why discoveries in sociology, economics, or psychology could not and should not have the same effect on entrenched patterns of thought and speech. It is important to remember, as Russell remarked, that our language sometimes enshrines the metaphysics of the Stone Age.

Consider one example: a man has been convicted of armed robbery. On investigation, we learn that he is an impoverished black whose whole life has been one of frustrating alienation from the prevailing socio-economic structure—no job, no transportation if he could get a job, substandard education for his children, terrible housing and inadequate health care for his whole family, condescending-tardy-inadequate welfare payments, harassment by the police but no real protection by them against the dangers in his community, and near total exclusion from the political process. Learning all this, would we still want to talk—as many do—of his suffering punishment under the rubric of "paying a debt to society"? Surely not. Debt for what? I do not, of course, pretend that all criminals can be so described. But I do think that this is a closer picture of the typical criminal than the picture that is presupposed in the retributive theory—i.e., the picture of an evil person who, of his own free will, intentionally acts against those just rules of society which he knows, as a rational man, benefit everyone including himself.

But what practical help does all this offer, one may ask. How should we design our punitive practices in the society in which we now live? This is the question we want to ask, and it does not seem to help simply to say that our society is built on deception and inequity. How can Marx help us with our real practical problem? The answer, I think, is that he cannot and obviously does not desire to do so. For Marx would say that we have not focused (as all piecemeal reform fails to focus) on what is truly the real problem. And this is changing the basic social relations. Marx is the last person from whom we can expect advice on how to make our intellectual and moral peace with bourgeois society. And this is surely his attraction and his value.

What does Bonger offer? He suggests, near the end of his book, that in a properly designed society all criminality would be a problem "for the physician rather than the judge." But this surely will not do. The therapeutic state, where prisons are called hospitals and jailers are called psychiatrists, simply raises again all the old problems about the justification of coercion and its reconciliation with autonomy that we faced in worrying about punishment. The only difference is that our coercive practices are now surrounded with a benevolent rhetoric which makes it even harder to raise the important issues. Thus the move to therapy, in my judgment, is only an illusory solution—alienation remains and the problem of reconciling coercion with autonomy remains unsolved. Indeed, if the alternative is having our personalities involuntarily restructured by some state psychiatrist, we might well want to claim the "right to be punished" that Hegel spoke of.[37]

Perhaps, then, we may really be forced seriously to consider a radical proposal. If we think that institutions of punishment are necessary and desirable, and if we are morally sensitive enough to want to be sure that we have the moral right to punish before we inflict it, then we had better first make sure that we have restructured society in such a way that criminals genuinely do correspond to the only model that will render punishment permissible—i.e., make sure that they are autonomous and that they do benefit in the requisite sense. Of course, if we did this then—if Marx and Bonger are right—crime itself and the need to punish would radically decrease if not disappear entirely.

37. This point is pursued in Herbert Morris, "Persons and Punishment." Bonger did not appreciate that "mental illness," like criminality, may also be a phenomenon of social class. On this, see August B. Hollingshead and Frederick C. Redlich, *Social Class and Mental Illness* (New York, 1958). On the general issue of punishment versus therapy, see my *Punishment and Rehabilitation* (Belmont, Cal., 1973).

ALAN GILBERT   Marx on Internationalism
                      and War

Most scholars adhere, sometimes inadvertently, to an economic determinist notion of Marx's politics, according to which the development
of capitalist productive forces would inevitably produce proletarian
revolution with minimal political organizing. This view overlooks the
distinctive role of politics in Marx's social theory and especially his
advocacy of internationalism—the hallmark of his political activity.[1]
I shall focus here on the international aspect of Marx's theory and
activity and suggest its relevance for a consideration of justice in
contemporary international distribution.

    1. See Alan Gilbert, "Salvaging Marx from Avineri," *Political Theory* 4, no. 1
(February 1976). Even Richard N. Hunt's recent *The Political Ideas of Marx
and Engels: Marxism and Totalitarian Democracy, 1848-50* (Pittsburgh, 1974),
which is more cognizant of Marx's political activity in 1848 than most works,
omits Marx's internationalism. Marx sought to further the mass movements of
"the present" (democratic revolutions, trade unions). Yet, at the same time,
dialectically, Marx argued that communists must take care of the "future" of
the movement and advocate the overall politics—internationalism, abolition of
private property, and after 1871, formation of a state modeled on the Paris
Commune—which would lead to proletarian revolution. Marx and Engels,
Selected Works, 2 vols. (Moscow, 1962), 1: 64-65, 22, 46. (Hereafter cited as
SW.) His defense of internationalism drew fierce attacks. For his support of
the Paris insurrection of June 1848, Cologne's leading newspaper, *Kölnische
Zeitung*, stigmatized Marx's journal, *Neue Rheinische Zeitung*, as an organ of
"red riot." As a result, Marx lost half the financial backing for his paper. In
1871 he wrote happily to Kugelmann that his support for the Paris Commune
had made "the devil of a noise, and I have the honour to be at this moment the
best calumniated and most menaced man in London." Oscar J. Hammen, *The
Red '48ers: Karl Marx and Friedrich Engels* (New York, 1969), p. 250. Karl
Marx, *Letters to Dr. Kugelmann* (New York, 1934), p. 126.

Today the problem of international distribution is apparent in the contrast between rich capitalist nations and nations so poor that large numbers of people live on the verge of starvation. Within poor countries during the United Nations' first "Development Decade," inequality of income shares worsened.[2] This deteriorating situation has caused philosophers such as Peter Singer to advocate a natural duty of individuals in the rich nations to help the starving elsewhere. Others, such as Charles Beitz, emphasizing international relation of dependency, have applied Rawls' difference principle to international affairs. Yet the actual social and political relations between at least the elites in the rich countries and the citizens of the poor countries offer little hope that such obligations will be fulfilled. If the conventional dichotomy between rich and poor nations holds, most citizens of the rich nations should benefit from the impoverishment of most citizens in the poor nations. The more accurately one depicts exploitative international relations of dependency, the weightier the moral obligations of the citizens of the rich nations to those of the poor will appear. At the same time, these obligations are less likely to be honored.[3] Marx argued that the interests of most people—at least those of working people—in the rich nations coincide with those of the majority of people in the poor nations and not with the elite of their own state. In this context, his position provides the basis for an important alternative strategy.

I. Marx's Internationalism

In the *Communist Manifesto*, Marx argued that their advocacy of internationalism distinguished communists from other working-class parties.

2. Joan Edelman Spero, *The Politics of International Economic Relations* (New York, 1977), p. 142. Hollis Chenery et al., *Redistribution with Growth* (Oxford, 1974), pp. xiv-xv.
3. For a discussion of Rawlsian views on justice in international distribution, see Alan Gilbert, "Equality and Social Theory in Rawls' *A Theory of Justice*," in the Spring 1978 *Occasional Review* on Rawls and Nozick; Peter Singer, "Famine, Affluence, and Morality," *Philosophy & Public Affairs* 1, no. 3, (Spring 1972); Charles R. Beitz, "Justice and International Relations," *Philosophy and Public Affairs* 4, no. 4 (Summer 1975).

In the national struggles of the proletarians of the different countries, they point out and bring to the front the common interests of
the entire proletariat independently of all nationality [Marx, *SW*
1: 46].

In the first sections of the *Manifesto*. Marx drew a general picture
of the capitalist transformation of the world which he thought might
lead to "common interests" among workers of different nationalities.
As capitalism develops within nations, it produces proletarians who
"know no country." These people, concentrated in large factories, have
only their own labor-power to sell. As capitalism expands internationally, it "batters down all Chinese walls" with the low prices of its
commodities, seeks out raw materials in the "remotest zones," and
finally, "creates a world after its own image" (*SW* 1: 37-38). Yet the
Manifesto does not fully explain either the nature of these common
interests or how radicals may pursue them in differing situations.
    In other writings, Marx argued that the proletarians have common
enemies. He saw the suppression of the Paris Commune of 1871 as a
leading example. In that case, fresh from fighting a war against each
other, the French and Prussian ruling classes put aside their differences and joined to crush the revolutionary government. In Marx's
critique of German Social Democracy's *Gotha Program*, he attacked
the influence of Lassallean patriotism which had deemphasized the
hostility of the bourgeoisie toward a proletarian movement.

Not a word . . . about the international functions of the German
working class! And it is thus [on the basis of a political development
limited to Germany alone] that it is to challenge its own bourgeoisie
—which is already linked up in brotherhood against it with the
bourgeoisie of all other countries . . . [*SW* 2: 11].

These common enemies created a common interest in international
unity among proletarians of different countries. Marx consistently
urged mutual support among radical working class or "red republican"
movements. For instance, he and his followers in Germany backed the
Paris insurrection of June 1848, and the International Workingmens'
Association (hereafter cited as IWA) supported the Paris Commune

of 1871. Such solidarity did not depend upon an advanced level of productive forces within countries, let alone a great degree of capitalist penetration into a foreign economy. Rather, such support depended on a political factor—the likelihood of a common response by the bourgeoisie of each European country to a revolutionary threat affecting any one of them. This response could be countered, Marx emphasized, by breaking down all divisions—internal and international—among the working classes. In Marx's "General Rules of the IWA," he stated that

> . . . all efforts aiming at that great end [the economic emancipation of the working class] have hitherto failed from want of solidarity between the manifold divisions of labor in each country, and from the absence of a fraternal bond of union between the working classes of the different countries [SW 1: 386, 384].

The previous argument clarifies the common interests between socialist movements, but how would these interests be pursued in differing situations? The fourth section of the *Manifesto* attempts to apply Marx's general theory, sketched in the opening section, to the specific international situation of 1848. Here he advocates mutual support, not only among incipient communist movements but also among democratic movements. The opening arguments of the *Manifesto* stress the rapid breakdown of national boundaries and the dissolution of national attachments, while the later section emphasizes the pivotal role of "national emancipation" in Poland in 1848. While the first sections picture the dispossession of small property-holding classes, particularly the peasantry, and characterize these classes as "reactionary" insofar as they "try to hold back the wheel of history," the later section looks to "agrarian revolution" in Poland (SW 1: 64). How did Marx reconcile these seemingly paradoxical conclusions?

To be applied in any specific historical situation, Marx's theory requires auxiliary statements which specify the international as well as the national historical context.[4]

4. For a discussion of the role of auxiliary statements in Marx's theory, see Alan Gilbert, "Changing the World: The Revolutionary Strategies of Marx and Lenin," *American Political Science Association Proceedings* (Michigan, 1976).

A look at the specific political situation of 1848 will clarify Marx's reasoning. Democratic revolutions loomed in many European countries, including Germany and Poland. These revolutions endangered the absolutist powers, especially tsarist Russia. English parliamentary capitalism also feared the shock of the European democratic revolution which would spur on its own working class movement—Chartism —just then at its peak. Since Chartism advocated universal suffrage for workers, the movement strongly sympathized with democracy on the Continent. Successful revolutions in Europe would strengthen Chartism in England as well. Thus, Marx argued, a political link existed between the interests of different oppressive social and political systems—tsarist Russia, the most backward; and capitalist England, the most advanced—which would oppose the European democratic revolution. Correspondingly, democratic and working-class "social republican" movements would have to unite in order to succeed. In this context Poland, previously divided between Prussia and Russia, would play a pivotal role. An independence movement there would cause revolutionary tremors throughout Europe.

In 1792, the duke of Brunswick's threat to raze revolutionary Paris resulted in the Jacobin Convention's *levée en masse*. For Marx, similarly, a new democratic revolution in 1848 would trigger counterrevolutionary invasion which would force the democratic movements to mobilize their populations and to wage war against absolutism and parliamentary capitalism. If the democratic movements became internally weak or failed to support each other internationally, their common enemies would divide and crush them one by one. The latter development, more or less, actually occurred.

Marx's analysis of the need for democratic internationalism in 1848 rested on a specific international configuration of reactionary powers, and not mainly on the development of productive forces (or on capitalist crisis) in a single country. Marx emphasized the setting of war and revolution. In this sense, his argument foreshadows the develop-

5. Marx and Engels, *The Revolution of 1848-49: Articles from the Neue Rheinische Zeitung*, trans. S. Ryanzanskaya, ed. Bernard Isaacs (New York, 1972), pp. 204-205; Karl Marx, *Politische Schriften*, ed. Hans-Joachin Lieber, 2 vols. (Stuttgart, 1960), 1: 398.

6. Marx and Engels, *Werke*, 39 vols. (Berlin, 1959), 5: 154.

ment of successful revolutions in the twentieth century in the context of massive world war. The Chinese Communist movement against Japanese imperialism in World War II provides the closest parallel to what Marx had hoped would be achieved in 1848.[7]

In addition, Marx argued in 1848, wars of conquest waged by the older monarchies played a vital role in maintaining their domination at home. Threatened with internal democratic revolution, for example, the Prussian government engaged in a series of expansionary attempts against democratic movements in Poland, Czechoslovakia, and Italy. It sought to rouse patriotic fervor among German democrats in order to divert their movement from its revolutionary course. At the same time, Prussia also sought to strengthen its army so that the revolution could be crushed.

Marx argued that these foreign campaigns were paradoxical "wars of restoration," often supported by the same German democrats who fought for liberty at home. The Prussian government sought to justify such expeditions with a wave of patriotic and racist propaganda. Through the newspaper *Die Neue Rheinische Zeitung*, edited by Marx, he and Engels waged an unremitting campaign within the German democratic movement against the Prussian government's nationalist justifications for its expansionary policies. As Engels argued, "A nation which throughout its history allowed itself to be used as a tool of oppression against all other nations must first of all [proclaim] the freedom of the nations hitherto suppressed by her."[8] Without opposing Prussian war efforts, the German democratic movement could not defeat absolutism.

English working-class support for the anti-slavery cause in the American Civil War provides another important example of the role of war in Marx's thinking on internationalism and of the difficult choices faced by workers in defending "the common interests of the proletariat independently of all nationality."

Marx saw the anti-slavery movement in the United States and the movement against serfdom in Russia as the two decisive political developments of the 1860s. At that time the United States possessed

7. The Russian Revolution of 1917 and the German Democratic Revolution of 1918 also took place during world war, but in response to defeat.
8. Marx and Engels, *Werke*, 5: 202.

"the only popular government" in existence.⁹ If the South should successfully secede, it would impose slavery in the border states, and
influence the entire future development of North America and Europe
in a profoundly conservative direction.

In the northern states, where Negro slavery is unworkable in
practice, the white working class would be gradually depressed to
the level of helotry. This would be in accord with the loudly proclaimed principle that only certain races are capable of freedom,
and that as in the South real labor is the lot of the Negro, so in the
North it is the lot of the German and the Irishman, or their direct
descendants.

The defeat of slavery, however, would strengthen the working-
class movement throughout the country, potentially unite black and
white laborers, and give an important impetus to the revival of the
working-class movement internationally. Within the United States,
Marx argued, "labor cannot be free in the white skin where in the
black it is branded."[10]

Due to the need for American cotton in English textile production,
the English capitalists and press favored the South. The English workers remained largely silent until the North took two Confederate
diplomats, Slidell and Mason, from the English ship H.M.S. *Trent.*
A major rift developed between the United States and England, where
pro-slavery agitation intensified.

The English workers might easily have been swept away in pro-war
sentiment by following their narrowly conceived economic interests.
In a newspaper dispatch, Marx vividly describes their misery:

The distress among workers in the northern manufacturing dis-
tricts, motivated by the blockade of the slave states which closed the

9. Saul K. Padover, ed., *Karl Marx on America and the Civil War* (New York,
1972), pp. 153, 247, 271, 272.

10. Padover, *Marx on America*, pp. 92-93, 237; Marx, *Capital*, trans. Samuel
Moore and Edward Aveling (New York, 1967), p. 301. Victory over slavery,
Marx argued, would trigger more radical developments. The violent suppression
of Reconstruction shows that the potential for such developments did exist. See
Allen W. Trelease, *White Terror* (New York, 1971).

factories or shortened the working hours, is unbelievable and increases daily. The other portions of the working class do not suffer to the same degree, but they suffer keenly from the repercussion of the crisis in the cotton industry on other branches of industry, from the reduction of exports of their own products to North America as a result of the Morrill Tariff and the destruction of this export to the southern United States as a result of the blockade. At the present moment, English intervention in America has therefore become a bread and butter question for the working class.

But despite the pro-slavery political campaign and this economic distress, no pressure to go to war emerged from below. Moreover, workers held mass anti-war meetings in Manchester, Sheffield, and London. Marx described the resolution passed by the London workers:

> Therefore this meeting considers it the particular duty of the workers since they are not represented in the senate of the nation, to declare their sympathy with the United States in its gigantic struggle for maintenance of the Union, to denounce the base dishonesty and advocacy of slaveholding indulged in by the *Times* and kindred aristocratic journals, to express themselves most emphatically in favor of a policy of strictest nonintervention in the affairs of the United States . . . and to manifest the warmest sympathy with the endeavours of the Abolitionists to bring about a final solution to the question of slavery.[11]

Though some pro-war sentiment existed in the English labor movement, pro-abolition sentiment predominated. As Royden Harrison notes, "The Sheffield workmen told Roebuck—who wanted to recognize the South: 'Never! We should have a Civil War in England.'"
In his 1864 "Inaugural Address of the IWA," Marx argued:

> It was not the wisdom of the ruling classes but the heroic resistance to their criminal folly by the working classes of England that saved the West of Europe from plunging headlong into an

11. Padover, *Marx on America*, pp. 112-113, 157-160, 266, 152-156, 161-163.

infamous crusade for the perpetuation and propagation of slavery on the other side of the Atlantic.[12]

This example raises two issues. First, internationalism involves a conflict of interest or a choice for the worker. The English textile worker who supported the war against slavery and the blockade suffered for it, to some extent. On the one hand, economic considerations gave him at least some interest in supporting the war. On the other hand, the international impact of a victory of a slave republic would worsen his own economic and social conditions. In addition, the English government would conscript him to fight in any war effort. Therefore, Marx argued, the worker's main interest lay in opposing slavery. His choice of the "common interest" over the narrow interest rested on understanding the larger political and economic consequences of the war. Given the conflict of interests, however, no guarantee existed that working class internationalism would win out. Only a political movement could defend the long-range common interests of the proletariat against short-lived economic gain.

Second, under some circumstances, internationalism may lead to redistribution of the means of production. The English workers helped prevent English intervention to aid an unjust cause, and thus supported a fundamental redistribution in the South as the former slaves gained property in their own persons. Marx's theory supports redistribution of the means of production through revolution. Within a given mode of production, however, he believed that no basic redistribution could occur (*SW* 1: 426).

As another important example of internationalism, Marx built the IWA around forms of solidarity specific to capitalism—international strike support and the fight for the shorter work week. This strike support consisted of stopping the importation of scabs from the Continent to England, and collecting funds for, and publicizing strikes on, the Continent. In the strike wave between 1864 and 1868, the IWA grew rapidly into a mass movement among European workers. In 1868 the Rouen manufacturers hoped to drive down wages and undersell their

12. Royden Harrison, *Before the Socialists* (London, 1965), pp. 66, 64, 76-77; Saul K. Padover, ed., *Karl Marx on the First International* (New York, 1973), pp. 35-36; Marx, *SW*, 1: 384.

competitors throughout Europe; the workers walked out. During the IWA's support of the Rouen strike, Marx formulated the principle of solidarity:

> This was a great opportunity to show the capitalists that their international industrial warfare, carried on by screwing wages down now in this country, now in that, would be checked at last by the international union of the working classes.

This widespread consciousness and organization among workers around union issues, Marx argued, could lead to support for such critical political developments as the abolition of slavery in the United States, independence for Ireland, and support of the Paris Commune. Marx looked mainly to international solidarity in the settings of socialist revolutions and movements for independence; he regarded union solidarity, though important, as secondary.[13]

At this point it might be objected that Marx's analysis of British rule in India and the historical role of colonialism is an important exception to his views on internationalism. As many scholars have noted, Marx "extenuated" British intervention in India by suggesting that British transformation of the "stagnant" Indian village and introduction of railways and capitalist production would prepare the way for eventual independence and socialism. These scholars, however, never consider the changes in Marx's views on the political role of colonialism within the context of his internationalism.[14] A comparison

13. Padover, *Marx on the First International,* p. 41. With the current development of multinational corporations, considerable possibilities exist for union solidarity in different countries. To take two current examples, the Colgate-Palmolive local in Oakland made the rehiring of ten black workers fired for union organizing at Colgate in Boksburg, South Africa, a main contract demand, and the convention of the International Boilermakers' Union has voted to refuse to work on ships contracted by South African companies as long as apartheid continues. The information is courtesy of Patrick Ryle, chief shop steward, ILWU, and Dwight Threepersons, member, International Boilermakers' Union.

14. Shlomo Avineri, ed., *Karl Marx on Colonialism and Modernization* (New York, 1968), pp. 132-134. Avineri's introduction omits any discussion of Marx's internationalism. The collection concentrates on the current "Third World" and, unfortunately, leaves out Marx's writings on the English in Ireland, which represent a fundamental change in Marx's interpretation of the role of colonialism.

of Marx's analysis of colonialism in India with his later views on
colonialism in Ireland will illustrate this development.

In 1853, Marx argued that a "sordid passion" for individual gain
at the expense of the Indian population accompanied even the positive
side of British rule in India, its breaking down of the old social forms
and introduction of a measure of capitalism.

> All the English bourgeoisie may be forced to do will neither
> emancipate nor materially mend the social condition of the mass
> of the people, depending not only on the development of the pro-
> ductive powers, but on their appropriation by the people. But what
> they will not fail to do is to lay down the natural premises for both.
> Has the bourgeoisie ever done more? Has it ever affected a progress
> without dragging individuals and peoples through blood and dirt,
> through misery and degradation?

At this time, Marx felt that liberation of India would come either from
a proletarian revolution in England or from an independence movement in India itself.

> The Indians will not reap the fruits of the new elements of society
> scattered among them by the British bourgeoisie, till in Great Brit-
> ain itself the now ruling classes shall have been supplanted by the
> industrial proletariat, or till the Hindoos themselves shall have
> grown strong enough to throw off the English yoke altogether.[15]

Far from extolling British paternalism as Mill did, Marx saw the main
positive role of colonialism as breaking down rural isolation and unit-
ing the Indian people to rebel against the British Raj. If a strong Indian independence movement emerged, Marx suggested, the European
socialist movement, then at a low ebb, should support it.

In 1857, the Sepoy mutiny erupted among Indian soldiers in the
British army. The British based their rule in India, Marx noted, on the
Roman precept, divide and rule. Yet in forging a national army, composed largely of Indian soldiers, they had created a "general center of
resistance" against themselves. The mutiny broke down the political

15. Avineri, *Marx on Colonialism*, p. 137.

divisions which provided the foundations of British rule: "Mussulmans and Hindoos, renouncing their mutual antipathies, have combined against their common masters" in a genuine "national revolt." For Marx, the revolt appeared all the more threatening to British rule because, unlike previous mutinies, it had spread beyond a few isolated localities; a revolt beginning with Hindus sought to restore a Moslem emperor in Delhi; Sepoy regiments for the first time murdered European officers; and Indian resistance to European supremacy coincided with resistance in China and Persia.[16] Marx may have overestimated the level of overall Asian resistance to colonialism at this time. Yet from Marx's point of view, the development of English colonialism undermined its own power.

Citing Indian reports of the "universal existence of torture as a financial institution" to extort newly imposed taxes, Marx even extenuated reported Indian atrocities against the British:

> In view of such facts, dispassionate and thoughtful men may perhaps be led to ask whether a people are not justified in attempting to expel the foreign conquerors who have so abused their subjects. And if the English could do these things in cold blood, is it surprising that the insurgent Hindoos should be guilty, in the fury of revolt and conflict, of the crimes and cruelties alleged against them?

Referring to the London *Times'* outcry against revolutionary "atrocities," Marx commented sardonically:

> The outrages committed by the revolted Sepoys in India are indeed appalling, hideous, ineffable—such as one is prepared to meet only in wars of insurrection, of nationalities, of races, and above all of religion; in one word, such as respectable England used to applaud when perpetrated by the Vendeans on the "Blues," by the Spanish guerillas on the infidel Frenchmen, by Serbians on their

16. Avineri, pp. 206, 443-444, 49-50. Marx produced an uncharacteristically negative evaluation of the massive Taiping rebellion in China for *Die Presse*. In this article, he relied entirely on the opinion of the English consul.

German and Hungarian neighbors, by Croats on Viennese rebels,
by Cavaignac's Garde Mobile or Bonaparte's Decembrists on the
sons and daughters of proletarian France.[17]

In addition, Marx argued, the bourgeoisie's economic and social
pressure on English workers was increased by raising taxes to maintain an army and by wars to defend English colonialism in India.
Marx estimated that the costs of British rule might outstrip the reve-
nues. The English people, however, paid the costs; the benefits went to
the East India Company, aristocratic military officers, and civil ser-
vants.[18] In this context, Marx saw the Indian revolt as a source of
increasing tension among English social classes and thus as an impetus for the reemergence of the working class movement. This workers' movement would have shared interests with the Indians in revolt.
He wrote to Engels in January 1858 that, "with the drain of men and
bullion which it must cost the English, India is now our best ally."[19]

Marx's sympathy with the Sepoy rebellion foreshadowed the fundamental transformation of his views on English colonialism in Ireland.
In 1867, the development of Fenianism made the issue of Ireland a
central one in English politics. Furthermore, the famine drove large
numbers of Irish emigrants into English cities, dividing the working
class between English and Irish laborers.

In the 1840s and 1850s, Marx believed that English socialism
would liberate the colonies. Though he stressed internationalism, he
saw it mainly as a political necessity among the democratic or socialist revolutionary movements in the relatively advanced European
states. His political experience in the IWA and the evident difficulties
of winning English workers from a trade union perspective—even an
internationalist one—to socialism caused Marx to reverse his earlier
estimate. He was now convinced that only a movement to support the
liberation of Ireland among English workers could lay the foundation
for a strong revolutionary movement in England.

17. Avineri, pp. 224-234. Though properly noting Marx's original skepticism
about the military chances of the revolt, Avineri's introduction incomprehensibly
ignores all of Marx's arguments in defense of the rebellion (see pp. 25-26, 29).
18. Avineri, pp. 238, 19, rightly emphasizes this point.
19. Avineri, p. 463.

For a long time I believed that it would be possible to overthrow the Irish regime by English working-class ascendance. I always expressed this point of view in the *New York Tribune*. Deeper study has now convinced me of the opposite. The English working class will *never accomplish anything* until it has got rid of Ireland. The lever must be applied in Ireland.

In Marx's analysis of the international situation in the 1860s the "material conditions for revolution," particularly a large proletariat which "had developed up to a certain degree of maturity," existed in England. A successful struggle there could trigger the entire socialist revolution internationally.[20] Yet further economic development—even an economic crisis—in England alone would not produce revolution, which was obstructed by the possession of Ireland and the resulting racist political attitudes among English workers. If socialism was to come to England in the 1860s, Ireland would serve as "the lever." As Marx put it in 1870:

. . . Every industrial and commercial centre in England now possesses a working class *divided* into two *hostile* camps, English proletarians and Irish proletarians. The ordinary English worker hates the Irish worker as a competitor who lowers his standard of life. In relation to the Irish worker he feels himself a member of the *ruling* nation and so turns himself into a tool of the aristocrats and capitalists of his country against *Ireland*, thus strengthening their domination *over himself*.

The religious, social, and national prejudices the English worker harbored against the Irish worker paralleled those of poor whites against blacks in the American south. The Irish worker responded by seeing the English worker as "at once the accomplice and the stupid tool of *English rule in Ireland*." The English ruling class, Marx argued, directed all of its ideological means to maintain this artificial antagonism, including "the press, the pulpit, the comic papers." The old po-

20. Marx and Engels, *Selected Correspondence*, trans. I. Lasker, ed. S. Ryazanskaya (Moscow, 1965), pp. 230, 232, 235, 236-237. Marx and Engels, *Ireland and the Irish Question*, ed. R. Dixon, (New York, 1972), pp. 290, 161-162.

litical tactic of divide and rule provided the bulwark for the political
and economic power of English capitalism.

   This antagonism is the secret of the impotence of the English
working class, despite its organization. It is the secret by which
the capitalist class maintains its power. And that class is fully aware
of it.[21]

During this period, Marx reevaluated the historical role of English
conquest of Ireland, starting with the Puritan Revolution. "By engaging in the conquest of Ireland, Cromwell threw the English republic
out the window. Thence the Irish mistrust of the English People's
party." On the basis of his new analysis, Marx led a campaign in the
first International to support independence for Ireland as its foremost
political objective.

   As Marx pictured it, the development of a strong working-class
movement in England, concurrent with an independence movement
in Ireland, would force the English government to withdraw. Then
an agrarian revolution of the starving Irish peasantry would promptly
dispossess both English and Irish landlords. The power of the aristocracy in England rested, in Marx's view, on its holdings in Ireland.
Consequently, the liberation of Ireland, based on the unity of English
and Irish proletarians, would destroy the influence of the landed aristocracy in England itself. In addition, independence for Ireland would
remove an essential justification "for retaining a big standing army"
in Britain. Without the army and the threat of its being "used against
the English workers after having done its military training in Ireland,"
a proletarian revolution would become much more likely. An English
revolutionary government and a democratic Ireland, possibly with a
strong socialist movement itself, might federate on a non-exploitative
basis.

   In estimating the potential for internationalism among English

   21. Marx and Engels, *Correspondence*, pp. 236-237; Marx and Engels, *Ireland*,
p. 162. Marx advocated Irish independence from the inception of the IWA, and
supported arrested Fenian leaders on many occasions. Though an advocate of
mass revolutionary violence, Marx opposed the conspiratorial and terrorist tendencies within the Fenian movement. Marx, *Correspondence*, pp. 513, 514.
Marx, *Ireland*, pp. 128, 143, 440-441, 145, 149, 281, 285.

workers, Marx again saw their interests as divided. The English worker, typically holding a slightly better job, feared the Irish worker "as a competitor who lowers his standard of life." On this fear rested the capacity of the bourgeoisie to exploit the English worker and to render the labor unions "impotent." Marx argued that the International could win English workers to support the Irish. He saw this support as arising mainly from common interests and not "humanitarian sentiment" or concern for "international justice."[22]

The cause of the Fenian prisoners and the activities of the IWA succeeded in evoking considerable English and international support for the Irish cause. However, support for the Paris Commune and subsequent repression of the IWA all over Europe ended the Irish campaign without major success.

Marx's new argument that the liberation of Ireland provided the lever for a socialist movement in England represented a fundamental change in his theory, in his political strategy for proletarian revolution, and in his overall estimate of colonialism. In 1848 he had argued that no nation could be free if it oppressed another. Yet he did not fully apply this analysis to the implications of colonialism for a socialist movement in an advanced capitalist country; he thought such movements could come to power before colonies were liberated. Now, however, Marx no longer believed this possible—at least for Ireland—and followed his internationalism of 1848 to its conclusion: only successful national revolt in Ireland, supported by the British workers, would permit the full development of socialism in England.[23] It seems but a short step from this argument to the notion that colonialism,

22. Marx never based his social theory or political strategies on appeals to justice. Nonetheless, he often used categories—exploitation, solidarity among workers, and the like—loaded with at least a rough moral conception.

23. In this, his argument still retained overtones of an economic determinist interpretation—proletarian revolution would inevitably come about through the development of capitalist productive forces in the advanced countries. An economic determinist interpretation, however, would make his later political argument completely incomprehensible. An economic determinist might conclude that English workers in the 1860s would not join a revolutionary movement because their economic conditions had improved. Marx thought that their economic conditions had not improved, and emphasized the politics of racism and patriotism as an explanation for the weakness of English socialism. Marx, *SW*, 1: pp. 377-381; Marx and Engels, *Ireland*, p. 163.

patriotism, and racism flourish together, and that any socialist movement should oppose them.

Marx commented on Indian independence once more in a letter of 1881 to the Russian N. F. Danielson. He argued that the English "bleeding" of India would probably produce a national revolt. In 1882, Engels wrote a letter to Kautsky which combined elements of Marx's old and new arguments. Following the 1848 analysis, Engels suggested that a socialist revolution in an advanced country would have to free the colonies as rapidly as possible. Yet at the same time, on the new argument, he expected a revolution in India, and pointed out that "the victorious proletariat can force no blessings of any kind upon any foreign nation without undermining its own victory by so doing." Lenin took up Marx's later view, and argued that revolutionary movements in advanced countries must oppose colonial enterprises and support the right of self-determination.[21]

II. SOME CONTEMPORARY IMPLICATIONS

Turning to contemporary international affairs, Marx's framework highlights certain unusual but important possibilities for redistribution to which most discussions have paid little attention. I would like to explore two of them: (1) cases of colonial—and by implication neo-colonial—wars waged by capitalist countries against independence or radical social movements, and (2) immigration of individuals from poor countries to rich ones. I shall then consider briefly the relevance of Marx's argument to the current discussion of unequal distribution between rich and poor nations.

In discussing colonial wars, I shall concentrate on two cases of great international impact—the French war in Algeria and the Portuguese wars in Africa.

Herbert Lüthy has described, in a style reminiscent of Marx's, the internal conflicts which raged in French society during the Algerian war.

24. Avineri, *Marx on Colonialism*, pp. 471, 473. V. I. Lenin, *Collected Works*, 45 vols. (Moscow, 1974), 22: 143-156, 320-360. The same tension, however, exists on Lenin's argument, between support for an independence movement led by a national bourgeoisie and socialism, as the one between democratic and proletarian revolution which troubled Marx in 1848. See Gilbert, "Changing the World," p. 20.

The empire was something with which the French people had nothing whatever to do, and its story was that of machinations of high finance, the Church and the military caste, which tirelessly re-erected overseas the Bastilles which had been overthrown in France.[25]

Similarly, the empire in Africa sustained fascism in Portugal. When serious resistance movements emerged in Algeria and in the Portuguese colonies, the costs to the French and Portuguese people in lives and taxes rose enormously. The impact of war, both in the colonies and on the population at home, underlined Marx's point about common interests of workers and peasants against oppressive or inegalitarian regimes and policies.[26] In Portugal, various forms of resistance emerged, ranging from massive emigration (one-third of the population, including many men of draft age, left the country) and widespread desertion, to the halting of all fighting months before the end of the war in Mozambique and Guinea-Bissau. An officer in the Armed Forces Movement summarized an attitude which became widespread during the lengthy campaigns abroad:

. . . the armed forces began to understand that the arms they had to defend the people were being used to destroy the people. Angola, Mozambique and Guinea were places where people had gone to get rich, and it was only a certain class who got anything from it . . .[27]

In addition to this type of opposition, contacts between servicemen, officers, and the African independence movements may have had a radical or internationalist impact. Eventually, the Armed Forces Movement, composed largely of officers, overthrew the fascist Portuguese regime and stopped these wars. As the turbulent post-coup

25. Herbert Lüthy, *France Against Herself* (New York, 1957), p. 205.

26. For differing criteria on the injustice of wars of this kind, see John Rawls, *A Theory of Justice* (Cambridge, MA, 1971), section 58; Beitz, "Justice and International Relations," pp. 386-387.

27. Three million people emigrated. Antonio de Figueiredo, *Portugal* (New York, 1976), p. 180. Rona M. Fields, *The Portuguese Revolution and the Armed Forces Movement* (New York, 1976), p. 73. Richard Hamilton, *Restraining Myths* (New York, 1975), p. 184, and chap. 5.

period showed, this Armed Forces Movement had considerable popular support. In this case, more strikingly than in Algeria, the internal
costs of a war against independence drove an important part of the
population into opposition. This resistance restricted the government's
maneuverability and ultimately overthrew it.

The Portuguese workers, soldiers, and peasants displayed only a
limited degree of conscious international working class or democratic
solidarity, and the Armed Forces Movement did not neatly fit a Marxian framework.²⁸ Nonetheless, the interconnected resistances in Africa
and Portugal provide a striking confirmation of Marx's internationalism. Colonialism and fascism fell together. The independence and
revolutionary movements, both in the colonies and the advanced country, created circumstances where new regimes, once they assumed
power, might achieve a certain degree of internal redistribution.²⁹

Let us now consider the second possibility for redistribution. Since
World War II, Western Europe and the United States have experienced an increasing immigration from the poorer nations of Europe,
Africa, and Latin America. In Western Europe, immigrants now account for 10 percent of the industrial work force in most countries.
Though not always the poorest individuals, many immigrants come
from the "least advantaged" backgrounds, and their remittances contribute directly to the support of the poorest segments of the population in their country of origin. According to one study, two million
rural inhabitants of Algeria receive income remitted from immigrants

28. See Figueiredo, *Portugal*, p. 251. In Marxian terms, the officers belonged
to the old ruling class. It seems far easier to explain the French officers' efforts
to maintain colonialism than the left-wing Portuguese movement to overthrow
it. In this case, the uneven development of Portugal in relation to the rest of
Europe is important. Portugal—the last empire—fought to hold on after stronger
colonial powers had met defeat. It was also almost the last fascist power in an
era when fascism had long been defeated, and was, simultaneously, the most
economically backward country in Europe. See Fields, *The Portuguese Revolution*, chap. 3. Under the impact of a long, costly, and losing war, many Portuguese officers decided that only democratic socialism would enable Portugal to
rid itself of unjust colonial wars and leap ahead of the rest of Europe.

29. Whether they do so depends upon decisions taken after the movements
come to power. The Algerian revolution produced relatively little redistribution.
Arnold Fraleigh, "The Algerian Revolution as a Case Study in International
Law," *The International Law of Civil War*, ed. Richard Falk (Baltimore, 1971),
p. 243. Arslan Humbaraci, *Algeria: A Revolution That Failed* (New York, 1966),
p. 271.

in France. In some villages such remittances amount to 80 percent of total money income.[30] In terms of the relations between the advanced countries and the least advantaged individuals internationally, the policies adopted toward immigrants represent an interesting test case. Yet most of the philosophical and social science literature on redistribution ignores this issue.[31]

Under current international law in states regarded as mainly self-sufficient, immigrants are entitled to be treated in accordance with the "ordinary standards of civilization."[32] Adopting the perspective of a natural duty to mutual aid or of Rawls' difference principle, one might look upon the presence of such individuals in the advanced countries (and the incomes they remit) as an important vehicle to further international redistribution. Given the fact that elites in poor nations benefit from increasingly unequal income distribution and do not use inter-governmental aid to improve the conditions of the poor, the presence of immigrants provides a special opportunity for the advanced countries—dealing with individuals under their direct jurisdiction—to guarantee fair treatment and a certain amount of economic support.

Unfortunately, current immigration policies have nothing to do with redistributing income to poor immigrants and their families; rather, immigration serves to recruit cheap labor. Castles and Kosack have aptly characterized current immigration policies as a form of development aid from the poor countries to the advanced ones.[33]

Legal immigration in Europe—for example, in West Germany—is restricted to "unmarried workers" allowed into the country for a limited period. The immigrants can expect a high rate of turnover in the hardest and lowest-paying jobs, with considerable harassment in return for temporary improvement in their living standards. In case

30. John Westergaard and Henrietta Resler, *Class in a Capitalist Society* (London, 1975), pp. 356-357. Stephen Castles and Godula Kosack, *Immigrant Workers and Class Structure in Western Europe* (Oxford, 1973), p. 418. Mexican immigrants to the United States remit an estimated three billion dollars per year. Richard R. Fagen, "The Realities of U.S.-Mexican Relations," *Foreign Affairs*, vol. 55, no. 4 (July, 1977), 689.

31. Suzanne Paine's *Exporting Workers* (Cambridge, 1974), is an important exception.

32. J. L. Brierly, *The Law of Nations* (Oxford, 1963), p. 279. Rawls, section 58.

33. Spero, *Politics of International Economic Relations*, chap. 6. Castles and Kosack, *Immigrant Workers*, pp. 427-429.

of recession, as in 1967, the government can require them to return
to their countries of origin. Where many immigrants are "illegal," as
in France or in the United States, the employers and government subject them to the worst conditions on the job as well as to harassment
and threat of deportation whether or not they organize to do anything
about it. As Marx suggested, the press often pillories immigrants.
Immigrants are also subjected to legal and extralegal campaigns of
harassment by reactionary groups such as the Schwarzenbach Initia-
tive in Switzerland, or the wave of murders of immigrants in Marseille
in 1973. Under present circumstances government, capitalist, and
media policies towards immigrants will probably not shift in a more
cosmopolitan, redistributive direction.

As in the case of the Irish in the nineteenth century, a Marxian
framework would suggest looking at the impact of immigration on
the working classes in the advanced countries. On one side (the one
most played up by the press and by some union leaders as well)[35]
immigration, as Marx put it, "lower(s) the standard of life" of citizen
workers through competition. Taking the given conditions between
classes as fixed, the ruling classes depict what is available to workers
themselves as a zero-sum game. On the other side, however, the workers might make an internationalist effort at organizing for better
conditions either as a greater share of growth or a cut in profits. Many
immigrants work in the same factories, though at lower pay and in
worse jobs, than citizen workers. For example, 46 percent of semi-
skilled auto workers in France are immigrants. In Europe immigrants
have frequently gone on strike or attempted to organize against re-
pressive conditions; they have also joined larger strike movements,
such as the May 1968 movement in France. Though some European
union federations have expressed sympathy with immigrant efforts,
only the CFDT in France has seriously and successfully organized
them. In a Marxian framework organizing immigrants would benefit
the citizen workers whose living standards—relative to the capitalists—

34. "Who Will Do the Dirty Work Tomorrow?" *Fortune*, January 1974. Manuel
Castells, "Immigrant Workers and Class Struggles in Advanced Capitalism:
The Western European Experience," *Politics and Society*, 5, no. 1 (January
1975): 56-57, 64. Castles and Kosack, *Immigrant Workers*, p. 341.

35. Alexander Saxton, *The Indispensable Enemy* (Berkeley, 1971), pp. 271-
282.

would otherwise decline. Thus, the case of immigration once again illustrates the economic and political connection between inequalities in the poor nations and inequalities in the advanced ones.[36]

A Marxian argument can justify cooperation among working-class democratic or socialist movements of different nations regardless of the degree of economic interconnection of their respective ruling classes. Does this theory provide any special insight into the current relationships between rich and poor nations?

International economic interconnection, especially through the investment of multinational corporations, has grown greatly since the nineteenth century when Marx examined it. On Marx's theory of surplus value, foreign corporations would benefit from processes of unequal exchange. In addition, they would take advantage of what Marx called the special "moral" or "historical" conditions of subsistence in these countries—the breaking of unions in Brazil or race laws in South Africa—which would increase the rate of exploitation.[37] At this point, however, some might object that under some conditions, the capital-intensive, multinational firm pays a relatively small number of workers higher wages than other more labor-intensive firms with domestic ownership. International exploitation may exist; multinational firms may even openly or tacitly (by their presence) support regimes which have race laws or destroy unions—but they are not the worst exploiters. In fact, the argument continues, they contribute strongly to economic growth.

To assess this argument, one would have to look—as Marx himself did—at the broader social, political, and economic consequences of

36. Castells, pp. 61-65. Castles and Kosack, *Immigrant Workers*, pp. 152-175, chap. 11. CFDT stands for *Confédération Française Démocratique du Travail*. The economist Michael Reich has studied the impact of racism toward blacks in the United States on the living standards of white workers. His work reveals that where the income of black workers is the lowest, the income of white workers is also the lowest, and the income differential between most whites and the top one percent of whites is at its highest. Michael Reich, "The Economics of Racism," *The Capitalist System*, ed. Richard C. Edwards, Michael Reich, Thomas E. Weisskopf (New York, 1972), pp. 313-325. If the same relationship exists between the incomes of citizens and immigrant workers, then despite the frequent racism among citizen workers, Marx's point about common interests would be well taken.

37. Marx, *Capital*, 1: 171, 236. Arghiri Emmanuel, *Unequal Exchange* (New York, 1972), chap. 3, especially pp. 116-120.

exploitative relationships. The Marxian argument against an exploitative class system rests not simply on an analysis of the relationship
of the non-producers who extract unpaid labor and the producers,
but also on the larger social and political consequences of this relationship. Under capitalism, for example, Marx indicted the alienation
of the worker in production, the capitalist's control of the government
and corruption of formal political equality, the propagation of racism
and divisions among workers, the recruitment of workers to fight in
and pay the other costs of wars to maintain despotism or exploitation,
economic crises and massive unemployment, and so forth. In many
dependent countries, to give a rough typical sketch, narrow growth in
production of raw materials and manufacturing occurs mainly
through highly technological multinational firms, which discourage
more labor-intensive local industry. Meanwhile the spread of capitalism to the countryside has undermined the old, comparatively reciprocal social relationships, and replaced them with more exploitative
ones.[38] Increasing numbers of unemployed agricultural laborers either
hang on in the villages or migrate to the cities to join a large, unemployed proletariat. Population growth magnifies this process. As a
result, a highly skewed system of income distribution develops, in
which the relationship of the wealthy to the urban and rural poor
grows more unequal as economic growth occurs. The political system,
especially a dictatorship relying on foreign military and economic
aid, maintains this unequal development. The broader consequences
of exploitation, in cases less extreme than South Africa, impose a
variety of severe economic, social, and political costs on the majortiy
of the people. These may amount to what Marx once referred to as
"a bleeding process with a vengeance" in examining the broader consequences of British rule in India. As Marx also argued, the increasingly intertwined political and now economic interests of (at least)
two elites—the ruling class of the country itself, and the multinational
corporations and governments of the advanced countries—reinforce
this process. Although the interests of these elites may sometimes conflict, investment by the multinationals creates an additional foreign

38. Hari P. Sharma, "The Green Revolution in India: Prelude to a Red One?"
in Hari P. Sharma and Kathleen Gough, *Imperialism and Revolution in South
Asia* (New York, 1973). James Scott, *The Moral Economy of the Peasant:
Rebellion and Subsistence in Southeast Asia* (New Haven, 1976), chap. 6.

interest in maintaining the stability of broad exploitative relationships, at least against radical social movements aiming at redistribution.[39]

Would a contemporary Marxian examination of international distribution conclude that the workers of the advanced countries and the exploited populations in the poor nations share significant common interests? Unjust war, as in the case of Portuguese colonialism in Africa, provides the best example. Given the class divisions within the advanced nations the government will send those who least benefit from the exploitation of the poor nations to fight. Because of the cost in lives and taxes, these situations provide the strongest basis for overriding narrow interests and producing internationalist activity. In other cases, such as the impact of the energy crisis or the slowdown in economic growth, the structure of advanced capitalism imposes differential costs which hurt mainly the workers and the middle classes. Whether, aside from war, such inequalities could generate a sufficiently strong radical movement to ally with radical movements in the poor nations is unclear. In the context of such a movement, however, one of Marx's basic points about internationalism—that the elite of the advanced country would use an appeal to foreign expansion in order to restore the nation's previous power to deflect the radical movement—might reappear. To succeed, Marx's argument suggests, an egalitarian or socialist movement in an advanced capitalist country would have to be internationalist.[40]

39. Michael T. Klare, "Pointing Fingers," *New York Times*, 10 August 1977; *War Without End* (New York, 1972), chaps. 9-10.

The intervention of ITT, the CIA, and international monetary institutions to undermine the Allende regime in Chile provides a vivid example of mutual support among elites given a radical threat. David Cusack, *Revolution and Counterrevolution in Chile* (Denver, 1977), p. 114.

40. A primary appeal to restoration of a nation's previous power could be mixed with others, for instance, the necessity to stop a rival "socialist" imperialism. Justifications for such policies to some sectors of the population could even include formulations much like an international difference principle: intervention in country X is justified because its elite refused to use foreign aid to help the least advantaged. Amdur argues that such intervention might be ideally justifiable from Rawls' original position. Robert Amdur, "Rawls' Theory of Justice: Domestic and International Perspectives," *World Politics* 29, no. 3, (April 1977). Given the actual network of relationships between rich nations and poor ones, such demands for intervention would not achieve the desired result.

PART II

MARX'S THEORY OF HISTORY

STANLEY MOORE # Marx and Lenin as Historical Materialists

Attacking Marxism in his *Statehood and Anarchy*, Bakunin asks what Marxists mean by calling their doctrines scientific. The expression indicates, he suggests, that since the mass of the people are incapable of science their emancipation will consist in accepting the despotic rule of an educated socialist elite. "A wonderful liberation!" he comments. "Government by intellectuals is the most oppressive, offensive, and despicable type of government in the world."

Marx's notes on Bakunin's book, written in 1874, contain an answer to this charge. Marxian socialism has been called scientific, he replies, only by contrast with utopian socialism, which seeks to impose upon the people new illusions instead of investigating the social movement created by the people themselves. The thrust of this defense is to shift the charge of elitism from scientific to utopian socialism.

Apart from the issue of elitism, what major differences does Marx discern between theories which seek to impose upon the people new illusions and theories which investigate the social movement created by the people themselves? One is the difference between empirical investigation and visionary speculation. Another is the difference between describing and prescribing.

Parts of this argument were presented to the Symposium on Science and Utopia, University of North Carolina at Chapel Hill, March 1972. Further discussion of the contrast between Marx's dialectic of liberation and his sociology of change can be found in my "Utopian Themes in Marx and Mao," *Monthly Review*, June 1969; reprinted in *Dissent*, March/April 1970. Further comparison of patterns of transition to socialism can be found in my *Three Tactics: The Background in Marx* (New York, 1963).

In *The Poverty of Philosophy*—to which he refers in answering Bakunin—Marx stresses the contrast between empirical investigation and visionary speculation. In his Seventh Observation on Method he divides socialist and communist theorists into two groups:

> When the proletariat has not yet developed sufficiently to constitute itself as a class and its struggle with the bourgeoisie has not yet assumed a political character, when the forces of production have not yet developed sufficiently to reveal the requisite material conditions for emancipation of the proletariat and formation of a new society, these theorists are simply utopians, who in order to do away with the poverty of the oppressed classes invent systems and seek a science of regeneration. But when in the course of historical development the struggle of the proletariat takes clearer form, socialist theorists need no longer seek for science in their minds: they need only describe what is happening before their eyes and become spokesmen of this movement. . . . From this moment science, produced by the historical movement and participating in it with full knowledge of its nature, is no longer doctrinaire but revolutionary.

In *The German Ideology*, Marx stresses the contrast between describing and prescribing. In the section of the first chapter entitled "History," he writes:

> Communism is not for us a state of affairs which ought to be established, an ideal in accordance with which reality should be transformed. For us communism is the real movement abolishing the present state of affairs, a movement whose necessary conditions exist as part of that same state of affairs.

How justified are Marx's claims that he has developed a socialist theory which is empirical and descriptive, by contrast with the speculative and prescriptive theories developed by his predecessors and his contemporaries? I propose to test these claims by examining critically his two most celebrated expositions of historical materialism: the one presented in *The Communist Manifesto* and the one presented in the Preface to *The Critique of Political Economy*. I shall consider first a set of problems centering upon the role of class conflict in history, then a set of problems centering upon the relation of political to eco-

nomic transformation. I shall argue that Marx's version of historical
materialism is an unstable combination of two conflicting approaches
to history—a dialectic of liberation and a sociology of change. I shall
conclude that the conflict between utopian and scientific—defined as
Marx himself defines it—is an internal conflict of Marxian socialism.

Concurrently indicating the position of Lenin on these issues, I shall
attempt to relate internal conflicts of Marx's historical materialism to
the split between communists and socialists after the Russian Revolution. The distinctive doctrines of Leninism, I shall argue, derive from
Marx's dialectic of liberation rather than his sociology of change.

Returning finally to Bakunin's account of the connection between
Marxism and elitism, I shall ask to what extent it has been confirmed
by half a century of Russian communism.

I

One set of problems presented by Marx's exposition of historical materialism centers upon the role of class conflict in history. Part One of
the *Manifesto* opens with the declaration that the history of all past
society is the history of class conflicts. The *Preface*, on the other hand,
explains past history in terms of conflicts between forces and relations of production—that is, between technology and institutions. In
this second account of historical materialism there is not a single mention of class.

It is true that there are cross references between the two accounts.
In the *Manifesto* Marx discusses the transition from feudalism to capitalism and the transition from capitalism to socialism in terms of the
interaction of forces and relations of production. In the *Preface*,
though there is no explicit reference to class conflict, there are two
oblique references. The first is Marx's characterization of political
economy as the anatomy of civil society. From a letter he wrote to
Weydemeyer in 1852 we can infer that he has in mind the services
of such theorists as Ricardo in exposing conflicts of class interest
within capitalist economies. The other oblique reference is Marx's
assertion that capitalism is the last antagonistic form of production.
From the concluding paragraph of Part Two of the *Manifesto* we can
infer that the antagonisms he has in mind are class conflicts.

It is also true that the contrasting aims of the two works, together with their contrasting circumstances of publication, might be expected to result in differences of emphasis. The *Critique of Political Economy* was written as a scientific treatise, the *Manifesto* as the program of a revolutionary party. Success for the former depended on acquiescence of the Prussian censors: success for the latter did not. It is accordingly understandable that Marx presented his doctrine of class conflict clearly and provocatively in the *Manifesto*, guardedly and obscurely in the *Preface*.

Yet apart from differences of emphasis, the two accounts differ radically in their range of application. To explain historical development in terms of class conflict is to present a theory that applies only to class societies. But explanation in terms of conflict between forces and relations of production applies to classless as well as class societies. Judged by the definition of class and the account of social evolution presented elsewhere in Marx's writings, his claim in the *Manifesto* that the history of all past society is the history of class conflict is indisputably false.

Forty years later—five years after the death of Marx—Engels attempted, in a footnote added to a new edition, to correct and explain this error. His correction consists in reducing the scope of Marx's statement from the history of all past society to the history of only those societies that have produced written history. His explanation of Marx's error is that in 1847 the organization of society before the emergence of written history was all but unknown. Examined critically, however, both the correction and the explanation raise more questions than they settle.

What types of society are covered by the corrected statement? In the *Preface* Marx divides evolution of the forces of production, together with their corresponding relations of production, into four major epochs: the Asiatic, the antique, the feudal, and the capitalist modes of production. In the *Manifesto* he mentions three main types of class society: ancient, based on exploitation of slaves; feudal, based on exploitation of serfs; and capitalist, based on exploitation of wage-workers. Clearly ancient, feudal, and capitalist societies fall within the scope of the corrected statement. But what about Asiatic society? If it is included, then even after Engels' qualification Marx's assertion remains false. From what Marx writes elsewhere about Asiatic society, it follows that in such societies the means of production are not privately owned. And from what he writes elsewhere about classes, it follows that private ownership of the means of production is a necessary condition for the existence of classes. Shall we then infer that Engels excludes Asiatic society from the scope of the corrected statement? In that case his explanation of Marx's error fails. Far from being all but unknown in 1847, the organization of Asiatic society had been discussed since the time of Herodotus. Hegel's account of Asiatic culture occupied a major portion of his *Lectures on the Philosophy of History*. Four years before writing the *Manifesto*, Marx himself had contrasted—in his *Critique of Hegel's Philosophy of Right* —the characteristics of political authority in Asiatic, ancient, feudal, and capitalist societies.

Primitive societies—such as those discussed by Engels in his *Origin of the Family*—are prehistorical, in the sense that they produce no written history. To characterize the economic systems of such societies as primitive communism precludes explaining their development in terms of class conflict. By reducing its scope in accordance with these considerations, Engels admits that Marx's original statement was false. But his explanation of Marx's error does not fit the facts. In 1847 the organization of primitive societies was not unknown, in any sense that could justify Marx's sweeping assertion about all past history. Speculation concerning prehistory extended back at least to Lucretius. Information about primitive societies was avidly collected and discussed during the Enlightenment. A few years before writing the *Manifesto*, Marx himself had commenced an account of social evolution—in the first chapter of *The German Ideology*—with the stage of tribal society, in which people lived by hunting and fishing, by raising animals, or (at a later period) by agriculture.

If we grant that Marx unjustifiably extends his theory of class conflict to cover all past history, we must reject the *Manifesto* as a guide to the remote past. Must we also question any of its arguments concerning the present or the future? One of these arguments rests on this false claim. It is Marx's defense of the prediction that triumph of communism will involve total disappearance of morality.

In Part Two of the *Manifesto* Marx considers the criticism that communists propose simply to abolish such universal ideals as freedom and justice, instead of establishing them on a new basis. Morality has been indispensable for all types of society, the critics argue, though in each it has taken a different form. In the society of the future it will not be abolished but transformed. Marx comments in reply:

What does this accusation amount to? The history of all past society has developed through class antagonisms, though in different epochs these have differed in type. . . . No wonder then that the social consciousness of past ages, despite all the multiplicity and variety it displays, has moved within certain common forms. Only with total disappearance of class antagonisms will these forms of consciousness completely vanish.

This passage belongs among what Lenin called the forgotten words of Marxism. Nowhere in the *Manifesto* is the prediction that morality will disappear supported by argument in terms of the interaction of forces and relations of production. Nowhere in Marx's subsequent writings is the topic even mentioned. Lenin, in chapter five of *State and Revolution*, explains Marx's prediction that the state will wither away in terms which flatly contradict the prediction that morality will completely vanish:

Only in communist society . . . will democracy itself begin to wither away, owing to the simple fact that . . . people will gradually become accustomed to observing the elementary rules of social life—which have been well known for centuries and reiterated in copy-book maxims for a thousand years—without force, without compulsion, without subordination, without the special apparatus for compulsion which is called the state.

This is the position Marx attributes to the critics of communism—that morality will not be abolished but transformed.

What is the significance of these forgotten words? The fact that in the *Manifesto* Marx defends so millenarian a prediction by a claim so obviously false points, I suggest, to a central tension in his version of historical materialism. On the one hand, his theory of history is a sociology of change, focused on analyzing the interaction of technology and institutions. On the other hand, it is a dialectic of libera-

tion, focused on exposing the sham freedoms of capitalist society in
terms of a millenarian vision of community. To develop this suggestion, I propose to contrast these two components in terms of their
theoretical antecedents and practical consequences.

II

Marx published his Preface to *The Critique of Political Economy* in
place of a longer and more comprehensive Introduction, which he had
written in part but failed to finish. His notes for continuing that
manuscript show that he planned to discuss the connection between
the materialism of his approach to history and what he calls nat-
uralistic materialism—that is, the philosophical materialism presented as a generalization of the methods and results of natural science.
In the *Preface* he does not consider this question. But he does discuss
it in *Capital*.

In the chapter of the first volume of *Capital* entitled "Machinery
and Modern Industry," Marx writes in a footnote:

Darwin has interested us in the history of nature's technology—that
is, in the formation of the organs of plants and animals as instruments of production for maintaining plant and animal life. Does
not the history of the productive organs of associated men, of the
material basis for the different forms of social organization, deserve
equal attention? . . . Technology discloses men's active relations
with nature, the basic process of production that sustains their
lives. Therewith it also discloses the relations structuring their social
life and the mental conceptions that derive from these.

The approach to history outlined in this passage could be called
scientific, in the sense that it proposes to investigate human history
as an outgrowth of biological evolution. The behavior of men, like
that of other animals, is to be explained in terms of interaction between organisms and environments. But the interaction of men with
their environment differs from that of all other animals. During recent stages of human evolution, changing the environment through
technology has played a far more important role than has biological
adaptation. This is because human technology differs from that of

other animals in being learned and cumulative rather than instinctive and repetitive. Furthermore, changes in human technology, because of its learned and cumulative character, affect the whole of human culture. From these considerations it follows that the distinctive pattern of human evolution is cultural rather than biological, and that the key to this cultural development is technological development. To the extent that this line of argument is accepted, it is plausible to view Marx's account of historical materialism in terms of forces and relations of production as a scientific approach to social change.

Marx was by no means the first to consider history from this standpoint. Among theorists of the Enlightenment, Rousseau in his *Discourse on the Origin of Inequality* and Adam Smith in his *Lectures on Justice, Police, Revenue and Arms* take this approach to social change. Among theorists of antiquity, Lucretius presents an account of cultural evolution centering upon technological innovation, which he treats as the key to institutional change. Cole, in his *Democritus and the Sources of Greek Anthropology*, has traced the ancestry of these ideas back to Democritus. What I have called Marx's sociology of change belongs to a tradition roughly as old as that of philosophical materialism.

By contrast, Marx's approach to history in terms of class conflict derives from a complex mixture of theoretical traditions. In a letter he wrote to Weydemeyer in 1852, he disclaims any credit for discovering class conflict in modern society. Bourgeois historians, such as Thierry and Guizot, have described the origins of this conflict. Bourgeois economists, such as Ricardo, have investigated the economic anatomy of classes. Marx continues:

> My contribution has been to prove: (1) that the existence of classes is confined to particular historical periods in the development of production; (2) that the class struggle necessarily leads to the dictatorship of the proletariat; and (3) that this dictatorship constitutes the transition to abolition of all classes, to a classless society.

The first item on this list seems redundant. If all past history is the history of class society, as Marx asserts in the *Manifesto*, then the first contribution is included in the third. But if class societies have developed from classless societies, as he recognizes in *The Critique of*

Political Economy, the same conclusion follows; for adherence to so
common an opinion could not be considered a separate contribution.
The distinctive features of Marx's attempt to understand social change
in terms of class conflict are accordingly reduced to two: his theory
of proletarian dictatorship and his theory of communist society. Both
theories are predictions of the future, rather than explanations of the
past.

What are the intellectual antecedents of these doctrines? The ancestry of Marx's theory of proletarian dictatorship can be traced
through Blanqui and Dezamy, Buonarroti and Babeuf, back to the
doctrine of revolutionary dictatorship formulated by Robespierre and
Saint-Just. Marx's theory of communist society derives from two intellectual currents—one acknowledged in the *Manifesto*, the other
not. In the section of Part Three entitled "Critical-Utopian Socialism
and Communism," after distinguishing his position from Babeuf's
equalitarian communism, he acknowledges his debt to Owen, Fourier,
and Saint-Simon. In the section entitled "German or 'True' Socialism"
he conceals his debt to the philosophical communism of Hess, which
is descended, through Cieszkowski and Feuerbach, from Hegel's theory of community.

Among these thinkers, Feuerbach is clearly influenced by philosophical materialism; and in *The Holy Family* Marx claims for this
tradition Fourier, Owen, Babeuf, Buonarroti, and Dezamy. Yet even
if it is justifiable to call these thinkers philosophical materialists, it
is not justifiable to conclude that they take a scientific approach to
social change. The antecedents of Marx's theory of communist society
are predominantly millenarian. As prophets of a New Jerusalem,
Babeuf, Cieszkowski, and Hess rival or surpass Fourier, Owen, and
Saint-Simon. To examine Marx's intellectual development is to discover that he had formulated his ideal of communism—through a
moral critique of capitalist culture and a call for a rebirth of community—before he adopted the position of philosophical materialism or
developed his sociology of change.

To trace the different sources of the two components of Marx's
theory of history arouses a strong suspicion that they are incompatible. But it does not amount to proof, because it does not eliminate
the possibility that Marx united these disparate elements in a complex

but consistent whole. For proof of incompatibility, it is necessary to turn from theoretical antecedents to practical consequences.

On one practical consequence of the first importance, the *Manifesto* and the *Preface* present opposing positions. The *Manifesto* supports the tactic of transforming bourgeois revolution into proletarian revolution—what Marx calls elsewhere the tactic of permanent revolution. But this tactic is incompatible with the account of historical materialism presented in the *Preface*.

Approaching the problem in terms of class conflict, Marx writes in Part Four of the *Manifesto*:

> The Communists turn their attention chiefly to Germany, because that country is on the eve of a bourgeois revolution that is bound to be carried out under more advanced conditions of European civilization, and with a much more developed proletariat, than the bourgeois revolution of England in the seventeenth century or that of France in the eighteenth century, and because therefore this bourgeois revolution can be but the prelude to an immediately following proletarian revolution.

This was the tactic Lenin advocated in his *April Theses*, when he returned to Russia after the February Revolution.

To consider this tactic of permanent revolution in terms of the connection between forces and relations of production is to deny it any prospect of success. Marx writes in the *Preface*:

> No social order ever disappears before all the productive forces it has room for have been developed. New, higher relations of production never appear before the material conditions for their existence have matured in the womb of the old society.

In a society on the eve of bourgeois revolution, can there be no further development of the forces of production within the framework of capitalist relations of production? Can a given level in the development of the forces of production provide simultaneously the material conditions for a bourgeois and a proletarian revolution? Of Babeuf's program for transforming bourgeois into proletarian revolution, Marx writes in Part Three of the *Manifesto*:

The first direct attempts of the proletariat to attain its own ends, made in times of general upheaval when feudal society was being overthrown, necessarily failed, owing to the undeveloped state of the proletariat and the absence of the economic conditions for its emancipation—conditions that had yet to be produced, and could only be produced, by the impending capitalist epoch.

Viewed in terms of Marx's sociology of change, how could his own program for transforming bourgeois into proletarian revolution be expected to escape a comparable frustration?

Three years before the Bolshevik Revolution, Lenin wrote a long encyclopedia article on Marx. In a section entitled "The Materialist Conception of History" he quotes verbatim almost the entire account presented in the *Preface*. In the following section, entitled "The Class Struggle," he quotes at length from the account presented in the *Manifesto*. But he neither quotes nor paraphrases the two passages cited above. They have no place in his version of historical materialism.

III

Entangled with the set of problems centering upon the role of class conflict in history is another set, centering upon the connection between economic and political transformation—or, as the issue is sometimes stated, between social and political revolution.

The account of historical materialism presented in the *Preface* outlines a discrete series of modes of production. Initially, relations of production—which Marx explicitly equates with property relations—harmonize with forces of production—which he tacitly equates with technology. Then, under the impact of technological change, this harmony gives way to conflict. "From forms of development of the forces of production, these relations turn into their fetters." When the conflict becomes intolerable, it is resolved by a period of revolution, during which new property relations are established in conformity with the new stage of technological development. Outside this revolutionary period, there is no overlap: one mode of production prevails, then another takes its place.

The account of the transition from capitalism to socialism presented in the *Manifesto* exemplifies this pattern. Marx argues that capitalist property relations have become fetters upon the forces of production. He predicts a revolution in which the proletariat will seize political power, replace capitalist property relations with communist property relations, and establish a new harmony between technology and institutions.

But the account of the transition from feudalism to capitalism presented in the same work exemplifies a different pattern. According to what Marx writes there and amplifies in *Capital*, capitalist property relations commenced to replace feudal property relations around 1500, though bourgeois revolution did not break out in England until 1640 or in France until 1789. This is a pattern of coexisting and competing modes of production, in which one gradually wins out over the other and in which seizure of political power follows a long process of economic transformation. While in the transition from capitalism to socialism political revolution precedes economic transformation, in the transition from feudalism to capitalism economic transformation precedes political revolution.

Marx's failure to make explicit this contrast in formulating his sociology of change results in serious ambiguities and inconsistencies. Some of these concern the connection between modes of production and relations of production. Others concern the line of demarcation between basis and superstructure. Still others concern the problem of predictability.

In the *Preface* relations of production are equated with property relations. A set of such relations, corresponding to a given set of forces of production, is an economic structure of society. An economic structure, together with its corresponding forces of production, is a mode of production. What in this context Marx calls a mode of production is what is ordinarily called an economic system.

But often in the *Manifesto* and in *Capital* what Marx calls a mode of production is only part of what is ordinarily called an economic system. Discussing the economic history of the bourgeoisie in Part One of the *Manifesto*, he writes that the capitalist class is the product of a series of revolutions in the modes of production and exchange. The aim of *Capital*, he writes in the Preface to the First Edition, is to

examine the capitalist mode of production and the relations of production and exchange corresponding to it. What is meant by a mode
of production in this narrower sense? A set of forces of production
unstructured by relations of any sort? Or a set of forces of production
structured by relations other than property relations?

In his notes for continuing the Introduction to his *Critique of Political Economy*, Marx includes the following topic for discussion:

> 5. Dialectic of forces of production (means of production) and
> relations of production—a dialectic whose limits must be established
> so that the real distinction is not annulled.

Nowhere in his writings is this dialectic explicitly developed. Yet,
with a hint from Hegel, we can conjecture its general pattern.

In the account presented in the *Preface*, Marx assimilates both his
contrast between forces and relations of production and his contrast
between basis and superstructure to the more general contrast between
matter and form. Hegel, developing in his *Logic* the dialectic of form
and matter, moves from contrasting abstract form with wholly form-
less matter to contrasting determinate form with matter possessing
a different determinate form of its own. Clearly, this second contrast
is the archetype of Marx's contrast between superstructure and base.
Is it also the archetype of his contrast between relations and forces
of production?

In the *Preface* Marx discusses forces of production without giving
any examples. In Part One of the *Manifesto*, however, he credits capitalism with creating the following forces of production: machinery,
application of chemistry to industry and agriculture, steam navigation,
railways, and the electric telegraph. Each item on this list points to
a process, involving both forces and relations.

Toward the end of the chapter entitled "Cooperation" in the first
volume of *Capital*, Marx writes:

> All combined labour on a large scale requires some degree of direc-
> tion to harmonize the activities of individuals, to perform general
> functions required for action of the entire productive body as dis-
> tinguished from action of its separate organs. A single violinist
> directs himself: an orchestra requires a conductor. This function

of controlling, superintending, and mediating becomes a function of capital from the moment cooperative labour is subordinated to it. . . . [But] control exercised by capitalists is not only a particular function arising from and belonging to the nature of the social labour process. It is at the same time a function of exploiting that social labour process, and is accordingly conditioned by the inevitable antagonism between an exploiter and the labourer he exploits.

Here Marx has in effect transformed his contrast between productive forces and relations into a contrast between two kinds of relations, the technologically conditioned and the property conditioned. What in this context he calls a mode of production is—as he makes clear in the opening paragraph of the same chapter—what is ordinarily called a technology.

How is the fact that Marx identifies a mode of production sometimes with a technology, sometimes with an entire economic system, connected with the contrast between bourgeois and proletarian revolution? All revolutions, according to the *Preface*, readjust a superstructure to a base. In all cases the base includes technology and the superstructure includes political institutions. The crucial difference between bourgeois and proletarian revolutions, as these are described in the *Manifesto*, concerns the role of property relations. In the transition from feudalism to capitalism, property relations constitute part of the base: bourgeois revolution consists primarily in adjusting political institutions to a changed economic system. This is the line of demarcation between basis and superstructure presented in the *Preface*. But in the transition from capitalism to socialism, property relations do not constitute part of the base: proletarian revolution consists primarily in adjusting both political and economic institutions to a changed technology. This is the line of demarcation presented in the footnote on technology already quoted from *Capital*. There Marx speaks of technology as the material basis for the different forms of social organization, without distinguishing economic from political forms.

Was it necessary for Marx to invent a terminology that obscures, rather than reveals, the contrast between bourgeois and proletarian revolution? Why not consistently equate mode of production with technology, and consistently include property relations in the super-structure? It would then be possible to contrast bourgeois and pro-letarian revolution in unambiguous terms. During the transition from feudalism to capitalism, the property relations in the superstructure change, on the whole, concurrently with transformation of the mode of production and before the bourgeois revolution. During the transi-tion from capitalism to socialism, the property relations in the super-structure change, on the whole, concurrently with the proletarian revolution and after transformation of the mode of production. Why not choose clarity, at the sacrifice of dialectic?

This suggestion understates the sacrifice involved. To formulate explicitly this contrast between bourgeois and proletarian revolution entails radically revising the claims Marx makes for the predictive power of his sociology of change.

Marx writes in the *Preface* that changes in the economic system can be determined with the precision of natural science, but changes in the political superstructure cannot. Such a distinction seems ap-plicable in the case of the transition from feudalism to capitalism, where changes in the economic system occur, on the whole, prior to and independently of the bourgeois revolution. But is it applicable in the case of the transition from capitalism to socialism, where changes in the economic system occur, on the whole, concurrently and inter-dependently with the proletarian revolution? Here it seems plausible to conclude that both economic and political changes can be deter-mined with the precision of natural science, or that neither can. Asserting in Part One of the *Manifesto* that the fall of the bourgeoisie and the victory of the proletariat are inevitable, Marx does not ascribe different degrees of predictability to the economic and the political changes involved.

On what grounds can Marx argue that the economic or the political changes constituting transition to socialism can be determined with the precision of natural science? A scientific prediction connects a particular statement with other particular statements through gen-eral laws supported by empirical evidence. On what general laws does Marx rely in forecasting the pattern of transition to socialism? And on what empirical evidence are these laws based? Nowhere in his writings does he describe a revolutionary transition from one precapitalist mode of production to another precapitalist mode of production. The only transition of which he writes the history is that from feudalism to capitalism. But the pattern he records differs radically from the pattern he predicts. His pattern for the transition from capitalism to socialism is not established from, but asserted against, the entire body of historical evidence that he himself presents.

IV

What pattern of transition from capitalism to socialism would parallel the pattern of transition from feudalism to capitalism? To organize cooperative associations within the framework of a capitalist economy, then to extend this cooperative sector at the expense of capitalist enterprise, would be to establish a pattern of competing systems. During the transitional period socialist economic institutions would oppose, permeate, and replace capitalist economic institutions, as in an earlier period capitalist economic institutions had opposed, permeated, and replaced feudal economic institutions. This is the general pattern of transition proposed by Fourier and Owen among Marx's predecessors and by Proudhon and Mill among his contemporaries. Marx himself seems to propose it in the *Inaugural Address* of the First International and in some passages in the third volume of *Capital*. In the chapter of the latter work entitled "The Role of Credit in Capitalist Production," he writes of cooperative associations:

> They show the way in which, at a certain level of development of the material forces of production and of the corresponding social forms of production, a new mode of production grows within and develops out of the old mode of production.

Why does he predict a radically different pattern of socialist transition in the *Preface* and the *Manifesto*?

Marx's contention that proletarian revolution must precede socialist transformation of the economy is not based upon his general theory of historical materialism, but upon his special theory of capitalist accumulation. His account of the law of motion of modern society—outlined in the *Manifesto*, elaborated in *Capital*—predicts a revolutionary situation resulting from two long-run tendencies of capitalist development. First, industrialization increasingly divides a capitalist

economy into a small minority of capitalists and a large majority of
wage-workers. Second, industrialization forces these wage-workers
into lives of increasing misery. Granted the correctness of these predictions, the cooperative movement could not acquire enough economic resources to compete successfully against capitalist enterprise.
In an economy dominated by class polarization and increasing misery,
cooperation can have only a symbolic or an educational influence. In
these circumstances, construction of a socialist economy must wait
until after the revolution.

Marx claims scientific status for his law of motion of capitalist
society—in the sense that it is empirical rather than speculative, descriptive rather than prescriptive. Commenting on Mikhailovsky's
interpretation of *Capital*, he writes in a letter to *Otechestvenniye
Zapiski*:

> The chapter on primitive accumulation does not pretend to do more
> than trace the path by which, in Western Europe, the capitalist
> economic order emerged from the womb of the feudal economic
> order. It therefore describes the historical movement which, by
> divorcing the producers from their means of production, converts
> them into wage-workers . . . while it converts those who possess the
> means of production into capitalists. . . . At the end of the chapter
> the historical tendency of capitalist production is summarized in
> the statement that it "begets its own negation with the inexorabil-
> ity which governs the metamorphoses of nature." . . . Now what
> application to Russia could my critic make of this historical sketch?
> Only this. If Russia is tending to become a capitalist nation after
> the example of the nations of Western Europe . . . she will not suc-
> ceed without first having transformed a large part of her peasants
> into proletarians; and after that, once taken to the bosom of the
> capitalist regime, she will experience its pitiless laws like profane
> peoples. That is all. But it is not enough for my critic. He feels he
> must transform my historical sketch of the genesis of capitalism in
> Western Europe into an historico-philosophical theory of the general
> path every people is destined to follow, whatever its historical cir-
> cumstances, in order ultimately to arrive at that form of economy
> which ensures, together with the greatest expansion of the produc-
> tive powers of social labour, the most complete development of man.

Such appeals to science, however, can cut both ways. To claim for a theory the support of empirical evidence and scientific method at one time is to risk at some later time rejection or radical revision of that theory on these same grounds. The law of motion Marx proposed for capitalist society has not escaped this fate. Considered as scientific predictions, his doctrines of class polarization and increasing misery have been tested and refuted by the history of every capitalist economy throughout the last one hundred years.

V

If the preceding analysis is correct, to abandon Marx's predictions of class polarization and increasing misery is to abandon the premises for his contention that proletarian revolution must precede development of a socialist economy. The way is cleared for adopting a different model of the transition to socialism, for replacing the pattern of increasing misery with a pattern of competing systems. This was the path taken in the period before the First World War by the revisionist movement within the Social Democratic Party of Germany, and afterwards by parties comprising the Socialist International. What was denounced by their opponents as a moral betrayal of revolutionary socialism seemed to them an adjustment of theory to facts and a complementary adjustment of tactics to theory.

It is less difficult to explain why some Marxian theorists became revisionists than to explain why the rest refused to join them. On what grounds could Lenin before the Bolshevik Revolution, and after it the parties comprising the Communist International, continue to assert that proletarian revolution must precede development of a socialist economy?

Lenin's writings on the Bolshevik Revolution revive and elaborate the pattern of permanent revolution that Marx proposed for Germany in 1848. This pattern presupposes the principle that proletarian revolution precedes development of a socialist economy. If bourgeoisie seize political power after the economic development of capitalism while proletarians seize political power before the economic development of socialism, it seems plausible to argue that under special circumstances a bourgeois revolution might develop uninterruptedly

into a proletarian revolution. Unless the two revolutions can occur
back to back, that plausibility disappears.

In his *Report on War and Peace* delivered in March 1918, Lenin
explicitly bases his theory of the Bolshevik Revolution upon this contrast between bourgeois and proletarian revolutions:

> One of the fundamental differences between bourgeois and prole-
> tarian revolutions is that in the bourgeois revolution, which grows
> out of feudalism, new economic organizations gradually develop
> within the womb of the old order and gradually change all aspects
> of feudal society. The bourgeois revolution has only one task—to
> sweep away, discard, destroy all the fetters of the preceding society.
> . . . The situation of the socialist revolution is altogether different.
> The more backward the country which, owing to the zigzags of his-
> tory, has started the socialist revolution, the more difficult is it to
> pass from the old capitalist relations to socialist relations. To the
> tasks of destruction are added novel, unprecedentedly difficult,
> tasks of organization.

But though this pattern of permanent revolution is consistent with
Marx's pattern of increasing misery in placing seizure of political
power before economic transformation, it is inconsistent—as I have
already pointed out—with the basic principles of Marx's sociology of
change. By implication, Lenin points this out himself. Later in the
same report he despairs of success for Russia's revolution without
support from a socialist revolution in a country at a much higher level
of technological and economic development. "At all events," he writes,
"under all conceivable circumstances, if the German Revolution does
not come, we are doomed." It was left for the utopian Stalin to impose
upon the people new illusions by proclaiming that backward Russia,
even in isolation, could complete the construction of a socialist economy and undertake the transition to communism.

Their reliance on the pattern of permanent revolution explains why
communists asserted that for backward countries, on the verge of
bourgeois revolution, proletarian revolution must precede development
of a socialist economy. Yet why did they maintain this claim for advanced capitalist countries, by refusing to abandon the pattern of

increasing misery? Of the different issues involved, I shall discuss only one: the connection between patterns of transition and ultimate goals.

In the fourth and fifth chapters of *State and Revolution*, Lenin proposes for his followers two revisions of prevailing terminology. He suggests that the Bolsheviks substitute "Communist" for "Social Democratic" in their party name; and he calls socialism that type of classless economy which Marx calls the first stage of communism. The theoretical interest of these proposals lies in the fact that Lenin asserts a connection between them. Disagreements between communists and social democrats concerning tactics are connected, he suggests, with disagreements concerning aims. That type of classless economy which for communists is a transitional stage is for socialists the ultimate goal.

How do the two stages which Lenin calls socialism and communism differ in economic organization? In both economies the means of production are collectively owned: no one lives on rent, interest, or profit. In a socialist economy individuals receive incomes, which they use to buy consumers' goods. In a communist economy no one receives an income: consumers' goods are rationed or free. Socialism abolishes exploitation: communism abolishes exchange. This is the contrast sketched by Marx in his *Critique of the Gotha Program* and amplified by Lenin in *State and Revolution*. It is consistent with the two-stage program presented in Part Two of the *Manifesto*.

If an exchange economy without exploitation is for communists a transitional stage but for socialists an ultimate goal, what bearing has this disagreement on disagreement as to whether proletarian revolution precedes development of a socialist economy? Consider, as extreme examples, two patterns of transition. According to one, the revolutionary vanguard seizes power, establishes a proletarian dictatorship, and controls economic development throughout the entire transitional period of socialism. Only with attainment of communism does the state—and the party—wither away. According to the other pattern, cooperatives are organized within the framework of a capitalist economy; they gradually expand in competition with capitalist enterprise; and they gradually change all aspects of capitalist society. Eventually transformation of the political superstructure follows this transformation of the economic base: peacefully or violently, capitalists and their agents lose their monopoly over the means of coercion. Legislation ending all private ownership of the means of production completes the transition to socialism. And then? Is it likely that a socialist society, established in this manner, would undertake the abolition of exchange?

VI

Though in Part Two of the *Manifesto* Marx indicates a two-stage pattern for postrevolutionary development, only in *The Critique of the Gotha Program* does he contrast the economies of the two stages and list the prerequisites for moving from the first to the second. After stating that in the lower stage workers will be paid with certificates which they will exchange for consumers' goods, he continues:

> In a higher phase of communist society, after the servitude of subordination to the division of labour has disappeared, and with it the opposition between mental and physical labour; after labour has become, not only a means of life, but the primary need of life; after each individual's productive power has increased with his all-round development and all the springs of cooperative wealth flow more freely—only then can the narrow limits of bourgeois right be wholly left behind, and can society inscribe upon its banners: From each according to his ability, to each according to his needs.

Three prerequisites are listed here: a change in the division of labor; a change in men's attitude toward labor; and continued economic growth. Marx's highly compressed formulations raise questions about his meaning, which can to some extent be clarified through reference to his other writings. The discussion of the division of labor in *The German Ideology* and *Capital* indicates that for Marx ending the servitude of subordination to the division of labor is not equivalent to ending all differentiation of social functions. What he seems to have in mind is ending specialization, the attachment of one individual to one function throughout his working life. The discussion of labor as an end in itself in *The German Ideology* and the *Grundrisse* indicates that for Marx labor becomes the primary need of life only through total fusion of labor and enjoyment in free activity. What he seems

to have in mind can be described, in current usage, as the atrophy of
material incentives. By contrast, his formulation of the third pre-
requisite is incorrigibly vague. All he says is that the forces of production reach a higher level of development; but presumably this condition is met almost continuously, both before and after the transition
to communism.

Is Marx predicting that at a certain level of development the productive forces of a socialist economy will come into conflict with its
relations of exchange? Why then does he write "can" instead of
"must"? Neither here nor in *Capital* does he present arguments to
show that in a socialist society continuing technological development
will at some time prove incompatible with earning wages and buying
consumers' goods. But in *The Economic-Philosophical Manuscripts*
and *The German Ideology* he argues that division of labor, commodity
exchange, and wages are at all times incompatible with the fusion
of labor and enjoyment in free activity. Throughout *The Economic-
Philosophical Manuscripts* this opposition is presented in explicitly
moral terms. Men's productive labor connects them with their fellow
men—with the universal, the species. To make this service of the universal not the unintended consequence, but the conscious motive, of
human activity is to achieve distinctively human status and dignity.
This requires transformation of productive work into an end in itself,
total fusion of labor and enjoyment. But the cleavage between labor
and enjoyment inherent in an exchange economy is incompatible
with this goal. Attaining economic abundance, ending specialization,
and ending exchange are material prerequisites for achieving a moral
ideal—transition from the abstract egoism of exchange society to the
mass fraternity of a new community, development of communist man.

Marx's account of the transition from socialism to communism
derives from his dialectic of liberation, rather than from his sociology
of change. The general pattern of that dialectic—wholly obscured in
the *Preface*, largely obscured in the *Manifesto*—is revealed almost
parenthetically in the *Grundrisse*. There, in a section of the second
chapter entitled "Money as a Social Relation," Marx writes:

> Relations of personal dependence (entirely spontaneous at the
> start) are the first forms of society in which human productivity

develops, though only at isolated points and to a limited extent. Personal independence, based upon dependence on *things*, is the second major form. Within it first develops a system of universal social metabolism, universal connections, varied needs, and universal wealth. Free individuality, based on universally developed individuals controlling their communal and social productivity as their social wealth, is the third stage. The second stage creates the conditions for the third.

This is an atheist's version of Hegel's philosophy of history.

Was Mikhailovsky then at least half right? The grounds for predicting the transition from socialism to communism are obscured in *Capital*, where this transition is conflated with the transition from capitalism to socialism. But in *The Critique of the Gotha Program*, where the two predictions are presented separately, the distinctive argument for predicting the transition to communism stands revealed. Apparently that prediction is grounded on an historico-philosophical theory of the general path mankind is destined to follow in order finally to arrive at that form of economy which ensures, together with the greatest expansion of the productive powers of social labor, the most complete development of man. Certainly Marx's prediction is speculative rather than empirical, prescriptive rather than descriptive—utopian rather than scientific, as he himself defines those terms.

VII

The preceding arguments can be summarized in two propositions. First, Marx's contrast between utopian and scientific can be used to expose a basic conflict in his own approach to socialism and to history. Second, Lenin's theories concerning the pattern of proletarian revolution and the nature of its ultimate goal derive from the utopian rather than the scientific side of Marx's thought. In conclusion, I propose to return—in the light of this analysis—to Bakunin's account of the connection between Marxism and elitism.

Have fifty years of Russian communism confirmed Bakunin's charges? To what extent have the majority been told that their emancipation consists in accepting the despotic rule of a socialist elite? To what extent has such rule been justified on the ground that only an educated minority are capable of understanding scientific socialism? And to what extent have the governed found such government oppressive, offensive, and despicable?

Stronger cases can be built for Bakunin's position on the first and third of these issues than on the second. Lenin's program for transforming bourgeois into proletarian revolution and Stalin's program for transforming socialism into communism both assigned crucial roles to dictatorship of a revolutionary minority. But neither Lenin nor Stalin equated proletarian dictatorship with government by an intellectual elite: and neither divided postrevolutionary society into an educated minority and an uneducable majority. The grounds on which they stressed the crucial role of revolutionary minorities had more affinities with Bakunin's own than with those that he ascribed to Marx.

To the extent that Marxian theory has been used to justify minority rule, the arguments have appealed to utopian elements of that theory. Neither the program of transforming bourgeois into proletarian revolution nor the program of transforming socialism into communism can be based, I have argued, upon Marx's sociology of change. Instead, critics of Lenin's revolutionary program could argue, from the principles of Marx's sociology of change, that such a revolution would entail for Russia an indefinite period of unstable and despotic minority rule. And critics of Stalin's program for transforming socialism into communism could argue, from the same principles, that proclaiming this unattainable goal would serve to justify perpetuation of such rule.

Today, what cure does Marxian theory prescribe for the bureaucratic stagnation of Russia's economic, political, and cultural institutions? For critics who approach the problem in terms of Marx's dialectic of liberation, the solution is to realize the ideal of communism. But for critics who approach the problem in terms of Marx's sociology of change, part of the solution is to reject the ideal of communism. The first is a utopian program: mobilizing for a great leap forward, to attempt the creation of communist man. Its alternative is a revisionist program: taking men as they are and making laws what they might be, to resume the long ascent toward social justice and individual freedom.

RICHARD W. MILLER   The Consistency of
                      Historical Materialism

In a recent article in this journal,[1] Stanley Moore argues that major
aspects of Marx's theory of social development are mutually incompatible. In particular, Moore perceives two major inconsistencies: a
contradiction between the theory of social development in the *Preface
to a Critique of Political Economy* and the theory of class struggle in
the *Communist Manifesto*; and a contradiction between the *Preface*
theory of social development and Marx's account of the transformation of feudalism into capitalism in *Capital*.

Moore's charges of inconsistency are based, I shall argue, on mis-
interpretations of Marx. But his mistakes are important, because the
texts to which he appeals are important, his interpretations are
plausible and widely current, and the approaches to Marx which lead
to these interpretations have guided many readers of Marx (including sympathetic ones) in their views of many passages not discussed
in Moore's short article. If my criticisms are valid, Moore's discussion
illustrates, by force of negative example, the importance of respecting
certain general principles in interpreting Marx, principles which I
shall subsequently describe.

Moore begins by arguing that there is a contradiction between the
discussion of forces of production and relations of production in the
Preface to a Critique of Political Economy and the discussion of class
struggle in the *Manifesto*.[2] In the *Preface*, Marx declares, "The gen-

1. "Marx and Lenin as Historical Materialists," above, pp. 211-234.
2. Ibid., part 2, pp. 217-221.

eral result at which I arrived after my formative investigations . . .
and which, once won, served as a guiding thread for my studies can
be formulated as follows:"

> In the social production of their life, men enter into definite rela-
> tions that are indispensable and independent of their will, relations
> of production which correspond to a definite stage of development
> of their material productive forces. The sum total of these relations
> of production constitutes the economic structure of society, the
> real foundation, on which rises a legal and political superstructure
> and to which correspond definite forms of social consciousness.
> The mode of production of material life conditions the social, polit-
> ical and intellectual life process in general. It is not the conscious-
> ness of men that determines their being, but on the contrary, their
> social being that determines their consciousness. At a certain stage
> of their development, the material productive forces of society
> come in conflict with the existing relations of production, or—what
> is but a legal expression for the same thing—with the property rela-
> tions within which they have been at work hitherto. From forms of
> development of the productive forces these relations turn into their
> fetters. Then begins an epoch of social revolution. With the change
> of the economic foundation the entire immense superstructure is
> more or less rapidly transformed.[3]

Two sentences after this summary of his "general result" (the passage quoted is widely accepted as the gist of the *Preface* and we shall
frequently return to it later on), Marx comments:

> No social order ever perishes before all the productive forces for
> which there is room in it have developed; and new, higher relations
> of production never appear before the material conditions of their
> existence have matured in the womb of the old society itself.[4]

It is this latter passage which, in Moore's view, contradicts the theory
of class struggle in the *Manifesto*.

Most of Moore's discussion of the *Manifesto* is concerned with the

3. Marx and Engels, *Selected Works in Three Volumes* (Moscow, 1969), vol.
1, pp. 503ff.
4. Ibid., p. 504.

renowned and crucial opening remark of the first substantive section:
"The history of all hitherto existing societies is the history of class
struggles."[5] But, it turns out, the contradiction Moore sees between the
Manifesto and the *Preface* is created by a particular application of
Marx's theory of class struggle to then current circumstances. For
late in the *Manifesto* Marx writes:

> The Communists turn their attention chiefly to Germany, because
> that country is on the eve of a bourgeois revolution that is bound
> to be carried out under more advanced conditions of European
> civilization, and with a much more developed proletariat, than the
> bourgeois revolution of England in the seventeenth century or that
> of France in the eighteenth century, and because therefore this
> bourgeois revolution can be but the prelude to an immediately
> following proletarian revolution.[6]

According to Moore, the *Preface* view of the role of productive forces
in social change precludes the possibility of a proletarian revolution's
immediately following a bourgeois one.

The inconsistency that Moore perceives disappears if one applies
to Marx's writings reasonably nonliteral interpretations of a sort that
are commonly applied to descriptions of complex processes. Quite
generally, when a scientist briefly describes a complex situation, he
indulges in simplifications, which are literally false. One needs to
understand to what extent and in what ways his statements are meant
to hold, in order to decide whether the description is true as intended
or is an invalid oversimplification. To take a simple example, a geologist might say, "The history of the earth's surface is the history of
continental drift." If he means to explain "the general idea guiding
his studies" in plate-tectonics, we would accept his statement as a
legitimate simplification of reality. This is true even though the earth
was once entirely covered with water (hence, there were no continents), and, before that, was molten (hence, there was nothing
like a continent). His statement would be true, as intended, even if
points of momentary equilibrium were sometimes reached during
which the continents, for a while, stopped moving.

5. Ibid., p. 108.   6. Ibid., p. 137.

In the *Preface*, Marx is explicitly giving a brief sketch of a "general idea" of a complex situation, a "guiding thread for my studies." Accordingly, when he speaks of how social systems (feudalism, capitalism, etc.) develop, his statements must be interpreted with the liberality we normally employ in understanding simplifications. In particular, in the *Preface* statements he is naturally understood as presenting a picture of the long-run development of a social system throughout all the interacting social units (e.g. countries) in which it is dominant. In addition, he can naturally be taken as describing the development of the whole system in terms of developments in the leading social units, the ones in which the economic processes in question are most advanced. Just as many general remarks about "the ills of modern society" are meant strictly to be applied only to typical features of the most thoroughly modern societies, so a Marxist sketch of the dynamics of capitalism (say) may well be meant strictly to apply only to long-term trends in the most advanced capitalist societies.[7]

Marx's remark that "no social order disappears until all the productive forces it has room for have been developed" requires a liberal interpretation of a related kind. Moore regards this statement as a declaration that significant technological advances must have become impossible on the eve of the radical transformation of social relations (e.g. the transformation of capitalism into socialism).[8] But Marx cannot have believed this. The discussions of technology in *Capital* make clear that Marx knew what is sufficiently obvious: that capitalism is able, at any point in its development, to create sig-

7. In the Preface to the first edition of *Capital*, Marx explicitly proposes to emphasize English phenomena in describing capitalism, on the ground that England is the "classic home" of capitalism. He compares his procedure with the physicist's effort to observe phenomena in their "most typical form." See *Capital* (Moscow, n.d.), vol. 1, p. 19.

8. After citing this remark, Moore asks, "In a society on the eve of bourgeois revolution, can there be no further development of the forces of production within the framework of capitalist relations of production?" The context makes it clear that he takes the *Preface* theory to require an affirmative answer (see p. 220). Throughout his essay, Moore equates productive forces and technology. Thus, on first alluding to this aspect of Marx, he speaks of "forces of production—which he [Marx] tacitly equates with technology."

nificantly new technology.[9] In later life, when he regarded England as economically ready for revolution, Marx also accepted the fact that technology was making strides there. Accordingly, Marx's formulation must be an exaggeration. It must be an example of the hyperbole which, Engels tells us, he and Marx sometimes engaged in, in the course of combating utopian or adventurist currents in socialism.[10] Marx's meaning must be something like this: Even though technological innovation is indefinitely available in certain social systems, a point is always reached at which the social relations characteristic of a system restrict its ability to expand its productive powers. ("Productive powers," I should note, is at least as good a translation of Marx's *"Produktivkraefte"* as the standard "productive forces," and much less technology-ridden.)[11] The proposed interpretation changes the remark in question from an absurdity to a somewhat exaggerated formulation of the idea of social relations as eventually "fettering productive forces" (or powers) that Marx previously raised.

With the interpretations I have proposed, Moore's alleged contradiction disappears. The *Preface* theory commits Marx to the view that capitalism as a whole (i.e. as an international system) will change into socialism in the long run, at some point after capitalist social relations (e.g. the competition between capitalists, the wage-labor system) have ceased, at least in the most advanced countries, to encourage the expansion of the productive powers of society and, instead, have become obstacles to expansion that otherwise would occur. None of this is inconsistent with the proposal that Germany, one among many interacting capitalist social units and (in Marx's time) one of the least advanced, might pass immediately from a bourgeois to a proletarian revolution.

Still, we have a right to demand more than mere consistency from Marx, at this point. He proposes, in the *Preface*, that economic phenomena are the leading factors, in the long run, in all important social changes. So, if the German situation can deviate from his sketch of

9. "Modern Industry never looks upon and treats the existing form of a process as final." *Capital*, vol. 1, p. 457.
10. Letter to Bloch, 21 September 1890, in *Selected Works*, vol. 3, p. 488.
11. David Levy first pointed this out to me.

the process of long-term change in capitalism as a whole (and especially in its most advanced representatives), he ought to be able to explain this important fact in appropriately materialist terms. Such an explanation was available to Marx and is often implicit in his discussions of capitalism as an international system. Germany, although economically backward, had long been part of the same world economy as Britain and France. As a result, German proletarians and intellectuals had absorbed and put into practice political and social ideas which had first arisen in the mature capitalism of Britain and the (more or less) mature capitalism of France, ideas which had been inevitably communicated as a result of the European-wide system of transportation, communication, and interdependence that capitalism created.[12] Thus, Marx sometimes regarded it as possible for German working people, having acquired the lessons that more advanced capitalism had originally taught, to respond to the superoppression and ruling-class divisions that accompanied German economic backwardness[13] by making a proletarian revolution soon after a bourgeois one had been effected. It is worth noting that Lenin makes a precisely analogous argument in answer to critics of the Bolshevik decision to lead a proletarian seizure of state power soon after the creation of the bourgeois Kerensky regime.[14]

The kind of unreasonably literal interpretation that leads Moore to think he sees a contradiction in Marx is often found in criticisms of

12. "The need for a constantly expanding market for its products chases the bourgeoisie over the whole surface of the globe. It must nestle everywhere, settle everywhere, establish connections everywhere. The bourgeoisie has through its exploitation of the world-market given a cosmopolitan character to production and consumption in every country . . . And as in material, so also in intellectual production. The intellectual creations of individual nations become common property." "Communist Manifesto," *Selected Works*, vol. 1, p. 112. See also *The German Ideology, Selected Works*, vol. 1, p. 39, and the discussions of the relation between German political economy and English economic developments in *Capital*, vol. 1, pp. 20, 23–26.

13. "In all other spheres we . . . suffer not only from the development of capitalist production, but also from the incompleteness of that development. Alongside of modern evils, a whole series of inherited evils oppress us. . . ." *Capital*, vol. 1, p. 20.

14. See "Our Revolution . . ." in Lenin, *Selected Works in Three Volumes* (Moscow, 1970), vol. 3, pp. 767ff.

Marxist writings. For example, it is sometimes claimed (despite Marx's explicit comments to the contrary), that Marx's theory of the class origins of social ideas and attitudes precludes any nonproletarian's siding with the proletariat.[15] Moore's mistake suggests the importance of alternative general assumptions in the interpretation of Marx. When Marx proposes a general description of a complex social process, his description can be a simplification without being an oversimplification, if it is literally true to the degree and in the ways that are appropriate to Marx's legitimate intentions. Often, what Marx says will only be true in the long run. Often, he will not take into account social forms which are understood not to be in question, given the issues at hand. Sometimes, he will describe the development of a social system in terms of the development of the most advanced embodiments of that system.

I hope I have shown that this reasonable nonliteralness is often extended to non-Marxist descriptions of social and of nonsocial reality. Moreover, it does not limit the significance of Marx's general ideas to the description of long-term trends in a few advanced embodiments of Marxist modes of production. For in Marx's view, if there is an important deviation from the general scheme in a specific case (important, that is, with respect to the needs of large numbers of people), it must be possible to explain this deviation as mainly due to the action of the factors mentioned in the general theories, e.g. class struggle and the development of productive forces.

The second major contradiction Moore sees in Marx is exemplified in an alleged contrast between the theory of social development in the *Preface* (embodied in the longer quotation I have given) and Marx's explanation of the transition from feudalism to capitalism in *Capital*.[16] According to Moore, the *Preface* theory requires that technology develop within an initially stable set of institutions of property ownership, until the point is reached at which the latter institutions inhibit

15. For example, in J.W.N. Watkins, "Methodological Individualism and Social Tendencies," *Readings in the Philosophy of the Social Sciences*, ed. May Brodbeck (New York, 1968), p. 274. Cf. "Communist Manifesto," *Selected Works*, vol. 1, p. 117.

16. See Moore, part 3, pp. 221-226.

the further development of technology. It is this conflict which ultimately gives rise to any radical change in institutions of property
ownership, and in the political and ideological institutions that accompany the latter. Moore claims that, in contrast, in the *Capital*
story of the destruction of feudalism, capitalist property relations are
seen as existing for centuries under feudalism, and gradually taking
over the economy, until a corresponding political revolution becomes
inevitable. "Economic transformation," in Moore's view "precedes
political revolution." He regards this as the realistic assessment of the
actual historical phenomena.

As Moore points out, this interpretation of *Capital* suggests a substantive argument against Marx's entire political strategy. Marx believed that a political revolution, instituting a dictatorship of the
proletariat, would be required before socialism could govern economic life on a broad scale. He also thought that the study of the
transition from feudalism to capitalism would provide evidence concerning the nature of the transition to socialism. But if Moore is
right, Marx's study of feudalism provides evidence that a gradual ac-
cretion of changes in relations of production, without substantial
political intervention, is a realistic means of bringing about the dominance of a new mode of production.

The contradiction which Moore discerns in Marx's writings depends
on a misinterpretation of important aspects of both the *Preface* and
Capital. First of all, in the *Preface* theory, "forces of production" are not
restricted, as Moore believes, to the results of technological advances.
The wider scope of the former concept is important, since, if the two
concepts were identical, the *Capital* account of the rise of capitalism
would indeed be incompatible with the *Preface* theory. For in *Capital*,
Marx notes the absence of significantly new technology as an important factor in capitalist development until the eighteenth century, well
after the main phases of the political revolution led by the bourgeoisie.

Moore quotes a passage from the *Manifesto* in which Marx does
describe the development of the steam engine and other familiar
episodes as instances of capitalism's enlarging the forces of production. But in *Capital*, Marx makes it clear that crucial advances in the
expansion of society's productive forces sometimes are matters of the

organization and rationalization of the ways people work, rather than
of technology in any strict or literal sense.[17] The organization of work
in factories did not, he emphasizes, originally involve the introduction
of new machinery. Rather, certain developments in financial resources
and markets made it rational for entrepreneurs to assemble workers
under a single roof, to divide work between them, and to coordinate
their diverse tasks in previously unheard-of ways.[18] Certain economies
resulted that led to a great increase in productive power. The seventeenth century "manufactory," in short, was a new productive force,
in Marx's view, though it initially involved no new technology.

Taking the other side of Marx's dichotomy, relations of production
are not, in themselves, institutions of property ownership.[19] In a
stable society, property relations will be, as Marx says in the *Preface*,
"the legal expression" of the dominant relations of production. But
Marx cannot, as Moore often implies, literally have equated the two
phenomena. For he explicitly distinguishes "economic conditions of
production" (there can be no doubt that relations of production are
included) from "legal" conditions, a few sentences later. And property
relations are a prime example of a legal condition of production. In
the *Preface* theory of social development, Marx's conception of relations of production is, roughly, this: the relations of production in a
society are the relations affecting access to the means of production
which are defined by a certain repertoire of social roles through which
people obtain the material means to live, namely, the repertoire which
the main ideological and coercive institutions of society tend to legiti-

17. This is the main theme of *Capital*, vol. 1, chap. 13, "On Cooperation."
For example, commenting on the results of merely organizing "many hands"
to "take part simultaneously in one and the same undivided operation," Marx
says, "Not only have we here an increase in the productive power of the individual but the creation of a new power, namely, the collective power of masses"
(p. 309). The phrase translated as "productive power," here, is one of those
normally translated as "productive force" or "force of production" in rendering
the Preface to the *Critique of Political Economy* into English.

18. See the previously cited chapter, "On Cooperation," and chapter 14, "Division of Labor and Manufacture."

19. Moore speaks of "relations of production—which Marx explicitly equates
with property relations" (p. 221), and thereafter uses the two phrases more or
less interchangeably.

mate and support. This is the most natural reading of the long passage from the *Preface* I first quoted.

If relations of production were always to be equated with forms of property ownership, then the *Preface* theory would be extremely hard to reconcile with the *Capital* account of the destruction of feudalism. The relation of production characteristic of feudalism is serfdom. If serfdom is defined in terms of property law, it will be taken to require a legal obligation on the part of farming families to remain on their farms and to give a fixed portion of their produce, income, or labor, to the head of a certain family, and a legal obligation of the latter to allow the farming families to work their land, so long as the customary rent is paid. As Marx was well aware, the form of property embodied in these laws, the classic manorial system, had become virtually extinct in England, long before the political revolutions of the seventeenth century, in which the bourgeoisie, in Marx's view, sought to achieve political dominance. In particular, most peasant families were under no legal obligation permanently to farm land under the control of a noble family.

On the other hand, if relations of production and property relations are distinguished, it becomes reasonable to adopt a broader conception of serfdom, the characteristic feudal relation of production, and to see it as an important economic phenomenon well into the eighteenth century. In particular, Dobb has proposed that serfdom consists of "an obligation laid on the producer by force and independently of his own volition to fulfill certain economic demands of an overlord. . . ."[20] By a "producer," Dobb means someone who is in control of his means of production (e.g. tools, animals), and typically controls enough of the output of his production to provide for his own subsistence. In this respect, serfdom differs from both slavery and wage-labor. By "force," Dobb means the coercive influence of the overlord, the government, or custom, as distinct from the operation of nominally uncoerced bargaining in the labor market that is characteristic of capitalism. A society is a feudal society, in this broader conception, if most of the income of those who do not directly participate in production derives

20. Maurice Dobb, *Studies in the Development of Capitalism* (New York, 1963), p. 35.

from the "overloard" status Dobb defines. It is feudal regardless of whether laws exist tying direct producers to their land. Dobb's description of feudalism is, in effect, a summary of Marx's own in "The Genesis of Capitalist Ground-rent," chapter 47 of the third volume of *Capital* (see especially pp. 782f.). Dobb argues that mid-seventeenth-century England was feudal in this broad sense.

In Dobb's analysis of late feudalism, property relations, in the literal sense of relations defined by property law, are seen as failing to express contemporary relations of production. Thus, if the broader conception of relations of production is adopted, Marx's side-comment, in the *Preface*, that property relations are a legal expression of relations of production, must be seen as a simplification. But that is a natural view to take, given Marx's intention of briefly sketching a general idea. For in the typical case of a relatively stable society, property relations *do* reflect relations of production. Marx's comment serves to clarify his talk of relations of production by indicating that the relations he has in mind are those which have typically been reflected in and legitimized by the main concepts of property law.

Given these interpretations, the *Preface* theory can be paraphrased as follows: When a society is stable, it legitimates and supports a fixed repertoire of social roles within which people can obtain the material means to live. But in working within these roles, at least some of the people are willing and able to develop the productive power of the means of production. This process leads to the destruction of the system of social roles around which production and, ultimately, the rest of society are organized. For, at a certain point, a group participating in the development of the forces of production will find that the roles society defines are a hindrance to the further expansion of these forces. One eventual result of this conflict is that such a group acquires the will to destroy this system of roles. And their access to the most advanced means of production will give them the ability to do so. (I should add that, for Marx, this is the general pattern. He apparently felt that the "Asiatic mode of production," for special reasons, would not give rise to the conflict just sketched.)

In addition to "productive force," "relation of production," and "feudalism," one other term in Marx's conceptual apparatus needs to be clarified if the *Preface* theory and the *Capital* account of the rise of capitalism are to be compared, namely, "capitalism" itself. In a number of common senses of this term, capitalism *can* be said (as Moore claims) to have dominated the English economy prior to bourgeois revolution, in Marx's later account. For, as the historical parts of *Capital* make clear, the pursuit of profit and the production of goods for sale (rather than for immediate consumption by producer or overlord) had come to dominate the English economy by the beginning of the seventeenth century. However, when Marx speaks of capitalism as the mode of production succeeding feudalism, he is not speaking simply of the pursuit of profit or the production of goods for subsequent sale. Rather, when Marx uses "capitalism" in the context that is crucial for Moore's thesis, he means the economic system in which nonproducers typically benefit from the results of the labor of others through the operation of a labor market in which the use of the labor power of those without control of the means of production is bought, like any other commodity, by those who have such control. Marx writes:

> In themselves money and commodities are no more capital than are the means of production and of subsistence. They want transforming into capital. But this transformation itself can only take place under certain circumstances that centre in this, viz., that two very different kinds of commodity-possessors must come face to face and into contact; on the one hand, the owners of money, means of production, means of subsistence, who are eager to increase the sum of values they possess, by buying other people's labour-power; on the other hand, free labourers, the sellers of their own labour-power, and therefore the sellers of labour. Free labourers, in the double sense that neither they themselves form part and parcel of the means of production, as in the case of slaves, bondsmen, etc., nor do the means of production belong to them, as in the case of peasant-proprietors; they are, therefore, free from, unencumbered by, any means of production of their own. With this polarisation of the market for commodities, the fundamental conditions of capitalist production are given. The capitalist system pre-supposes the complete separation of the labourers from all property as the means by which they can realise their labour. . . . The process, therefore,

that clears the way for the capitalist system, can be none other than the process which takes away from the labourer the possession of his means of production; a process that transforms, on the one hand, the social means of subsistence and of production into capital, on the other, the immediate producers into wage-labourers.[21]

At times, Marx uses "capitalism" in a broader sense, encompassing all economic activities guided by the pursuit of profits realized through the sale of commodities. And capitalism, in this broad sense, might well be taken to have dominated the English economy before 1640. But, as the previously cited remark and his discussion of "merchant capitalism" under feudalism make clear,[22] the "capitalist *mode of production*" in his sense of the phrase is dominated by a particular kind of commodity market (reflecting particular relations of production), namely, the labor market. In a capitalist society, production is dominated by the employment of wage-laborers by those who do not directly take part in the productive process.

Marx's rejection of the pursuit of profit and the production of goods for sale as a basis for defining capitalist production is an example of a principle of sociological analysis that was extremely important for him. In his general theories, his main concepts always have to do with relations within the sphere of production, not with relations within the sphere of distribution (e.g. the buying and selling of goods).[23] I shall subsequently suggest that Moore's charge of contradiction is only plausible if one understands "capitalism" in the latter fashion. Here, then, is another general interpretative principle, the importance of which Moore illustrates by force of negative example.

According to Moore, *Capital* presents a picture of the downfall of feudalism according to which capitalist relations of production had gradually come to dominate the English economy, before the bourgeoisie fought for state power and started to use it to suit its purposes. We have seen how misconstruals of some of Marx's key concepts, at least some of which are Moore's construals (i.e. the interpretations of "productive forces" and "relations of production") suggest such a

21. *Capital*, vol. 1, p. 668.
22. Ibid., vol. 3, chap. 20, "Historical Facts about Merchants' Capital," especially p. 334.
23. See Marx, *Grundrisse* (New York, 1973), p. 99.

judgment. But our analyses of "productive force," "relation of production," "feudalism," and "capitalism," provide the basis for a stronger claim: Moore is simply wrong in his estimate of the relation between economic transformation and political revolution in the historical part of *Capital*.

According to Marx, the English Civil War was the first of a series of political revolutions in which the English bourgeoisie gained increasing control of state power and used this power to advance its class interests.[24] If Moore's idea of economic transformation preceding political revolution is correct, then the English economy around 1640, on the eve of the Civil War, ought to have been predominantly capitalist. Feudal social relations would be secondary, though perhaps significant, features of the economy. The seizure of state power would be a means of completing and expanding a transition to capitalism which had already, in essence, been accomplished. In any case, this is the natural interpretation of Moore's idea of "economic transformation" preceding a political revolution.

Marx never says, in *Capital*, that economic transformation preceded political revolution in this way. Quite to the contrary. At several points he comes close to explicitly rejecting Moore's conception of a pre-English Civil War triumph of capitalism:

> The different momenta of primitive accumulation distribute themselves now, more or less in chronological order, particularly over Spain, Portugal, Holland, France, and England. In England at the end of the 17th century, they arrive at a systematical combination, embracing the colonies, the national debt, the modern mode of taxation, and the protectionist system. These methods depend in part on brute force, e.g., the colonial system. But they all employ the power of the State, the concentrated and organised force of society, to hasten, hot-house fashion, the process of transformation

24. "The revolutions of 1648 and 1789 were not English and French revolutions, they were revolutions of European significance. . . . In them the bourgeoisie was victorious; but the victory of the bourgeoisie meant at the time the victory of a new social order." Marx, "The Bourgeoisie and the Counter-Revolution," *Selected Works*, vol. 1, p. 139. The same point is made in *The German Ideology*, p. 61, and in "The Communist Manifesto," p. 137, both found in *Selected Works*, vol. 1.

of the feudal mode of production into the capitalist mode, and to shorten the transition. Force is the midwife of every old society, pregnant with a new one. It is itself an economic power.[25]

The transition from the feudal mode of production is two-fold. The producer becomes merchant and capitalist, in contrast to the natural agricultural economy and the guild-bound handicrafts of the medieval urban industries. This is the really revolutionising path. Or else, the merchant establishes direct sway over production. However much this serves historically as a stepping-stone—witness the English 17th century clothier, who brings the weavers, independent as they are, under his control by selling their wool to them and buying their cloth—it cannot by itself contribute to the overthrow of the old mode of production, but tends rather to preserve and retain it as its precondition. The manufacturer in the French silk industry and in the English hosiery and lace industries, for example, was thus mostly but nominally a manufacturer until the middle of the 19th century. In point of fact, he was merely a merchant, who let the weavers carry on in their old unorganised way and exerted only a merchant's control, for that was for whom they really worked. This system presents everywhere an obstacle to the real capitalist mode of production and goes under with its development.[26] In the relevant chapter as a whole, Marx makes it clear that English production was still dominated by merchant capital in the mid-seventeenth century.

Presumably, Moore feels that concrete historical facts presented in *Capital* embody his conception of prerevolutionary economic transformation, even if Marx sometimes rejects it, in that work. But once Marx's concepts are understood in the ways I have proposed, there is no basis for this claim. In particular, Marx presents no evidence that production in the mid-seventeenth-century English economy was dominated by wage-laborers in the employ of nonlaborers.

Still, Moore could be wrong in detail in his criticism of Marx, but right in substance. For Moore's general claim is that it is impossible to accommodate the rise of capitalism to the *Preface* model, given the

25. *Capital*, vol. 1, p. 703.
26. Ibid., vol. 3, p. 334.

historical facts that Marx admits in *Capital*. This general claim could be right, even if Moore were wrong in his specific estimate of the timing of the transformation of feudalism.

Moore would be right if "productive forces," "relations of production," "feudalism," and "capitalism" were understood in the ways I have criticized. On a proper understanding of these terms, Moore is wrong. One can construct a plausible, if controversial, account of the rise of capitalism which is compatible with (indeed, largely derived from) concrete historical facts presented in *Capital* and other writings of Marx, and which embodies the *Preface* model of social change.

Under the Tudors and the early Stuarts, the mode of production in England was still predominantly feudal. Most goods, both agricultural and nonagricultural, were produced through what Marx calls "small production," in which the typical productive unit consists of someone who controls the means of production and most of their output, and directly participates in production, sometimes helped by one or two hired hands. The exploitation of wage-laborers by nonproductive property-owners which is essential to capitalism, in the relevant sense of the word, is not characteristic of such an economy. The dominant mode of production was also feudal in the broad sense explicated by Dobb, since most of the income extracted from the labor of producers by nonproducers took the form of fixed, customary rents or of merchants' profits derived from monopolistic advantages artificially supported by the state.[27]

Under the Tudors and the early Stuarts, the productive powers of English society were expanding. In particular, while small production was dominant, there were more and more instances of specialized, relatively large-scale production using wage-labor. As Marx emphasizes in the chapter on "Cooperation" in *Capital*, such production leads to economies of scale and increasingly efficient specialization and coordination, even when it is not accompanied by significant technological innovation. While Marx seems to have regarded agriculture as

27. See *Capital*, vol. 1, p. 700; Dobb, *Development of Capitalism*, pp. 20f., 151, 166ff., 199, 230; Christopher Hill in *The Century of Revolution* (New York, 1970), pp. 28–42; Hill, "Comment" in P. Sweezy et al., *The Transition from Feudalism to Capitalism* (New York, 1967), p. 75; and Arnold Toynbee, *Lectures on the Eighteenth Century in England* (London, 1884), pp. 52f.

in the forefront of this development of productive forces he was also aware of the growth of capitalist production in manufacturing and mining.[28] By the time of the early Stuarts, however, feudal relations of production, in the extended sense explicated by Dobb, had come to inhibit the further expansion of the productive powers of English society. Production, innovation, and internal commerce were inhibited by the extensive granting of royal monopolies and the general fear that court favorites might be given a monopoly over any as yet un-monopolized field. The Stuarts' personal and unpredictable initiatives in finance and taxation (extending to the wholesale cancellation of state debts) created an atmosphere unfavorable to the growth of investment resources. Much territory was controlled by aristocratic and ecclesiastical landlords who were not inclined to organize production in new and more efficient ways. Many small farmers paid fixed rents, or had long or lifetime land-tenure, inhibiting the expansion of the wage-earning labor force and the development of capitalist production on the countryside. These are some of the fetters on production which the bourgeoisie was to attack politically, starting in the middle of the seventeenth century.[29]

As Marx says in the *Preface*, these fetters were broken in the course of "an epoch of social revolution . . . a period of transformation." Stretching over almost two centuries, this period was the epoch of a series of political struggles in which the bourgeoisie used state power to transform the English mode of production. The first, most violent, and in Marx's view, most important of these struggles was the English Civil War of the mid-seventeenth century, as a result of which many of the "fetters on production" that I have described were broken during the Cromwell regime. In its attacks on feudalism at this time, the bourgeoisie relied on an alliance with small tradesmen, small farmers, and wage-earners. The instability of this alliance led the bourgeoisie to accept the Restoration, and the minor setbacks to the creation of capitalism that the Restoration entailed. But when feudal

28. "Genesis of the Capitalist Farmer," *Capital*, vol. 1, chap. 29; "Communist Manifesto," *Selected Works*, vol. 1, pp. 109f.

29. See *The German Ideology, Selected Works*, vol. 1, p. 61; "The Bourgeoisie and the Counter-Revolution," *Selected Works*, vol. 1, pp. 139f.; and "Moralizing Criticism and Critical Morality," in Marx, *Selected Essays* (New York, 1926), p. 142.

restrictions seemed about to be strengthened under Charles II, the bourgeoisie in 1688 once again seized state power, as senior partners in an alliance with the more progressive wing of the aristocracy. In the eighteenth century, the bourgeoisie employed this state power to eliminate most remnants of feudalism and to provide resources for the expansion of capitalism. Crucial examples of the impact of political power on economic transformations in this period are the Enclosure Acts, the basis for an attack on feudal land-tenure among small farmers which far exceeded, in scope, the initial enclosure movements of the Tudor period, and, of course, the economic expansion of the British empire. Finally, in the early nineteenth century, the bourgeoisie broke its partnership with the aristocracy, in order to abolish a tariff system, including a high tariff on foodstuffs, the Corn Law, that inhibited the development of domestic industry. In this last progressive political struggle, the bourgeoisie entered into a highly temporary alliance with the proletariat. In sum, through an extended process of political struggle, the bourgeoisie transformed the English economy from a predominantly feudal one to a classic example of the capitalist mode of production.[30]

Of course, I would not claim to have established the validity of the picture of the rise of capitalism that I have just sketched. My claim is that this account is compatible both with everything said by Marx in *Capital* and with the *Preface* theory of social development. It is worthy of serious consideration in light of historical research, rather than dismissal on the grounds of alleged inconsistencies.

In the *Preface*, does Marx provide a valid description of how capitalism, once it triumphs, comes to be succeeded by socialism? Moore offers no direct argument against Marx's views on this subject, aside from claiming, without argument, that Marx's conception of the dynamics of capitalism has been refuted in every capitalist country in the last hundred years. So detailed consideration of this aspect of Marx's writings is beyond the scope of this essay. But it is worth

30. This process is described in Marx's review of Guizot's book, *Why Has the English Revolution Been Successful?* in *Articles on Britain* (Moscow, 1971), pp. 89f. and (in connection with the anti-Corn Law campaign) in Marx's "Speech on Free Trade," in *Articles on Britain*, pp. 74ff. Engels gives a lucid summary of Marx's views in the Introduction to the 1892 English edition of *Socialism: "Utopian and Scientific," Selected Works*, vol. 3, pp. 105–112.

noting that a *Preface*-type theory of the development of capitalism is only worth serious consideration if one adopts a broader conception of productive forces than the one Moore assumes. At crucial points in Marx's account, new productive forces come into being that are not primarily technological, e.g. the development of mass literacy among workers and the coordination of production on a nationwide and even a worldwide scale. Also, in removing fetters on productive forces, socialism is not imagined as primarily removing fetters on technological improvement. For example, in Marx's view, the collective orientation, discipline, and coordination which develop among the proletariat as a result of capitalism and which deepen in the fight against capitalism, make it possible to organize work on a more self-motivated, more flexible, and hence, more productive basis—but only when capitalist rule has been overthrown and socialism is being created.

Productive forces must not be equated with technology, and relations of production must not be equated with institutions of property ownership if Marx's views on the rise of capitalism and the rise of socialism are to be understood and evaluated fairly. The rejection of these equations has significance for many other issues in Marxist theory as well. For example, if relations of production are distinguished from forms of property ownership, the question of whether Russia or China is socialist becomes at least a matter for debate. Thus, the questions Moore raises again suggest a general premise for the interpretation of Marx: the phenomena that have the greatest underlying importance for Marx cannot be reduced to technology and are not described by the legal or political concepts ruling classes have used to legitimize and maintain the status quo. I have argued for the importance of locating productive forces and relations of production in this intermediate realm between the technological and the "juridical." Similar points can, I think, be made concerning Marx's concepts of class and of the State.

In the course of this essay, my interpretations of Marx have sometimes departed from a strict and literal reading. But the interpretative freedom I have claimed is extremely limited compared with that required by standard interpretations of many philosophers (e.g. Rousseau, Kant, or Plato). Perhaps the time has come to interpret

Marxist texts with the reasonable liberty taken for granted in the reading of all other philosophers. More precisely, this liberty might be allowed here, as everywhere else, in those cases where it might free the author from inconsistency or obvious error. If this is done, we will find, I think, that Marx is not inconsistent or obviously wrong. This will encourage political theorists to examine a question of great political and intellectual importance; whether Marxism, in addition to being consistent and plausible, fits the facts of present-day society.

STANLEY MOORE A Consistency Proof for
Historical Materialism

In a recent issue of *Philosophy & Public Affairs* (Winter 1975), I
published an article entitled "Marx and Lenin as Historical Materialists."[1] In a subsequent issue (Summer 1975), Richard W. Miller published a critique of that article, opposing to some of my interpretations
of what Marx wrote interpretations of his own—which admittedly
depart from "a strict and literal meaning," on the ground that such
departures free Marx "from inconsistency or obvious error."[2] In my
opinion these nonliteral interpretations exemplify a fault all too
common among writers on Marxian theory—the vice, as R.M. Hare
describes it, of trying to settle substantive questions by verbal maneu-
ver. To support this opinion, I shall examine the nonliteral interpretations upon which Miller's arguments turn, then indicate the substantive issues they obscure.

Miller's initial justification for what he calls "reasonably nonliteral"
interpretation is based upon a single hypothetical example from natural science: a geologist's statement that the history of the earth's surface is the history of continental drift. Such a statement is acceptable
as "a legitimate simplification of reality," according to Miller, even
though the earth's surface was once molten and then entirely covered
with water.

Used as an attention-provoking introduction, this false statement
is perhaps excusable. Yet instead of describing it as a legitimate sim-

1. See above, pp. 211-234.
2. See above, pp. 235-254.

plification, it seems more accurate to describe it, in this use, as a careless though harmless exaggeration. It is careless because the geologist's exposition would lose nothing if he inserted "recent" or "since the emergence of dry land" to make his statement true. It is harmless because of the way it is used.

The importance of use is illustrated by Marx's statement that the history of all past society is the history of class conflicts—which, in the abstract, resembles the geologist's statement. At its first occurrence in the *Manifesto* Marx's claim might be excused as a harmless exaggeration, sacrificing pedantic accuracy for emotional impact in a call for proletarian revolution. Yet at its second occurrence, my article points out, Marx uses this false statement to defend the prediction that after communism triumphs morality will disappear. Here the historical claim is not a harmless exaggeration. Qualified sufficiently to become defensible as true, it reverses the argument.

Sidestepping my discussion of this point of conflict between the *Preface* and the *Manifesto*, Miller suggests that the only contrast I draw between them concerns the tactic of permanent revolution. The passage in the *Preface* which I interpret as a general repudiation of that tactic includes the statement that no social order disappears before all the productive forces it has room for have been developed. This statement Miller considers a simplification, to be understood through a double application of the Principle of Nonliteral Interpretation. He suggests replacing "before all the productive forces it has room for have been developed" with "before its relations of production have become fetters upon the development of its forces of production." Yet this revision does not end the incompatibility. Miller further suggests that when Marx writes that no social order disappears before certain conditions are met, "he can naturally be taken as describing the development of the whole system in terms of developments in the leading social units, the ones in which the economic processes in question are most advanced." If these interpretations are accepted, he concludes, the alleged contradiction between the *Preface* and the *Manifesto* disappears. Presumably he also interprets nonliterally the corresponding passage in the Preface to *Capital*—which denies for each separate nation the possibility of skipping stages.

What Marx wrote in the *Preface*, applied to a set of economies of

the same type at different levels of development, yields different conclusions according to the degree of interdependence assumed. Assuming a high degree of interdependence, we can infer from Marx's statement that revolution cannot occur in any of the countries until its
objective prerequisites are present in all. Assuming less interdependence, we can infer that revolution cannot occur in any country until
its objective prerequisites are present in that country. The wording of
the statement, however, provides no justification at all for inferring
that, though revolution cannot occur in the most advanced countries
unless its objective prerequisites are present in those countries, revolution can occur in less advanced countries though its objective prerequisites are absent in those countries. To weaken in this fashion
Marx's strong statement concerning the objective prerequisites for
revolution is certainly a nonliteral interpretation. But it is natural only
for a reader who has closed his mind to the possibility that what Marx
wrote in the *Preface* could disagree with what he wrote in the
Manifesto.

To explain away, by nonliteral interpretation, the incompatibility
of what Marx wrote on this topic at the beginning of 1848 and what
he wrote on it at the beginning of 1859 is to miss a set of interesting
problems. Miller seems not to have asked himself whether during the
intervening period—which included the Revolution of 1848—Marx
might have changed his mind. I believe Marx did change his mind;
and I have stated my reasons in the first chapter of *Three Tactics*.
In 1871, the general question of prematurity was reopened by Marx's
support of the Paris Commune. At that time, I believe, his public
defense did not fully reflect his private views: my reasons are stated
in the second chapter of the same book.

(When this reply was first published, I pointed out that the discussion of permanent revolution was distorted by a typographical
error that has been corrected for this Reader.)

The bulk of Miller's critique is devoted to attacking the contrast I
draw between Marx's program for the transition from capitalism to
socialism, as presented in the *Manifesto* and implied in the *Preface*,
and his account of the transition from feudalism to capitalism, as

presented in the *Manifesto* and amplified in *Capital*. Miller rejects my account of the pattern of social revolution presented in the *Preface* on the ground that I have incorrectly interpreted what Marx meant by forces and relations of production. He rejects my account of the pattern of transition from feudalism to capitalism presented in *Capital* on the ground that I have incorrectly interpreted what Marx meant by feudalism and capitalism. On the basis of his own analysis of these four Marxian concepts, he concludes that I am "simply wrong" in my summary of what Marx wrote on the relation between economic trans-formation and political revolution in the transition from feudalism to capitalism.

In my account of the *Preface* I state that Marx explicitly equates relations of production with property relations. My evidence is that he writes there of forces of production coming into conflict with exist-ing relations of production or with—"it is merely a legal expression of the same thing"—existing property relations. But Miller contends that Marx cannot "literally" have equated the two because shortly after-ward he distinguishes economic conditions of production from legal forms. A few paragraphs later Miller concludes that Marx's "side-comment" that property relations are merely a legal expression of relations of production must be seen as a simplification. Is it untrue that Marx literally equated them? Or did he literally equate them, in a simplification which is justifiable by the Principle of Nonliteral Inter-pretation? Miller's answer seems to be that he both did and didn't.

In my account of the *Preface* I state that Marx tacitly equates forces of production with technology. My evidence is that this expression, at its first two occurrences there, is qualified by the adjective "material." But Miller denies that in the *Preface* Marx equates forces of produc-tion with technology, on the ground that in *Capital* he describes the collective power of cooperative labor as a force of production. If what Marx published in 1859, literally interpreted, seems inconsistent with what he published in 1867, literally interpreted, it follows that one of the passages must be nonliterally interpreted to render them con-sistent. Miller does not tell us why.

In reporting what Marx wrote about forces and relations of produc-tion in the *Preface*, I had no intention of providing definitions for these terms that would fit Marx's use of them at every other time and place. Instead, my discussion suggests that his account in the *Preface* later turned out to provide an inadequate framework for his concrete analysis of capitalist production. Citing a passage from *Capital*, I assert that here Marx has in effect transformed his contrast between productive forces and relations into a contrast between two kinds of relations, the technologically conditioned and the property conditioned. In a parallel discussion—presented in the third chapter of *Three Tactics*—I add that though Marx continued to attack Mill's contrast between laws of production and laws of distribution, his own contrast between productive forces and productive relations developed definitely in that direction.

My article did not attempt to formulate Marx's definitions of feudalism and capitalism. For the argument at hand it was sufficient to summarize what he wrote when describing in the *Manifesto* and *Capital* the transition from one to the other. This I attempted in the following three sentences:

> According to what Marx writes there [in the *Manifesto*] and amplifies in *Capital*, capitalist property relations commenced to replace feudal property relations around 1500, though bourgeois revolution did not break out in England until 1640 or in France until 1789. This is a pattern of coexisting and competing modes of production, in which one gradually wins out over the other and in which seizure of political power follows a long process of economic transformation. While in the transition from capitalism to socialism political revolution precedes economic transformation, in the transition from feudalism to capitalism economic transformation precedes political revolution.

This summary Miller claims is simply wrong. But is it?

In the first volume of *Capital*, in the chapter entitled "The Secret of Primitive Accumulation," Marx writes:

> Although we come across the first beginnings of capitalist production as early as the 14th or 15th century, sporadically, in certain towns of the Mediterranean, the capitalist era dates from the 16th century.

In the chapter entitled "Expropriation of the Agricultural Population from the Land," he writes:

> The prelude of the revolution that laid the foundation of the capitalist mode of production [in England] was played in the last third of the 15th, and the first decade of the 16th century.

In the chapter entitled "Genesis of the Capitalist Farmer," he writes:

> . . . England, at the end of the 16th century, had a class of capitalist farmers, rich, considering the circumstances of the time.

And in the chapter entitled "Genesis of the Industrial Capitalist," he writes:

> In the infancy of capitalist production, things often happened as in the infancy of medieval towns, where the question, which of the escaped serfs should be master and which servant, was in great part decided by the earlier or later date of their flight. The snail's pace of this method corresponded in no wise with the commercial requirements of the new world-market that the great discoveries at the end of the 15th century created. . . . The discovery of gold and silver in America, the extirpation, enslavement and entombment in mines of the aboriginal population, the beginning of the conquest and looting of the East Indies, the turning of Africa into a warren for the commercial hunting of black-skins, signalized the rosy dawn of the era of capitalist production.

Although Miller ignores the fact, my summary refers also to the *Manifesto*. In the first section, entitled "Bourgeois and Proletarians," Marx writes:

> The discovery of America, the rounding of the Cape, opened up fresh ground for the rising bourgeoisie. The East-Indian and Chinese markets, the colonisation of America, trade with the colonies, the increase in the means of exchange and in commodities generally, gave to commerce, to navigation, to industry, an impulse never before known, and thereby, to the revolutionary element in the tottering feudal society, a rapid development.

And later in the same section, he writes:

An oppressed class under the sway of the feudal nobility, an armed and self-governing association in the medieval commune: here independent urban republic (as in Italy and Germany), there taxable "third estate" of the monarchy (as in France): afterwards, in the period of manufacturing proper, serving either the semi-feudal or the absolute monarchy as a counterpoise against the nobility, and, in fact, cornerstone of the great monarchies in general, the bourgeoisie has at last, since the establishment of modern industry and of the world market, conquered for itself, in the modern parliamentary state, exclusive political sway.

Instead of dealing with these texts and others like them to demonstrate the incorrectness of my summary, Miller follows an indirect strategy. He first rejects, on Marxian principles, the wider of the two definitions of capitalism he finds in Marx. He next argues that in 1640 the economy of England was not predominantly capitalist, because a majority of the direct producers were not wage workers. He then asserts that if my summary is correct, in 1640 the economy of England was predominantly capitalist in the sense defined. He concludes that therefore my summary is wrong.

To justify his pivotal claim that my summary entails the statement that in 1640 the economy of England was predominantly capitalist in the sense defined, Miller contends that this is the "natural interpretation" of my formula that economic transformation precedes political revolution. Yet this interpretation has no justification if that formula is read in conjunction with the two sentences it follows and summarizes. These sentences include the following statements: capitalist property relations commenced to replace feudal property relations around 1500; the capitalist mode of production gradually won out over the feudal mode of production; bourgeois revolution followed a long process of economic transformation; bourgeois revolution broke out in England in 1640. These statements do not entail the conclusion Miller draws from them if "won out" is interpreted literally as "became decisively stronger." They entail it only if "won out" is interpreted nonliterally as "became numerically predominant." This time the Principle of Nonliteral Interpretation has been applied, in a somewhat different spirit, to me.

The significance of Marx's contrast between bourgeois and proletarian revolution can be clarified by stating it in terms of power. According to the *Manifesto*, the power of the revolutionary bourgeoisie is based on expansion of the capitalist economy within the framework of feudal society. According to the same work, the power of the revolutionary proletariat is based on expansion of the trade union movement within the framework of capitalist society. Some twenty years later, in his *Instructions* for the Geneva Congress of the International, Marx summarized this contrast in the statement that trade unions are the organizational centers of the working class, as medieval municipalities and communes were the organizational centers of the bourgeoisie.

To state the contrast in these terms is to stress its importance for theories of transition to socialism. Not only does it provide such theorists as Lenin and Stalin with a starting point from which to develop the Bolshevik doctrine of proletarian dictatorship. It also provides such theorists as Bernstein and Jaurès with a starting point for opposing to the revolutionary pattern of socialist transition a reformist pattern. Arguing that the transition from capitalism to socialism, like the transition from feudalism to capitalism, will follow what I have called the pattern of competing systems, Jaurès states that this pattern exemplifies the law of such great transformations. Rejecting what he calls Marx's catastrophism and asserting that socialism is developing inside capitalist society, Bernstein substitutes for Marx's theory of transition to socialism a theory closer to Marx's theory of transition to capitalism. I have discussed this set of issues twice: from a standpoint sympathetic to reformist socialism in the third chapter of *Three Tactics*, from a standpoint sympathetic to Leninism in the third chapter of *The Critique of Capitalist Democracy*. Both discussions demonstrate, I believe, the value of Marx's contrast for clarifying tactical disputes among socialist theorists, inside and outside the Marxian tradition.

I shall conclude with a general comment on Miller's method. His critique is entitled "The Consistency of Historical Materialism." In that critique he is not content to claim that his alternative interpretations are as plausible as mine. Instead he claims, by exposing the error of my interpretations, to establish the consistency of statements I contrast. But how is this accomplished? In each case where I have shown that two statements of Marx are inconsistent when interpreted literally, Miller considers this sufficient reason for interpreting one nonliterally to make them consistent. Each argument, in other words, assumes the truth of the thesis it purports to prove.

ALLEN BUCHANAN   Revolutionary Motivation
                              and Rationality

I

Much recent literature concentrates on the question of whether Marx's analysis of capitalism uses moral concepts, especially a concept of justice, or whether it is a non-moral, strictly scientific analysis. Less attention has been paid, however, to what role, if any, Marx assigns to moral principles in his account of revolutionary motivation.

Marx repeatedly asserts the superiority of his views to those of moralizing socialists, who appeal to moral principles to spur the masses to revolt.[1] Thus Marx's claim to a non-moral, strictly scientific analysis of capitalism would seem to be in harmony with his account of revolutionary motivation. I shall argue, however, that Marx's account of revolutionary motivation is extremely weak and that remedying its defects may require significant revisions in his social theory.

II

We can begin by outlining the main features of Marx's account of the revolutionary motivation of the proletariat. At a certain stage in the development of capitalism, what Marx calls the "contradictions" of the system become so extreme that they become plain to any but

1. See, for example, Marx's scathing criticism of the "true socialists'" conception of a Republic based on the idea of humanity, in *Karl Marx: Selected Writings*, ed. D. McLellan (New York: Oxford University Press, 1977), pp. 216-218. Note also Marx's admonition to the German socialists to cease their preoccupation with "obsolete verbal rubbish" about justice and right, p. 569.

the most abject bourgeois hypocrite.[2] A contracting minority of propertied non-workers stands in undisguised opposition to an expanding
majority of propertyless workers. Caught in the toils of worsening
business cycles, workers are laid off because they have been too productive. Wealth accumulates in the hands of the minority, while accelerating impoverishment and mental and physical degradation are
the lot of the majority. Once the proletarian recognizes these basic
facts of the class struggle (which Marx articulates and systematizes
in his materialistic conception of history and his analysis of capitalism), he will realize that his own interest, as well as that of every
other proletarian, requires the overthrow of the system.[3]

It is something of an understatement to say that for Marx the proletarian's revolutionary motivation is self-interest or class interest. For
at times Marx goes so far as to identify the interest as the most basic
one of all—the interest in survival. For Marx the phrase "class war" is
no hyberbole. In the *Communist Manifesto* he declares that the existence of society itself is no longer compatible with the rule of the
bourgeoisie.[4]

What is striking about Marx's conception of proletarian revolutionary motivation is that it makes any motivational role for moral principles otiose. Where self-interest—indeed the interest in survival—is
adequate, there is no need to appeal to a sense of justice or to any

2. In the Preface to the Second German Edition of *Capital*, vol. I, Marx states
that ". . . [bourgeois] political economy [could] remain a science only so long
as the class struggle remains latent . . ." and that once it became overt—after
1830—bourgeois political economy became the trade of "hired prize-fighters" who
no longer asked "whether this theorem or that is true, but whether it was useful
to capital. . . ." *Capital*, vol. 1 (New York: International Publishers, 1967),
p. 15. All subsequent references to *Capital* are to this edition.

3. In the *Communist Manifesto* Marx describes the proletarian revolution as
the ". . . movement of the immense majority, in the interests of the immense
majority." *Karl Marx: Selected Writings*, p. 230. The role of the communist
party, Marx says on p. 231, is simply to make the proletariat aware that its
interest lies in the overthrow of the system and to guide the resulting revolutionary action so as to maximize its efficacy. Additional textual evidence that
Marx held what I shall call an interest theory of revolutionary motivation will
be marshalled as my argument unfolds.

4. *Karl Marx: Selected Writings*, p. 230. In *Capital*, I: 269. Marx writes of
"the depopulation of the human race" by capitalism.

moral standard. Marx believes this is all to the good, since every un-scientific socialist sect has its own conception of justice or fairness. There is no need for a careful analysis of these moral conceptions, since effective revolutionary motivation in no way depends upon them. Marx concludes that talk about justice is "obsolete verbal rubbish."[5]

According to Marx, the motivation of previous revolutionary classes has also been self-interest. The rising bourgeoisie in France, for instance, found it necessary to destroy the *ancien régime* to achieve its own good. There is, however, a crucial difference between the way in which the bourgeois revolutionaries presented their struggle and the way in which the proletariat presents its attack on the social order. In every revolution in the past, including the French, the revolutionary class, not being a majority, found it necessary to present its own special interests as universal rights in order to enlist the support of other classes.[6] Granted Marx's assumption that the intermediate classes become "proletarianized," so that the proletariat becomes the vast majority, with only one tiny class confronting it as its implacable foe, such ideological window-dressing is no longer necessary. The proletariat, like previous revolutionary classes, is motivated by its own interests; but unlike its predecessors, it can boldly acknowledge this fact. And granted the confusion and divisiveness Marx associates with appeals to moral principles, there is something to be gained by insisting upon the self-interested character of the proletarian struggle.

III

Criticisms of Marx's account of revolutionary motivation have often focused on its apparent inapplicability to non-proletarians who strive for socialist revolution. The most notorious instances of this puzzling phenomenon are Marx and Engels themselves—the one a petty bour-

5. *Karl Marx: Selected Writings*, p. 569. See also p. 566: "What is 'a fair distribution' [*gerechte, fair* or *just*]? Do not the bourgeois assert that the present-day distribution is 'fair'? . . . Have not also the socialist sectarians the most varied notions of a 'fair' distribution?"

6. "A particular class can only vindicate for itself general supremacy in the name of the general rights of society." *Karl Marx: Selected Writings*, p. 71.

geois, the other a big bourgeois, both dedicated to the cause of the proletariat. Though such cases pose problems for Marx's account of revolutionary motivation, they are not the most interesting ones. The most interesting challenge for Marx's theory is to see if it can respond to the much more radical charge that it is unsatisfactory even as an account of the *proletarian's* revolutionary motivation.

This more radical type of criticism may impugn either the *descriptive* accuracy of Marx's account or its *normative* adequacy. Descriptive criticisms purport to show that Marx's theory is inaccurate as an explanation of how proletarian revolutionaries are in fact motivated. Normative criticisms contend that Marx has not shown that a proletarian has adequate reason to become a revolutionary, whether in fact he becomes one or not.

Some have argued that Marx's theory is normatively adequate but descriptively inaccurate. The overthrow of capitalism is in the interest of the proletariat, and if its members believed this and acted rationally on this belief, they would undertake revolutionary action. But, in fact, many workers, still in the thrall of bourgeois ideology, fail to perceive what is in their own best interests. Their motivational failure has a cognitive root.

Another standard objection is that the theory fails both normatively and descriptively. Marx underestimated the resilience of capitalism and its potential for reform. Many workers have not become revolutionaries for the simple reason that their lot has improved significantly since Marx's day. The crushing contradictions of capitalism have given way to the tolerable tensions of the welfare state. The normative inadequacy of Marx's view seems to follow as a matter of course: granted the proletariat's improved condition, it is no longer obvious that revolutionary activity is rational.

IV

There is, however, a much more radical objection which has received little scrutiny.[7] The purpose of this essay is to articulate this objec-

7. M. Olson in *The Logic of Collective Action* (Cambridge: Harvard University Press, 1965), pp. 105-106, states very briefly the public goods objec-

tion, to elicit its implications for Marx's social theory as a whole, and to evaluate its force. Stated in the baldest and boldest form, it is the charge that even if revolution is in the best interest of the proletariat, and even if every member of the proletariat realizes that this is so, so far as its members act rationally, this class will *not* achieve concerted revolutionary action.[8] This shocking conclusion rests on the premise that concerted revolutionary action is for the proletariat a public good in the technical sense. By a public good is meant any object or state of affairs such that if it is available to anyone in a group it is available to every other member of the group, including those who have not shared in the costs of producing it.[9]

There are five features of public goods which together result in a basic problem of social coordination. (i) Action by some but not all members of the group is sufficient to provide each member with the good. (ii) If the good is produced, it will be available to all, even to those who did not contribute to its production. (iii) There is no practical way, or no way not involving excessive costs, to prevent those who did not contribute from enjoying the good.[10] (iv) The individual's contribution is a cost to that individual. (v) The value of what

---

tion I develop in detail in this essay. Olson does not explore the relation between Marx's theory of revolutionary motivation and Marx's views on coercion and moral principles. Nor does he consider the problematic relationship between Marx's assumptions about proletarian cooperation and the failure to cooperate which Marx attributes to capitalists. Finally, Olson does not consider Marxian replies to the public goods objection. None of this is surprising, since Olson's reference to Marx is only a brief but suggestive digression on the application of Olson's general theory to Marx's views on revolution.

8. In Section VII, I respond to the charge that rationality is not to be identified either with individual or with group utility-maximization. Even if this charge is correct, the main points of my argument are unaffected.

9. My presentation of the concept of a public good and my analysis of the public goods problem borrow heavily from R. Sartorius's discussion in his forthcoming paper "The Limits of Libertarianism," in *Law and Liberty* (College Station: Texas A & M Press, 1978).

10. Item (ii), jointness of supply, must be distinguished from (iii), non-excludability. A good may be produced in joint supply, yet it still may be possible to exclude certain persons from partaking of it. "Non-excludability," as I shall use it, is a dispositional term referring to the practical or political infeasibility of exclusion. "Jointness" is a manifest or non-dispositional term referring to the way in which a good is in fact produced.

each individual would gain from the good outweighs his share of the costs of producing it.

Granted these five features, provision of the public good in question is threatened by the free-rider problem. Each member of the group, if rational, will reason as follows. Regardless of whether I contribute or not, either enough others will contribute to provide good G or they will not. If the former, then the good will be available to me free of charge and my contribution would be wasted. If the latter, then my contribution would again be a loss to me. So rational self-interest requires that I not contribute and go for a "free ride" on the efforts of others.

The free-rider problem arises for such public goods as clean air, energy conservation, population control, and preventing inflation. The situation can be illustrated by the following matrix, M.

OTHERS

	Contribute	Don't Contribute
Contribute	Benefits of G 2 Costs of Contribution	No Benefits of G 4 Costs of Contribution
Don't Contribute	Benefits of G 1 No Costs of Contribution	No Benefits of G 3 No Costs of Contribution

INDIVIDUAL

The numbers in the four cells of M represent the individual's preferences among the outcomes: the lower left cell is most preferred, the upper right is least preferred.

It is often assumed that the public goods problem arises only for rational egoists—individuals who seek to maximize their own utility. This is not the case, however, as matrix M shows. Assume that the individual contemplating contribution or non-contribution is not a maximizer of his own utility but a maximizer of overall utility for the group. Matrix M still captures this situation accurately and reveals the same free-rider problem. Each maximizer of group utility would reason as follows. Regardless of whether I contribute or not, either enough others will contribute or they won't. If the former, then my costs of contribution would do no good, while constituting a subtraction from the utility the group gains from G. If the latter, then my costs of contribution are again a subtraction from the group's utility. So maximizing group utility requires that I be a free rider. And again, since every other maximizer of group utility reasons in the same way, the good G will not be secured. Matrix M, then, represents the problem for the maximizer of group utility as well as for the maximizer of individual utility, since the result is the same whether "costs" and "benefits" are calculated solely for the individual or for the group as a whole.[11]

Application to the case of the proletarian is straightforward. Concerted revolutionary action is a public good for the proletariat as a

11. In *Sociologists, Economists, and Democracy* (London: Collier-Macmillan, 1970), B. Barry argues that the cases of the individual and the group utility-maximizer differ crucially. The difference, he thinks, is that the group utility-maximizer will not view his contribution as negligible because it will affect a large number of people. In "The Limits of Libertarianism," (p. 6), R. Sartorius points out that this will only be true where so-called *threshold effects* are not present. The idea is that in many of the more important public goods cases the likelihood of the individual's contribution occurring at the threshold of contribution which must be crossed if the good is to be produced is virtually nil. It seems clear that in the case of concerted revolutionary action a rational individual would regard the likelihood of his contribution occurring at a "threshold" as negligible. If this is so, then Barry's point is inapplicable and the public goods problem arises regardless of whether the proletarian maximizes individual or group utility. A Marxian who is still convinced that the cases are different and who wishes to argue that the public goods problem is avoided because each proletarian maximizes group utility would have to provide an account of how the proletarian comes to desire to maximize his class's interest rather than his own.

group. Yet each proletarian, whether he seeks to maximize his own interests or those of his class, will refrain from revolutionary action. The radical character of this objection must not be underestimated. The point is not that inaction is *compatible* with rationality. Rationality *requires* inaction. Further, the problem does not depend upon an assumption that the costs of contribution for the individual are very high, much less sacrificial. The phenomenon of revolutionary self-sacrifice presents interesting problems for the moral psychologists, but they are not the problems I shall deal with here.

The public goods objection to Marx's account of proletarian revolutionary motivation can be understood either descriptively or normatively. As a normative objection, it is the claim that the proletarian, far from having conclusive reasons to join the revolutionary struggle, has conclusive reasons to withhold his support from it. Granted the assumption that the proletarian is in fact either a maximizer of his own utility or of his group's, the descriptivist objection follows.

V

The seriousness of the public goods objection to Marx's theory of revolutionary motivation is enhanced once it is related to Marx's views on the role of capitalist competition in the downfall of capitalism. According to Marx, the capitalists, by producing an impoverished, exploited proletariat whose only salvation lies in the overthrow of the system, produce "their own gravediggers."[12] The mechanics of the capitalists' self-destruction is an integral part of Marx's economic theory and the details are quite complex. For our purposes, however, a simple sketch will suffice.

Each capitalist must either compete successfully or eventually lose his capital. To compete successfully he must extract more and more surplus value from his workers; he must increase what Marx calls the degree of exploitation.[13] But this increasing pressure on the proletariat

12. *Karl Marx: Selected Writings*, p. 231.

13. Surplus value, for Marx, is the value the worker produces in excess of the value of the commodities needed for his subsistence as a worker. *Capital*, I: 177-198, 331. "The rate of surplus-value is . . . an exact expression for the de-

eventually makes its condition unbearable: the victims become revolutionaries. It is compellingly rational for each capitalist to squeeze more and more surplus from his workers, since to moderate his efforts unilaterally would be disastrous for him. Rationality on the part of each capitalist, however, brings the death of the capitalist class.

The structural similarities between the predicament of the capitalists and that of the proletariat are striking. In each case there is an interest common to all members of the group. In the case of the proletariat there is the common interest in winning control over the means of production; for the capitalists, preservation of their control over the means of production and the power and wealth which go with it. Yet in each case, rational assessment by each member of the group apparently leads to inaction. What is rational for each is disastrous for all.

Marx, however, assumes that the needed cooperation will be forthcoming in the case of the proletariat, but not in the case of the capitalists. We have already seen that Marx's confidence in proletarian cooperation may be misplaced—he seems to have simply overlooked the possibility that a public goods problem arises for the proletariat. In the case of the capitalists, however, it seems that Marx has not only identified a public goods problem—he has also made its insolubility a cornerstone of his theory of revolution. An adequate response to the public goods objection to Marx's theory of proletarian revolutionary motivation therefore must show either (i) that the problem faced by the capitalists and by the proletariat are dissimilar or, if similarity is admitted, must explain (ii) why the problem is soluble in the one case but not in the other.

The task facing the Marxian here is a strenuous one, especially if alternative (ii) is chosen. As we shall see later, the most common response to the public goods problem is to invoke coercively backed regulation to restructure the individual's preferences by making noncooperation more costly than cooperation. The prospects of a coercive

---

gree of exploitation of labour-power by capital or of the labourer by the capitalist." *Capital*, I: 218. Marx defines the rate of surplus value as the ratio of surplus value to the value of the commodities necessary for the worker's subsistence as a worker. *Capital*, I: 218-219.

solution, however, seem much brighter for the capitalists than for the proletariat. For on Marx's view it is the capitalists who control the dominant coercive apparatus in society—the state. It can be plausibly argued that since Marx's day the capitalist class has in fact effectively used its control over the state to make the condition of workers bearable enough to cool their revolutionary ardor. Indeed the modern welfare state—which alleviates the condition of the propertyless, while preserving a large sphere of private ownership of the means of production—is the ideal candidate for a solution to the capitalists' Hobbesian predicament. Redistributive programs prevent the formation of an impoverished revolutionary mass, while the fact that these programs are financed through *compulsory* taxation diminishes the temptation for the individual capitalist to be a free rider and assures him that his contribution to averting the revolution will be matched by those of his fellows.

VI

There are two types of strategies which might be used to rebut the public goods objection to Marx's account of proletarian revolutionary motivation. The first acknowledges that there is a public goods problem but attempts to show that it can be solved. The second tries to show that there is no public goods problem for the proletariat. If either strategy is to serve as a defense of *Marx's* account of proletarian motivation it must square both with other features of that account and with Marx's social theory as a whole. In this Section, I shall pursue and evaluate the first strategy. In Section VII, I consider the second.

There are three generally recognized types of solutions to the public goods problems. The first relies upon (1) *coercion*, the second upon what I shall call (2) *in-process* benefits, and the third upon (3) *moral principles*. The first solution, as noted earlier, is to use coercion to restructure the individual's preferences by making non-contribution more costly than contribution. The second contends that the individual will gain certain benefits from the process of participation itself, regardless of the outcome of the process, and that these in-process benefits well outweigh his costs of contribution. The third type of

solution argues that adherence to certain internalized moral principles will solve the problem by precluding the individual from making
those cost-benefit calculations which would lead him to go for a free
ride. An example would be a principle requiring one to attempt to
overthrow an unjust or inhumane social order. Each of the three types
of solution will be examined in detail. In each case I shall argue that
even if the proposed solution is promising, it is not available to Marx
because it conflicts with some of his most basic views on the nature
of socialist revolution.

(1) Coercively backed penalties for pollution provide a contemporary example of the coercive solution; Hobbes' sovereign, as the dominant coercive power in society, is the classical case in political theory.
The coercive solution can be applied to the case of the proletariat in
either of two ways, depending upon the time period in which force is
to be applied. Force might be applied either during the revolutionary
struggle or after it. In the former case, some group would threaten
the imminent use of violence against those proletarians who refrain
from revolutionary activity. In the latter, some group would threaten
to use violence against non-contributors once the proletariat achieves
power.

Though both versions of the coercive solution may be descriptively
accurate as accounts of revolutions which have actually occurred, neither squares with Marx's views on the role of coercion in socialist revolution. Marx nowhere, to my knowledge, even suggests that the
threat of either imminent or postrevolutionary violence plays a role
in motivating the proletariat to action. It is, of course, true that Marx
predicts that violence will be used during the revolution against the
bourgeoisie and against those *lumpenproletarians* whom it hires to
fight its battles.[14] Further, his doctrine of the *dictatorship* of the proletariat implies that for some time after it has come to power the proletariat will find it necessary to employ coercion against the remnants

14. Though Marx's dominant view was that proletarian revolution will be
violent, he considered the possibility of peaceful revolution in certain countries
under certain conditions. See Engels' Preface to the English translation of *Capital*, I:6.

of the bourgeoisie.[15] But in neither case does Marx so much as hint
that coercion will be needed in order to spur the proletariat to action.

Additional problems arise when one asks, *Who* is it who is supposed
to use coercion against the proletarians to secure their participation
and, more importantly, what motivates these motivators and how does
their motivation achieve collective action? If the motivators are themselves proletarians motivated either by the desire to maximize their
own utility or that of their class, then the public goods problem reiterates. If, on the other hand, the motivators are not members of the
proletariat but, say, non-proletarian intellectuals, then two problems
remain for the Marxian. First, some account of their motivation is
still needed. If that account holds that these non-proletarians somehow come to identify with the proletariat's interests, then the nature
of this identification must be explored. Second, even granted such
identification, the public goods problem again reiterates at the level
of the cooperation needed to form a convincing group of coercive motivators. The formation of such a group is itself a public good for the
persons who wish to form it for purposes of solving the proletariat's
public goods problem.

It is important to note that Marx's doctrine that the communist
party is the "vanguard" of the proletariat does *not* provide textual support for any version of the coercive solution.[16] Marx's point is not that
the communists are revolutionary police whose function is to bully
the proletariat into action; his idea, rather, is that they are the *educational* and *tactical* elite of the movement. They "point out and bring
to the front the common interests of the entire proletariat, independently of all nationality,"[17] and they insure that the revolutionary efforts of the masses achieve their most effective expression. The first,
educational function assigns a crucial role to the elite in *forming* a
revolutionary class, but provides no solution to the public goods problem, since it assumes that the mere recognition of a common interest
is sufficient for contribution to its achievement. This, of course, is pre-

15. *Karl Marx: Selected Writings*, p. 565.
16. Though Lenin popularized the term "vanguard" in this connection, it fits
Marx's conception of the role of the communist party accurately.
17. *Karl Marx: Selected Works*, p. 231.

cisely what the public goods objection denies. The second, tactical
function again provides no solution since it assumes the existence of
a revolutionary proletariat and addresses only the question of its tactical deployment. And neither the educational nor the tactical function even suggests the use of coercion by a revolutionary elite against
the proletariat. It is important to re-emphasize that if the Marxian
chooses to revise Marx on this issue by assigning a coercive role to
the "vanguard," he must still explain the motivation which produces
an effective coercive group.

(2) According to the in-process benefits solution, certain goods intrinsic to the process of contribution offset the costs of contribution.
Plausible examples of this phenomenon may not be hard to find. Not
only revolutionary terrorists but also Red Cross volunteers and peace
demonstrators may set great store by the community, fraternity, and
solidarity which they experience as participants in a common struggle.
There appear to be, however, three rather severe limitations on the
force of this solution to the problem. First, Marx nowhere suggests
that such derivative goods of association, rather than the proletariat's
interest in the overthrow of the system, are a major factor in the revolutionary motivation of the proletariat.[18]

18. In the following passage from the *1844 Manuscripts* (cited by Shlomo
Avineri, in *The Social and Political Thought of Karl Marx*, Cambridge: Cambridge University Press, 1971, p. 141), Marx shows that he is aware of what I
have called in-process benefits.

> When communist artisans [*Handwerker*] form associations, teaching and
> propaganda are their first aims. But their association itself creates a new
> need—the need for society—and what appeared to be a means has become an
> end. The most striking results of this practical development are to be seen
> when French socialist workers meet together. Smoking, eating and drinking
> are no longer simply means of bringing people together. Society, association,
> entertainment which also has society as its aim, is sufficient for them; the
> brotherhood of man is no empty phrase but a reality. . . .

Nonetheless, Marx fails to develop an account of how the competitive, egoistic
barriers to these goods of association can ultimately be overcome. Nor does he
attempt to assign a significant role to them by integrating the idea of in-process
benefits into the rational interest theory of revolutionary motivation which
dominates the theory of the breakdown of capitalism in his middle and late
works.

The second difficulty with this solution is that a theory of proletarian revolution which did assign such a crucial role to in-process benefits would have to provide an account of the conditions under which such benefits are a sufficient motivating factor. For it is clear that these intrinsic benefits of association are not always forthcoming nor, even if forthcoming, always effective. History provides numerous examples of peoples who failed to achieve effective resistance to their oppressors, even though they shared a common form of life and a common experience of persecution. A Marxian who relies on the in-process benefits solution must explain, for instance, how the case of the proletariat differs from that of Ghetto Jews in Nazi Europe. On the face of it, one would have thought that the resources of community, fraternity, and solidarity would have been richest in such closeknit ethnic groups.

There is a third, more serious difficulty which is independent of the first and second. Where an ongoing process of common struggle already exists, it is plausible to appeal to in-process benefits to explain the continual existence of cooperation. But the mere possibility of in-process benefits in the future, if the process gets underway, is of dubious merit as an explanation of how the process gets started. This problem is greatly exacerbated by Marx's insistence that the capitalist system fosters competition and egoism in all its members and thoroughly undermines all genuine forms of community. In addition to the general climate of competitive egoism and individualism in capitalism, Marx emphasizes two related barriers to proletarian cooperation: competition for jobs between employed workers and the "industrial reserve army" of the unemployed and competition between employed workers for managerial positions. At one point he goes so far as to say that relations among workers are even more competitive than among capitalists. Yet Marx provides no adequate account of how these barriers to community and its benefits can be overcome within capitalism, offering instead only the following unenlightening remarks.

Competition separates individuals from one another, not only the bourgeois but still more the workers, in spite of the fact that it brings them together. Hence it is a long time before these individuals can unite, apart from the fact that for the purpose of this union—if it is not to be merely local—the necessary means, the big industrial cities and cheap and quick communications, have first to be produced by large-scale industry. Hence every organized power standing over and against these isolated individuals, who live in conditions daily reproducing this isolation, can only be overcome after long struggle.[19]

Here the problem is recognized and some *necessary* conditions (concentrations of workers, improved means of communications) for its solution are listed. Yet no solution is offered. We are only comforted with the observation that the solution will take a long time. Marx maintains that the eradication of egoism, competition, and individualism, and the transformation of man into a "communal being" begins with the process of revolution and is completed only when human beings grow up in communism.[20] Unfortunately, the psychological transformation produced by a process of revolutionary cooperation cannot explain how untransformed individuals came to participate in the process in the first place.

3. It can be argued that a distinctive function of certain moral principles is to provide a solution to public goods problems as well as other problems of social coordination. Among the moral principles to which this function might be attributed are various types of generalization principles, principles imposing a duty to keep promises, and principles requiring us to help establish just or humane or free social institutions.[21] The idea is that adherence to such principles produces

19. *The German Ideology, Collected Works: Marx and Engels*, vol. 5 (New York: International Publishers, 1976), p. 75.

20. See, for example, *Economic and Philosophic Manuscripts*, pp. 87-96, and *Critique of the Gotha Programme*, pp. 568-69, in *Karl Marx: Selected Writings*.

21. Generalization principles include, for example, Kant's Universal Law Formula of the Categorical Imperative and the Principle of Utilitarian Generalization. The former states that one is to act only on that maxim one can at the same time will to be a universal law. The latter requires one to do that action which is such that the consequences of everyone doing that kind of action in similar circumstances would maximize utility.

In Section 51 of *A Theory of Justice* (Cambridge: Harvard University Press, cooperation in cases where none would be forthcoming if individuals acted to maximize individual or group utility. In the case at hand it might be argued that adherence to a principle imposing a duty to help establish humane institutions would serve this needed function for the proletariat.[22]

If we set aside, for a moment, the question of whether Marx himself accepts such a role for moral principles, there is at least one reason why this solution to the proletariat's public goods problem is more plausible than the coercive solution. As I argued earlier, the proletariat, unlike the capitalist class, does not exert control over an antecedently existing coercive apparatus. Hence, the coercive solution, in the case of the proletariat, simply pushes the public goods problem back to a deeper level—the problem then becomes that of achieving the cooperation needed to create a convincing coercive apparatus. For this reason the moral principles solution is worth considering.

The immediate difficulty in appealing to moral principles as a *Marxian* response to the public goods problem is, of course, that it requires a wholesale rejection of Marx's fundamental claim that the proletarian's motive is self-interest or the interest of his class. Before we proceed further, however, it is important to make a distinction which is often neglected in the perennial debate over whether Marx's theory includes moral elements or is "strictly scientific." We must distinguish two questions. (a) Do moral concepts play a significant role in Marx's analysis of capitalism and of history in general? (b) Do moral concepts play a significant role in Marx's theory of proletarian revolutionary motivation? At the outset of this essay I noted that the answer to

---

1971), J. Rawls proposes a principle requiring one to support just social institutions. Rawls' principle is not designed to solve what he calls the assurance problem: it operates where the individual can already count on the cooperation of others in supporting just institutions. A principle of justice capable of solving the public goods problem, therefore, would have to be stronger than Rawls' principle. Different degrees of strength are possible. The principle could require that one direct one's efforts to the establishment of just institutions, if one can do so without great cost to oneself. A much stronger principle would exact such a duty even if its fulfillment meant one's own destruction.

22. Such a principle would be consistent with Marx's refusal to rely upon a conception of *justice* and is consonant with his vision of communism as a humane social order.

the latter question is negative: Marx repeatedly scoffs at socialists who
rely on moral exhortation to move the masses to revolt. The answer
to the former question is much more problematic. Some have argued
that Marx's analysis of capitalism does not employ the concept of
justice.[23] Yet Marx's charges that capitalism is exploitative, that it
alienates man from his nature as a communal being, that it is an inhuman system, and a disguised form of slavery all rest upon moral
or at least normative concepts—whether they are concepts of justice or
not. What solution is available to a consistent Marxian who wishes to
preserve Marx's denial of a motivating role for moral principles in his
account of proletarian revolution, while acknowledging that Marx's
analysis of capitalism employs moral concepts? Such a position would
hold that though the moral condemnation of capitalism and the proletarian's self-interest both dictate the overthrow of the system, appeal
to moral principles would be superfluous, since self-interest will suffice. Where one's self-interest—indeed one's survival—dictate revolutionary action, the exhortation that one ought morally to revolt is an
otiose echo. This way of harmonizing the claim that Marx's analysis
of capitalism employs moral concepts with the claim that his account
of revolutionary motivation assigns no significant role to such concepts leaves the public goods problem untouched. It simply assumes
that the proletarian's recognition of his own interest or of that of his
class will itself produce effective revolutionary action. Marx seems to
have overlooked the possibility that even where morality and interest
speak as with one voice, morality may still have an ineliminable
function.

It was noted earlier that there are two main strategies for the Marxian who seeks to rebut the public goods objection. The first is to acknowledge that the problem exists and to attempt to solve it, either
by appeal to coercion, in-process benefits, or moral principles. I have
just argued that none of these solutions is compatible with some of
Marx's most basic views on revolutionary motivation.[24] The second

23. A. Wood, "The Marxian Critique of Justice," See above, pp. 3-41, and
R. Tucker, *The Marxian Revolutionary Idea* (New York: Norton Publishers,
1969), pp. 37-48.
24. There may be still other alternatives. For instance, one might use the

main strategy available to the Marxian is to attempt to show that no
public goods problem exists for the proletariat. It is this second type
of reply we must now examine.

VII

There are, it seems, only three versions of the second strategy worth
considering. The first appeals to a certain interpretation of Marx's materialism; the second to an extreme version of the doctrine of the immiseration of the proletariat; and the third to Marx's historicist critique of concepts of rationality.[25]

In briefest form, the first version goes like this. The objection that
the proletariat faces a public goods problem is based on a misconception. The misconception is that the revolutionary movement is produced through deliberation and calculation on the part of individual
proletarians. But Marx's view—the correct view—is that the individual's participation in the revolutionary struggle is simply a response
to changes in the material base of society.[26] To emphasize individual
decision-making is to neglect the material forces which shape history
—it is to flirt with idealism. Even if individual reasoning about inter-

---

notion of leadership by example or rely upon the motivation of resentment. In
the first case one would develop a theory of revolutionary motivation which
assigns a pivotal role to the ability of leaders to inspire the masses to emulate
their personal example, without calculating costs and benefits. In the second
case, the crucial motivating factor would be the resentment of the masses
toward their oppressors. In this essay I shall not pursue either of these alternative solutions for two reasons. First, neither of them seems to be at all plausible
as a Marxian solution, since Marx nowhere assigns a significant role to either
factor. Second, unlike the three solutions I do consider, the theory of leadership
by example and the theory of the motivation of resentment are not *rational
solutions* to the proletariat's public goods problem. Instead, they remove the
problem from the theory of rational decision and treat it as a problem of
empirical psychological explanation.

25. For purposes of the argument I will assume that Marx intends his historicist views about concepts in general to apply to concepts of rationality, while
acknowledging that there may be no conclusive textual evidence to support this
assumption.

26. The material base, for Marx, is the set of processes by which a society
produces the material means of life—food, shelter, and so on. *Karl Marx: Selected Works*, p. 165.

ests is present, it is present only as a reflection, an epiphenomenal overlay: the moving force of history lies in the transformation of a society's mode of production.

A consistent Marxian should be reluctant to embrace this reply because it rests on a very dubious interpretation of Marx's materialism. To emphasize the crucial importance of the processes by which a society produces the material means of life is not to deny that individuals deliberate, calculate, and act on their interests or the interests of their group as they perceive them. Marx never denied that the individual's behavior is a purposive expression of his needs and interests as he perceives them. Marx's thesis, rather, is that the needs and interests an individual has, as well as his awareness of them, are conditioned by his location in the social structure, and that the material processes of production are the foundation of that structure.[27] Marx's materialism, then, is not a substitute for a theory relating the proletarian's needs and interests to his actions. It is an explanation of how those interests and needs come to be and of how the proletarian comes to see them for what they are, without the benefit of ideological cosmetics. More importantly, though I shall not argue the point here, this version of materialism is much more plausible than the epiphenomenalist interpretation, regardless of which version enjoys the strongest textual support. Perhaps the most unattractive feature of the materialist reply to the public goods problem is that it forces one to deny any sense to the question of what reasons there are for a proletarian to become a revolutionary.

A second way of arguing that there is no public goods problem for the proletariat is to deny that condition (iv) above is satisfied. The Marxian could argue that the proletariat's condition deteriorates until a point is reached at which the burdens of continuing to live under

27. In the Preface to *A Contribution to the Critique of Political Economy,* Marx distinguishes between "the material transformation of the economic conditions of production . . . and the legal, political, religious, aesthetic, or philosophic—in short, ideological forms in which men become conscious of this conflict and fight it out." *Karl Marx: Selected Writings,* pp. 389-390. The crucial point here is that even though men's interests and their consciousness of those interests depend upon conflicts in the material base, nonetheless men *do* "fight out" the conflict at the level of conscious purposive behavior.

capitalism become so overwhelming that the worker no longer counts his revolutionary effort as a cost. This strategy for avoiding the public goods problem, however, comes at an excessive price. It rests upon the most extreme version of Marx's prophecy of the accelerating immiseration of the proletariat, and that prophecy has so far proved false.

The third, somewhat more plausible attempt to show that there is no public goods problem for the proletariat can be sketched as follows. According to Marx, our most basic concepts, including our concept of rationality, are historically conditioned social products. The concept of rationality as individual or group utility-maximization is the *bourgeois* concept of rationality. The public goods objection makes the mistake of identifying bourgeois rationality with rationality *per se*. Thus even if bourgeois rationality thwarts revolutionary action, it does not follow that rationality (*per se*) requires that the proletarian refrain from participating in the revolution.

There are several reasons why this reply will not do. First, the main force of the public goods objection does not depend upon whether individual or group utility-maximization is accorded the honorific title of "rationality." Call it what you will, the problem is to show either that such maximization will produce the desired cooperation, or, if it will not, to provide some alternative account of effective revolutionary motivation.

Second, it seems most plausible to interpret Marx's claim that the revolutionary action of the proletariat is motivated by the interests of the proletariat as the claim that in revolting, the proletarians seek to maximize their individual or class interests. It is difficult to imagine how else one could interpret the former claim.[28]

Third, the historicist reply can be turned against itself. Suppose we

28. It might be replied that Marx's point is that the proletarian does not ask "What should *I* do to maximize my own or my class's utility?" Instead he identifies himself as a member of the proletariat and asks, "What should *we* do?" He avoids the public goods problem by calculating the cost of *our* not participating relative to the benefits of *our* participating. The difficulty with this reply, however, is that it *assumes* what the Marxian must establish, namely, that, in spite of the isolating, egoistic environment of capitalism, the proletarian can arrive at a new way of conceiving of his decisions which avoids the public goods problem. As I argue below, Marx assumes that this transformation will emerge within the capitalist factory, but he gives no account of how it does occur.

grant that the concept of rationality as individual or group utility-maximization is that historically conditioned concept of rationality which arose and which will fall with the bourgeois mode of production. Suppose also that we grant the further claim, not made explicit in the historicist reply, that there is a different concept of rationality peculiar to the socialist mode of production. Each of these claims requires support—support which I believe is not to be found either in Marx's writings or in those of later Marxians. But let us set that problem aside. Instead we ask, granted these claims about rationality, what is the correct Marxian account of the proletarian's motivation?

If the historicist reply is to be effective, it must establish two theses: (i) that proletarians are rational according to the socialist, not the bourgeois concept of rationality; and (ii) that the public goods problem does not arise for individuals who are rational in the socialist sense.

The latter thesis cannot of course be established until a coherent concept of socialist rationality is articulated. Further, there are important restrictions on what such a concept of rationality could include, if recourse to it is to be compatible with Marx's rejection of a significant role for moral principles in revolutionary motivation. In particular, a socialist concept of rationality cannot include those sorts of principles—for example, principles of justice—scorned by Marx in his attacks on the moralizing socialists.

Whatever the content of the socialist concept of rationality turns out to be, recourse to it as an explanation of proletarian revolutionary activity appears to be illegitimate for Marx. It must be remembered that for Marx the bourgeois concept of rationality would be that concept of rationality which is dominant *throughout* capitalism, not just among the bourgeois—as Marx himself emphasizes, "the ruling ideas of each age have ever been the ideas of its ruling class."[29] A distinctive socialist concept of rationality would have to be one, then, which *emerges* in the course of the revolutionary struggle: the process of revolutionary cooperation transforms the proletarian from one who is rational in the bourgeois sense to one who is rational in the socialist

29. *Karl Marx: Selected Writings*, p. 236.

sense. Yet the new form of rationality which emerges from the proletarian struggle cannot explain how individuals come to participate in
that struggle.

It might be replied that the new socialist form of rational cooperation is emerging within the capitalist factory and that this phenomenon explains how individuals come to participate in the revolutionary process. The following passages from *Capital* might be invoked
as rather tenuous support for this view.

> When the labourer [in the capitalist factory] cooperates systemat-
> ically with others, he strips off the fetters of his individuality and
> develops the capacities of his species. . . .
>   [The working class] is being disciplined, unified, and organized
> by the very mechanism of the capitalist mode of production.[30]

There are two immediate problems with this reply. First, the notion
of a new form of rationality emerging within the capitalist factory
must somehow be made to square with Marx's repeated charges that
factory work in capitalism turns worker against worker in the competition for jobs, alienates man from his communal nature, mortifies his
body, and ruins his mind.[31] This will, be no small task. Second, it is
not enough to say that a new form of rational cooperation capable of
solving the public goods problem will emerge in the capitalist factory
—empirical investigation to support this thesis is required. Marx nowhere executed such an investigation.

More recent researchers have studied the processes by which successful union activity emerges within the context of the factory. A
Marxian who wishes to use the fruits of such research must do so
with care. Granted Marx's rejection of reliance upon coercion and
moral motivation, some of the more obvious and common explanations of how unions overcome public goods problems cannot be
adopted by the Marxian. Explanations which assign a fundamental

---

30. *Capital*, I: 329, 763.
31. For Marx's most extended discussion of the alienation of the worker from
his fellows, see *Karl Marx: Selected Writings*, pp. 75-112. For his account of the
debilitating effects of factory work see chapter 14 "Division of Labour and
Manufacture, *Capital*, I.

role to the coercion of workers (for example, the closed shop) or to the motivational power of the call for a "fair wage" or for a just social order are not available to the Marxian. My point is not that it is impossible to provide an account of how a new form of rational cooperation—one which relies neither upon coercion nor moral principles—could arise in the capitalist factory. I am only urging that such an account must be produced and confirmed by empirical research if it is to serve as an adequate reply to the public goods objection.

VIII

The foregoing analysis may help account for the persistence of two phenomena that adherents of Marx's interest theory of proletarian motivation find it difficult to explain but equally difficult to ignore: the revolutionary's use of violence against members of the proletariat and his reliance upon what Marx called "obsolete verbal rubbish" about justice and rights. The use of violence against members of the proletariat is usually explained away as an exception due to the underdeveloped class consciousness of backward countries. But if, as I have argued, there is a public goods problem for the proletariat, coercion of proletarians by a dedicated elite may be needed even where the entire proletariat is convinced that its own interests dictate the overthrow of the system. Further, the Marxian who believes that concepts of justice or of the rights of man are muddled, obsolete notions which cannot withstand Marx's ruthless scientific analysis must consider the possibility that appeal to these spurious notions is nonetheless necessary for the success of the revolution. The dedicated revolutionary would then be faced with the prospect of maintaining two contradictory views about moral principles—the one esoteric, the other exoteric.

The Marxian who wishes to rehabilitate Marx's theory of revolutionary motivation by conceding a significant role to moral principles commits himself to an onerous task. He must produce an adequate moral principle or set of moral principles. There is reason to believe, however, that the most broadly acknowledged moral principles are not capable of solving the more serious public goods problems.[32] Consider, for example, a principle requiring one to help establish a just or humane or free social order, granted that one has assurance that others will also put forth effort. On the one hand, it is the assurance clause of this principle which makes it so plausible, yet this same clause makes it ineffective in solving public goods problems without recourse to coercion. Rawls acknowledges this by stating that the duty to help establish and support just institutions applies only where a coercive apparatus assures one that others will reciprocate.[33] On the other hand, if the assurance clause is excised, the resulting principle may be strong enough to solve the public goods problem without recourse to coercion, but its very strength will make it implausible. It is one thing to say that one ought to help establish just or humane or free institutions, if one has reasonable assurance that others will reciprocate. It is quite another to demand that one ought to help establish such institutions no matter what others do and regardless of whether one's own destruction may result. Though I cannot argue the point here, I suspect that many, if not all, of the moral principles a Marxian might plausibly invoke are either too weak to solve the proletariat's public goods problem or too strong to enjoy independent plausibility. At any rate, the Marxian who invokes moral principles must show that they do solve the problem and that they are principles to which a proletarian could reasonably commit himself.

There is, however, yet another serious obstacle for a revised Marxian account to overcome. It is not enough to show that there are moral principles which the proletariat could plausibly embrace and which would solve their problem of coordination. The revised Marxian account must also show that the capitalists are incapable of achieving a similar solution.

32. For some of these reasons see Sartorius, "The Limits of Libertarianism."
33. Rawls, *A Theory of Justice*, pp. 268-69.

An earlier version of this paper was presented at the University of Pittsburgh Philosophy Department. I would like to thank Annette Baier, Kurt Baier, John Cooper, N. J. McClennan, and T. Seidenfeld for their helpful comments. I am also indebted to the Editors of *Philosophy & Public Affairs* for several helpful suggestions.

G. A. Cohen   Karl Marx and
                 the Withering Away of
                 Social Science[1]

When presented with evidence against one of the propositions it is
their business to believe, professional communists sometimes accuse
their opponents of looking at the surface of things only, at appearances. They invoke the words of Marx: "If there were no difference
between essence and appearance, there would be no need for science."
Thus armed, they claim, for example, that he who thinks the apparently uneven distribution of power in East European countries proves that
they are not classless societies is bewitched by seemings. What appear to be classes are really strata, or, to take other instances, what
appears to be competition is really emulation, what appears to be a
crime is really a distortion of socialist development, and so on.

The present paper concerns not the thought of professional communists but that of Karl Marx, and the ramifications of the dictum
communists are prone to quote. In section 1 I try to explain what Marx
intended by it. I then (section 2) display discrepancies between essence and appearance in feudal and in bourgeois society, by stating
some differences between exploitation on the medieval manor and
exploitation in the capitalist factory. Next (section 3) I demonstrate
that the dictum entails, for Marx, that socialism and social science
are incompatible, that as socialism develops, social science must
wither away. In section 4 I relate the antagonism between socialism
and social science to the doctrine of the unity of theory and practice.

1. In preparing this article for publication I benefited from the comments of
Robert Black, Gerald Dworkin, Russell Keat, Frank Sibley, Richard Wollheim,
and above all the Editors of *Philosophy & Public Affairs*. A revised version of
this essay appears as Appendix I in G. A. Cohen, *Karl Marx's Theory of History:
A Defence* (Princeton, 1978), pp. 326-344.

Finally (section 5), I criticize Marx's idea of science, but I endorse
his belief in the desirability of a society whose intelligibility does not
depend upon it.

1. Marx frequently pronounced his dictum on essence and appearance when he was at work on *Capital*, which he conceived as an
attempt to lay bare the reality underlying and controlling the appearance of capitalist relations of production. He was aware that the
theories offered in *Capital* are abstruse. In Volume II[2] of the work he
identifies the "really scientific" explanation of a phenomenon with
the "esoteric" view of it. In Volume III he declares that "all science
would be superfluous if the manifest form [Erscheinungsform] and
the essence of things directly coincided";[3] and in a lecture to workers
in 1865 he warns that "scientific truth is always paradox, if judged
by everyday experience, which catches only the delusive appearance of
things."[4] He often crowns his demonstrations in *Capital* by glorying
in the fact that common observation contradicts his analysis;[5] and
in the course of a letter to Dr. Kugelmann (11 July 1868) he complains that recent bourgeois economists (unlike their classical predecessors)[6] use only the ordinary concepts of price and profit with
which every merchant is familiar. He finds no virtue in economic
studies which fail to penetrate beneath the phenomena a businessman
can see.[7]

Marx mentions achievements of natural science which help us to
gauge what he means when he distinguishes appearance from essence

2. Pp. 212, *183*. Page references to *Capital* in ordinary type are to the English
version published in Moscow by the Institute of Marxism-Leninism, which my
translations follow closely. Accompanying references in italics are to the German text, in the relevant volume of the Hamburg edition (Meissners Verlag).
(Elsewhere I quote the translations cited exactly. All translations published in
Moscow were prepared by the Institute of Marxism-Leninism.)

3. Pp. 797, *352*.

4. *Value, Price and Profit*, in *Marx-Engels Selected Works* (Moscow, 1958),
I, 424. (Marx wrote this work in English.)

5. See, e.g., I, 307, *270*: "This law clearly contradicts all experience based
on appearance [Augenschein]." See also III, 205, *188*; 846-847, *404-405*.

6. Notably Smith and Ricardo. For a fascinating comparison of the two,
see *Theories of Surplus Value* (Moscow, 1969), II, 164-169. See also pp. 106,
191, 347, 351, 437 of this volume.

7. See also *Capital*, III, 760, *312*, where Hegel is credited with the insight
that genuine science thrives on paradox.

and maintains that science discovers the latter. The air we breathe appears to be elemental, but chemistry discloses that it is composed of distinct substances, which are not detected by the nose. The sun appears to move across the heavens, but science replaces this proposition, which experience supports, with the thesis that the earth is the moving body.[8]

These cases provide analogues of the relation between capitalism as Marx analyzes it and capitalism as it appears to those who live inside it.

It is a cardinal tenet of Marx's theory that only the expenditure of labor creates economic value, and in proportion to the amount of labor that is expended. It follows that because workers do not receive the whole value of what they produce they are not paid for all the labor they have performed. It also follows that capital investment enables the creation of profit only to the extent that it is investment in labor power.

Notwithstanding these theorems, the wage worker appears to receive payment, whether high or low, for every unit of labor time he completes. If his wage is eight shillings for each hour and he works ten hours, he will receive four pounds, which is the exact product of ten times eight shillings. But in the reality divulged by the theory of surplus value, the four pounds compensate the worker for only part of his time, and the unremunerated remainder creates what is appropriated as profit. Yet since the worker appears to be rewarded for all the effort he expends, the profit appears to have a source other than his labor. Economists in the thrall of appearance therefore attribute it to capitalist's decision to invest instead of consume his wealth, or to his entrepreneurial ingenuity, or to the power of the machines he owns. They tend to impute to capital itself the faculty of profit-creation.

This imputation is encouraged by the unavailability to those who inspect appearances alone of a critical distinction between the locus of profit-creation and the locus of profit-allocation. Although the amount of profit *created* in an enterprise depends entirely on the amount of capital it has invested in labor power (as opposed to machines, raw materials, etc.), the amount of profit that *redounds* to the enterprise is, in a competitive economy, directly proportional to the *total* capital

8. *Capital*, I, 316, 280; 74, 41.

invested in it, in all factors of production.[9] Labor-intensive industries have a higher rate of profit-creation but the same rate of profit-appropriation as other industries. Competition induces an equalizing flow of profit through the economy from high-profit to low-profit industries. It is therefore irrelevant to the capitalist's practice that labor alone creates value and profit. He will not be most tempted by the opportunity of investing in a labor-intensive industry. He cares about the volume of his return, not the dynamics of its creation. He therefore regards what determines the share of profit he will receive as tantamount to what creates it, and the economist who does not penetrate below the surface, on which the distinction between profit-creation and profit-allocation is not exhibited, follows him.[10]

Let us now return to the rudimentary illustrations from natural science. For Marx the senses mislead us with respect to the constitution of the air and the movements of heavenly bodies. Yet a person who managed in ordinary breathing to detect different components in the air would have a nose that did not function as healthy human noses do. And a person who sincerely claimed to perceive a stationary sun and a rotating earth would be suffering from some disorder of vision, or of motor control. Perceiving the air as elemental and the sun as in motion are experiences more akin to seeing mirages than to having hallucinations. For if a man does not see a mirage under the appropriate conditions, there is something wrong with his vision. His eyes have failed to register the play of light in the distance.

The ideas of the air as a uniform substance and of the sun rising and setting do not result from faulty perception. That is how the air and the sun present themselves. The notion that the worker's labor is fully rewarded, or that every unit of capital invested by his employer participates in the creation of profit—these are not a result of misperceiving the shape of capitalist arrangements. They record surface features of capitalist society. But anyone who thinks the fundamental lineaments of that society are present on its surface and open to observation fails to apprehend its nature.

9. See *Capital*, III, part 2; *Theories of Surplus Value*, II, chap. 10.

10. "To the unscientific observer" things appear just as they do "to him who is actually involved and interested in the process of bourgeois production" (*Theories of Surplus Value*, II, 165; see also pp. 218-219, 266-267, 318, 333, 427).

The appearances just reviewed are, like mirages, part of the world around us. They comprise the outer form of things, which enjoys an objective status, and which only science can strip away. To express the thought with less imagery, let us say that *there is a gulf between appearance and reality when and only when the explanation of a state of affairs renders unacceptable the description that it is natural to give of it if one lacks the explanation.* Gulfs exist only when things appear as they would appear if reality were different from what it is, and only when they exist is science required for a state of affairs to be intelligible.

(The italicized formulation allows that a *theory* may describe appearance and not reality if it is replaceable by a "deeper" theory which falsifies it. But Marx accepted a two-dimensional contrast between observation and theory, and in expounding him I follow him. Hence the description mentioned in the italicized formulation is to be understood as based on pretheoretical observation. I shall ignore challenges to the absolute distinction here presupposed between the world of experience and the world of theory.)[11]

Now if the nose channeled nitrogen through one nostril and oxygen through the other, and if the respirer sensed a difference between the gases, he would not need science to inform him that the air is heterogeneous. (Science might still outdo the nose by revealing the proportions of nitrogen and oxygen in the air and the chemical structure of each; but not by asserting the fact of atmospheric diversity.) If there were enormous periscopes attached to our eyes, which we could control as snails do their horns, then the Copernican revolution might never have occurred.

But it is fortunate that we do not always perceive the essential natural phenomena, for we probably would not survive if we did. Nasal sifting of nitrogen and oxygen might be taxing and distracting, and periscopes would reduce our mobility. The gulf in nature between essence and appearance benefits the human organism. And

11. Skepticism about Marx's use of the contrast between observation and theory may be based on the view that theoretical concepts serve to connect observation statements without denoting constituents of a reality underlying experience; or on the contention that experience is always shaped by a theoretical perspective; or on the distinct contention that the contrast in question is always relative to a context of inquiry.

we shall see that, for Marx, the survival of a class society, and in particular of capitalism, also depends on a disparity between what it really is and the appearance it displays to its members, rulers and ruled alike.

Giambattista Vico said that society is more intelligible to man than nature, because it is his creation. And certainly a schism between essence and appearance in society provokes more disquiet than a similar gap in nature. But according to Marx, man's creation is riddled with mystery: curious theoretical constructions are required to grasp what men are doing. There arises the desire to establish a social order which eliminates the gulf between essence and appearance, in which things are as they appear to be. We shall see that socialism is expected to satisfy this desire. But we must first ask why class societies present themselves in a guise that differs from the shape a correct social theory must attribute to them.

2. Part of the answer is that they rest on the exploitation of man by man. If the exploited were to see that they are exploited, they would resent their subjection and threaten social stability. And if the exploiters were to see that they exploit, the composure they need to rule confidently would be disturbed. Being social animals, exploiters want to feel that their social behavior is justifiable.[12] When the feeling is difficult to reconcile with the truth, the truth must be hidden from them as much as from those they oppress, and so illusion must be constitutive of class societies.

I say "constitutive" because Marx is not claiming merely that the members of a class society will acquire false beliefs about it. The falsehood maintains its grip by permeating the world they experience; their perceptions are false because what they perceive is a distortion of reality. The philosophical tradition out of which Marx grew insists on the prevalence of such cognitive situations. For Plato (according to some interpretations) men observing the empirical world are under illusions not because their thoughts fail to correspond to it, but because they accurately reflect an illusory world. Marx accordingly

12. Though Marx never explicitly states this essentially psychological thesis, it must be attributed to him if we are to make sense of a great deal of his theory of ideology. I have explored some of its consequences in "The Workers and the Word: Why Marx Had the Right To Think He Was Right," *Praxis* (Zagreb) 3-4 (1968): 376-390.

writes that workers take seriously the appearance (*Schein*) that their labor is fully rewarded. His phrasing[13] shows that he thinks of the appearance as an attribute of the reality. It is only derivatively a reflection of reality in men's minds.

Hence the discovery of the labor theory of value does not "dissipate the mist"[14] through which commodity relations are observed. Those who know the theory continue to "move about in forms of illusion [Gestaltungen des Scheins]."[15] Things do not seem different to a worker who knows Marxism. He knows they *are* different from what they continue to seem to be. A man who can explain mirages does not thereby cease to see them.

The table below purports to display what is obvious and what is hidden under two regimes of exploitation, feudalism and capitalism. Before turning to the table, I shall briefly expound two analytical constructs which enable us to identify some general differences between the societies.

Nineteenth-century German sociology, drawing on Marx and Hegel and Sir Henry Maine, established a distinction between two ideal types of human society, the *Gemeinschaft* and the *Gesellschaft*. No pair of English nouns adequately conveys the intended contrast, but it is customary to translate *Gemeinschaft* as "community" and *Gesellschaft* as "association." They are distinguished by the different relations between people characteristic of each. In an association men connect with one another only when each expects private advantage

13. The text in question is at *Capital*, I, 558, 521. Other passages demand the same construal. Thus "everything appears reversed in competition, and *thus* in the consciousness of the agents of competition" (III, 220, 205; italics mine). "The mystification . . . lies in the nature of capital" (*Grundrisse* [Berlin, 1953], p. 534; translation mine). Cf. also *Capital*, I, 550, 512; III, 165-166, 147-148; 802, 357-358; 845, 403; *Critique of Political Economy*, trans. N. I. Stone (Chicago, 1904), p. 302; *Theories of Surplus Value*, II, 69, 165, 217.

I cite only Marx's later writings here. A list of passages is not required to prove that he conceived of reality and appearance in this manner in his earlier work. In his response to Feuerbach he took the view that the "inversions" the latter had identified in consciousness occurred because consciousness was of an inverted world. (See, for example, the first page of the Introduction to *A Contribution to the Critique of Hegel's "Philosophy of Right,"* in *On Religion* [Moscow, 1957]. See, further, section 4 below.)

14. *Capital*, I, 74, 41. The translation is free here.

15. *Capital*, III, 810, 366.

from the connection. Links between people are impersonal and contractual. The perfect capitalist market embodies this idea. But the feudal manor *looks*[16] more like the opposite social type, a community, in which relations flow from personal status. The bond between lord and serf does not derive from a freely entered contract: it is conceived in the imagery of kinship. The lord fights for the sake of his manorial dependents. He is their paternal protector. The serf labors in a spirit of filial homage to provision the lord's household. Ties between master and servant, it seems, are not utilitarian, not rooted in prudential calculation. Each appears concerned for the welfare of the other, not interested in the other merely as protector or as provider of consumables.[17] The incursion of commerce dissolves these bonds and reduces human contact to patently cash-determined transactions. A man is merely a means to another man under capitalism, but in the *Gemeinschaft* (and, to all appearances, under feudalism) his position is respected by his fellows. It restricts the uses they are prepared to make of him, and the uses he is prepared to make of them.

Now neither a *Gemeinschaft* nor a *Gesellschaft* is of necessity exploitative. To be sure, in a market society, in the pure association, men make use of one another, but mutual use is not exploitation unless it yields unequal rewards.[18] The content of Marx's concept of simple commodity production is a *Gesellschaft* which is not exploitative. In simple commodity production men meet at a market to exchange their wares, but the marketeers themselves produce the commodities they bring. No one is subordinated to them in the productive process. The simple commodity market may not be an enthralling ideal of social organization,[19] but where it prevails there is no unjust treatment.

16. See, e.g., *Grundrisse*, p. 82.
17. See *Grundrisse*, pp. 873-874, 913. Ferdinand Tönnies developed the contrast in his *Gemeinschaft und Gesellschaft*. See *Community and Society*, trans. Charles Loomis (New York, 1963), *passim* and, e.g., p. 59.
18. See *Grundrisse*, pp. 911-912.
19. It was a component in the ideals of Sismondi, Proudhon, and some anarchists, but Marx spurned it because it was incompatible with modern technology, and because even if it were possible to install it, it would inevitably lead to capitalist commodity production again. It was with some plausibility that he derided it as a futile petty-bourgeois aspiration. See, for example, *Grundrisse*, p. 916.

Again, the ideal manor I have sketched, though it involves exploitation in the technical Marxian sense (a surplus product is extracted), contains no serious injustice. My neighbor does not exploit me if in friendship I help him dig his garden, particularly if he loyally defends my garden against marauders. If capitalism were simple commodity production, and if feudalism had measured up to its *gemeinschaftliche* ideology, then neither could be deemed exploitative, if exploitation entails oppression. But both societies are in fact oppressively exploitative, because the stipulated conditions are not fulfilled. Capitalism is not simple commodity production. Its propertied marketeers exert power over propertyless producers. And feudalism, according to Marx, is not the intimate community it presents itself as being. The relation between lord and serf is utilitarian in basis, however much the parties to it are unaware of the fact.

The following table captures the difference between the two societies.

	Under Feudalism	*Under Capitalism*
That surplus product is extracted	is evident	is concealed
That human relations are utilitarian	is concealed	is evident

Both societies really have the two features noticed in the table, but in each society only one of them is immediately observable.

Consider the first feature. It is obvious to all concerned that the serf spends a part of his time working for the benefit of his lord. If labor rent is exacted, that part is spent tilling the lord's demesne, instead of his own plot; alternatively, or in addition, some of the effort the serf expends on his own and on the common land is directed to raising produce he will deliver to the lord's table or sell to provide money for the lord's coffers. Nothing is more obvious than that a definite quantity of the fruits of his labor belongs not to him but to his master.[20] But under capitalism the manner in which a portion of the product of the worker's toil is retained by the capitalist obscures

20. *Capital*, I, 77, 44.

the fact that he keeps it. The working day and the working year are
not manifestly divided into stretches of time for which the worker is
compensated and stretches for which he is not. It is false that at any
given moment the worker is either producing the product-equivalent
of wages or producing the product-equivalent of profit, yet theory
enforces a division of his total time into those two segments.[21] Nor
is the palpable physical product divided between capitalist and worker. They share only the money it fetches on the market, and this
mystifies the entire transaction. So what feudal rent reveals, the wage
system conceals.[22] "A child could tell the sources of wealth of an
ancient slave-holder or medieval feudal baron. Not so with our non-
producing classes. The sources of the wealth of our merchant-princes
are shrouded in mystery."[23]

Now consider the second feature. Under capitalism, production
relations are obviously utilitarian. Capitalists pretend no affection
for their workers, and the indifference is reciprocated.[24] But, Marx
believed, manorial relations only appear to be otherwise. Though men
seem bound by noneconomic ties of tradition and loyalty, historical
materialism entails that it is really economic necessity that glues them
together. The level of productivity characteristic of the medieval period made the manorial scheme an appropriate device for provisioning
the species. A patina of *Gemeinschaftlichkeit* is required to reconcile
men to the scheme, whose ground is utilitarian. If the members of the
manor knew that it was founded on interest rather than sentiment,
then the peasants would not serve the lord, and the lord could not
sustain his patriarchal posture. In his early *Manuscripts* Marx goes
so far as to treat the fact that feudalism is a *Gesellschaft* masquerad-
ing as a *Gemeinschaft* as the reason for its demise. The economic
reality underpinning the superstructure of quasifamilial relations
must reveal itself. Capitalism supersedes feudalism because the truth

21. "The product is always divisible in its value form, if not always in its
natural form" (*Grundrisse*, p. 330; translation mine. Cf. p. 888).

22. See *Grundrisse*, pp. 194, 487, 658; *Capital*, I, 236-237, *196-198*; 539-540,
502; 568-569, 530-531; III, chap. 47, part 2; *Theories of Surplus Value*, I, 46.

23. Louis Boudin, *The Theoretical System of Karl Marx* (New York, 1967),
p. 59.

24. See Marx and Engels, *The German Ideology* (London, 1965), p. 448.

must come into view.[25] Marx later abandoned this Hegelianizing explanation of the transition to capitalism, but he retained the contrast on which the explanation relies.[26]

To conclude. Feudalism and capitalism have two features. One is veiled under feudalism, the other under capitalism. It is a plausible suggestion that in any society qualified by those features it is necessary[27] that one of them be concealed for the society to persist. If serfs knew that the communality of the manor was a sham, they would not do what they in fact do, for they knowingly surrender a part of their produce to the lord. If factory workers knew they were not recompensed for all their labor, they would cease working for the capitalist, since their sole motive for doing so is self-interest. No traditional bonds inhibit them from revolting against the system, so when they become apprised of the truths of Marxist science they do revolt. But they must learn those truths to become revolutionaries. They must penetrate through the mirage of the wage form.

IT MAY be objected that even if historical materialism committed Marx to the thesis that economic necessity generated the manorial structure, there is no evidence that he accepted it. I therefore offer some documentation. According to *The Communist Manifesto*, only capitalism compels man "to face with sober senses his real conditions of life, and his relations with his kind."[28] The relations obtained under feudalism, but men were blind to them because they did not "surface." Under capitalism men are "no longer bound to other men even by the *semblance* of common ties."[29] Marx did believe that the second feature, concealed though it was, characterized feudalism.

25. "In general, movement must triumph over immobility, overt self-conscious baseness over concealed, unconscious baseness, . . . and money over the other forms of private property" (*ibid.*, p. 143; cf. p. 115).

26. For its retention see *The German Ideology*, p. 239; *The Poverty of Philosophy* (Moscow, n.d.), pp. 178-181; *The Communist Manifesto*, in *Selected Works*, I, 36-38; *The Critique of Political Economy*, p. 267; *Capital*, III, 603-604, 157. See also my "Bourgeois and Proletarians," *Journal of the History of Ideas* 29, no. 2 (April-June 1968): 224-225.

27. The stated condition is not sufficient, if only because the concealed feature may become known while continuing to appear to be absent. See p. 188, above.

28. *Selected Works*, I, 37.

29. *The Holy Family* (Moscow, 1956), p. 156.

But did he believe, as I have claimed, that under feudalism the first feature was a matter of observation? A statement in the *Manifesto* may seem to refute my interpretation: "In one word, for exploitation, veiled by religious and political illusions, [the bourgeoisie] has substituted naked, shameless, direct, brutal exploitation."[30] If this is inconsistent with my presentation, it is equally inconsistent with the texts[31] on which I based it. But there is in fact no inconsistency, or even tension. Exploitation in the technical sense (the first feature of the table) is not at issue here: it is not asserted that the extraction of surplus product was made more evident by the bourgeoisie. The passage patently means that capitalism made the utilitarian treatment of men by their masters more obvious, and that is something I affirmed.

Marx also contrasted the illusions of capitalism and slavery. Whereas the wage worker seems to perform no unpaid labor, the slave seems to perform unpaid labor only. But the latter is as much a false appearance as the former, since the slave is allowed to consume part of his product. Worker and slave are both paid because they both receive necessities of life in return for labor. Yet "since no bargain is struck between [the slave] and his master, and no acts of selling and buying go on between the two parties, all his labour seems to be given away for nothing."[32] "The ownership-relation conceals the labour of the slave for himself; . . . the money-relation conceals the unrequited labour of the wage-labourer."[33]

3. One corollary of the dictum regarding essence and appearance is that science may study a social formation only if it is held together by mechanisms that disguise its basic anatomy. The true content of human interaction must be hidden for social science to assume a role.

When a capitalist hires a worker, neither, in a flourishing capital-

---

30. *Selected Works*, I, 36.   31. Listed in note 22.

32. *Value, Price and Profit*, in *Selected Works*, I, 429. Cf. *Capital*, I, 574, 536; III, 30, 5. M. Ernest Mandel is therefore guilty of deviation when he writes that under slavery "the mere idea of a necessary product, of a subsistence minimum, is completely deprived of meaning" (*Marxist Economic Theory* [London, 1968], p. 537).

33. *Capital*, I, 539-540, 502. The three major regimes of exploitation (slavery, feudalism, capitalism) are compared in the latter passage, and also in *Value, Price and Profit, Selected Works*, I, 429.

ism, is aware of the nature of the exchange they enact. The worker lacks the facilities needed in a market society to produce and sell goods. These are monopolized by the capitalist class. He is therefore constrained to submit himself to some member of that class. But he appears to dispose of his labor freely, because he can bargain and reject what one capitalist offers in favor of a deal offered by another. In essence bound to capital, he appears to be a free agent. This appearance, generated by the opportunity to bargain, is the form his bondage takes, and under which it is concealed.[34]

One more example. According to Marxian theory, the market values of commodities are determined by the quantities of socially necessary labor time required for their production. But those values appear to be independent of human effort. They seem to inhere in commodities, like natural properties such as size or weight. The capitalist reasons that because a commodity has a high market value, it is worth hiring a large number of workers to produce it, whereas in reality it is because a large amount of labor is needed to produce it that its value is high. But again, the idea that economic values are unrelated to the expenditure of energy by human beings is nourished by ordinary experience. For in the day-to-day flux of supply and demand prices do vary independently of expended labor time, and their ultimate determination by it is concealed from those who do not reach beyond daily experience to theory.

Now Marx says that relations between human beings under socialism are "transparent" and "intelligible." Economic agents whose actions are integrated by a democratically formulated plan understand what they are doing. The rationale and the import of economic activity become publicly manifest. If we conjoin Marx's conceptions of socialism and science, we obtain the conclusion that socialism renders social science superfluous. It has no function in a world which has surpassed the discrepancy between the surface of things and their true character.

The mysteries of capitalism, its inaccessibility to the ordinary

34. See *Grundrisse*, pp. 565-566; *Capital*, I, 574, 536; 577-578, 541; 613-614, 578; II, 440, 416. See also Engels, *The Condition of the Working-Class in England in 1844*, trans. Florence Wischnewetzky (London, 1892), pp. 79-80, 185-186.

mind, result in one way or another from the fact that capitalist production aims at the expansion of exchange value, expressed in the
accumulation of money. Socialism dissolves the mysteries by abolishing the market. For it thereby eliminates money, the medium of market exchange, and without money there can be no accumulation of
abstract wealth,[35] as opposed to wealth in particular, useful, percep-
tible forms. Marx writes that "if we conceive society as being not
capitalistic but communistic, there will be no money-capital at all
. . . nor the disguises cloaking the transactions arising on account of
it."[36] There will, for example, never be that disparity between the
apparent and the real performance of an enterprise which the stock
market systematically promotes.

If Marx supposed that socialism would be immune to social science,
did he think all economists would be fired after the revolution? We
know that he accused post-Ricardian bourgeois economists of redun-
dancy when they spoke the language of ordinary economic agents.[37]
But in their day ordinary economic language was necessarily inadequate, because it could be applied only to surface phenomena which
covered the real state of affairs. Socialist economists, or many-sided
socialist men who sometimes engage in economics, will have no
occasion to employ a specialized conceptual apparatus. But they
will still have tasks to perform. For though the rationality and thus
the intelligibility of socialist production are immediately accessible,
it is not the case that all the facts of the socialist economy are com-

35. So abstract is the wealth of capitalists that many of them cannot say
what they own, but only how much, and some cannot be even that specific.
See my "Bourgeois and Proletarians."

36. *Capital*, II, 315, 287. He adds that "in capitalist society . . . social reason
asserts itself only *post festum*" and therefore "great disturbances may and must
constantly occur" (315, 288). Note the kinship between the idea that rationality comes in only after the event (*"post festum"*) and Hegel's owl of Minerva
figure, discussed below.

Mandel explains Marx's meaning: if something which has been produced
remains unsold, there has been a waste of "social labour time. This waste, in
a consciously co-ordinated society would have been realised in advance," and
therefore prevented. "On the market, the law of value reveals it only after the
event . . ." (*Marxist Economic Theory*, p. 68).

See *Grundrisse*, p. 277, for similar remarks. For more on the rationality of
socialism, see *Capital*, II, 358, 331; 424-425, 400; 451, 427.

37. See p. 183, above.

present to perception. No peak in the Urals is so high that it affords a view of every factory, field, and office in the Soviet Union. Data-gathering and data-processing are requisites of socialist planning, at any rate in the centralized socialism Marx envisaged when he emphasized the rationality of the future society in Volume II of *Capital*. But while the findings of socialist economics will exceed those of unaided observation, there is no reason to think they will subvert them. They will therefore not constitute science, if Marx's account of science is correct.

For Marx socialist economics is not science because it does not use specifically scientific concepts, which *are* needed to make capitalism intelligible. Above all, it dispenses with the concept of exchange value, which is heavily impregnated with theory. It needs the concept labor time, but that is different. Labor time is not a theoretical entity, and calculations of it are performed in all economies, including Robinson Crusoe's,[38] according to principles derived not from theory but from common sense. Only under capitalism does labor time take the mystifying form of exchange value, of which it is the secret content.[39]

By unifying social theory and social practice, socialism suppresses social science. It makes intelligible in practice spheres of human contact which had been intelligible only through theory. When social science is necessary, men do not understand themselves. A society in which men do not understand themselves is a defective society. Socialism is not a defective society, and therefore social-scientific theory is foreign to it. Capitalism is obscure. Only science can illuminate it. But in the bright light of socialism the torch of the specialized investigator is invisible.

4. Philosophy is not identical with social science. Nevertheless, in his early response to the work of Feuerbach, Marx called for a repeal of philosophy comparable to the repeal of social science entailed by his mature views of science and socialism. In each case the abolition

38. *Capital*, I, 76-77, 43.
39. "The mystical character of commodities does not . . . proceed from the content of the determining factors of value" (*Capital*, I, 71, 37-38). Cf. *Critique of the Gotha Programme*, in *Selected Works*, II, 22-23.

is a consequence of the extinction of those "illusiogenic" properties of social reality which give life to philosophy and social science alike.

In the present section I propose a somewhat novel account of Marx's Eleventh Thesis on Feuerbach. It suggests a close connection between the dictum on essence and appearance and the Marxist emphasis on the unity of theory and practice.

The concept of the unity of theory and practice has borne a number of meanings in Marxist theory and practice. In its popular use, it advances a policy for revolutionaries. In its crudest accentuation, it enjoins the revolutionary to spend half his day up in the library, and the rest down at the docks or the factory gates. But this life-style does not in itself deserve the description *unity* of theory and practice, for it is merely their juxtaposition. A further demand is that the teaching of the library be carried into the docks and the experience of the docks be applied at the library desk. And still more sophisticated recommendations regarding correct revolutionary conduct are available.

But the unity of theory and practice may also refer not to a policy but to a feature of an established socialist society. The integration of intellectual and manual labor is one such feature, but I have in mind something of a higher metaphysical grade, which may be expressed as a supplement to Marx's last thesis on Feuerbach. He wrote that "the philosophers have only interpreted the world, in various ways; the point is to change it." I suggest that we may add: "to change it so that interpretation of it is no longer necessary." When Engels opined that the German working-class movement was the rightful heir to German philosophy,[40] he intended that the proletariat would fulfill in practice the project of making the world intelligible that the philosophers had attempted within theory. The unity of theory and practice as a policy relates to the task of instituting a rational world. The unity of theory and practice in the present sense is a constituent of the revolutionized rational world that policy achieves. It is a world in which the theory explaining the practice of socialist man appears in his practice, and needs no separate elaboration in a theorist's head.

40. *Ludwig Feuerbach and the End of Classical German Philosophy*, in *Selected Works*, II, 402.

A certain line of reflection underlies a[41] conception of the unity of theory and practice in Marx's *Contribution to the Critique of Hegel's "Philosophy of Right"* and *Theses on Feuerbach*. It runs as follows: Theory aims at the production of thoughts which accord with reality. Practice aims at the production of realities which accord with thought. Therefore common to theory and practice is an aspiration to establish congruity between thought and reality. Now a person might consider himself as fundamentally neither a theorist nor an activist, but as primarily dedicated to arranging a correspondence between thought and reality, by theorizing or by action or by both. He might say: "The method of securing the correspondence is a secondary question. It is whatever, in the given circumstances, eliminates illusion."

It was from this (unstated) point of view that Marx judged Feuerbach's program for rescuing men from illusion to be inadequate. In certain domains thought could maintain a correspondence with reality only if reality were changed. Feuerbach demanded that people give up their illusions about their condition. He should have demanded that they give up the condition which continues to produce illusions, even after these illusions have been theoretically exposed.[42] When social circumstances inevitably generate discord between thought and reality, the enemy of illusion must operate on reality, not in thought alone. There are certain problems which only practice can solve.[43]

Consider the Fourth Thesis on Feuerbach: "Feuerbach starts out from the fact of religious self-alienation, the duplication of the world into a religious, imaginary world and a real one. His work consists of the dissolution of the religious world into its secular basis. He overlooks the fact that after completing this work, the chief thing still remains to be done. . . ."[44]

It would be superficial to read Marx as expressing an activist's

41. I use the indefinite article because I believe several semi-independent conceptions of the unity of theory and practice may be found in these documents, and I am here discussing only one of them.

42. *Contribution to the Critique*, in *On Religion*, p. 42.

43. See *ibid.*, p. 50. See also the portion of the Fourth Thesis on Feuerbach not quoted below.

44. I give Engels' version of the thesis (*The German Ideology*, p. 652) because it makes explicit the Marxian thought to which I draw attention here. I believe that in this instance Engels interpolated words but not thoughts.

impatience with the analytical response to illusion. He is not merely announcing his unwillingness to rest content with intellectual victories. It is false that whereas Feuerbach's concern is theory, his is practice. Their primary interest is the same. Both want to suppress illusion, and Marx's complaint is that theory alone will not do so.[45] The goal with respect to which "the chief thing still remains to be done" is to secure intelligibility. Only by bearing in mind that common aim can we understand the critique of Feuerbach as motivated by something beyond a difference of temper.[46] There is a genuine disagreement with Feuerbach, arising out of a shared desire to destroy illusion and initiate a harmony between reality and thought.

The illusions that occupy both thinkers survive theoretical exposé because theory does not cure the conditions which produce them. And this is because they are not, in the first instance, errors of thought, but distortions in the world, which theory is impotent to rectify. Marx thought social conditions must themselves be conflicted to be capable of generating a conflict between reality and appearance. But he did not oppose them only because he deplored the conflicts inherent in them. That they generated illusions was an independent evil. They were offenses against both epistemic and social harmony.

THERE appears to be a straightforward clash between the Eleventh Thesis on Feuerbach and the counsel of passivity Hegel dispensed to philosophers in the Preface to *The Philosophy of Right*. Philosophy, he said, is unable to contribute actively to history. It is its office to discern the rationale of historic endeavor in the afterglow of the fire of events. The owl of Minerva, emblem of wisdom, flies in the evening, when the day's work is over.[47] The Eleventh Thesis sets the tasks of the new day.

But it is not clear that Hegel thought the diurnal self-restraint of

45. See p. 188, above.
46. Cf. *The German Ideology*, p. 54: "[Feuerbach] wants . . . like the other theorists, merely to produce a correct consciousness about an *existing* fact; whereas for the real communist it is a question of overthrowing the existing state of things." I maintain that "it" here refers to the question of securing intelligibility.
47. *Hegel's "Philosophy of Right,"* trans. T. M. Knox (Oxford, 1958), pp. 13-14.

Minerva's owl permanently necessary, and if we turn to his concept of Absolute Knowledge, we may see less opposition between him and Marx than the last paragraph suggests. For Marxian socialism, depicted from the epistemic standpoint which has dominated this essay, is the fruition of Absolute Knowledge, since to have that knowledge is to know immediately, without ratiocination, the nature of the total spiritual world. Marx runs this conception to earth by projecting a community of human beings who appreciate without theory the sense of both their own actions and the actions of other men.

5. I have brought together Marx's views of reality and appearance, science and society, and theory and practice. I shall now criticize Marx's conception of science, but I shall defend his belief in the desirability of a society immune to social science.

We saw that Marx's concept of a gulf between appearance and reality depends upon an unrefined distinction between observation and theory. I shall continue to accept the distinction in its naïve form. I shall not challenge the concept of a theory-free observation report, which, moreover, counts as an observation report no matter what its context of utterance is. I shall also not question the coherence of the characterization of a discrepancy between reality and appearance provided earlier. To repeat it: there is a gulf between appearance and reality when and only when the explanation of a state of affairs renders unacceptable the description that it is natural to give of it if one lacks the explanation, this description being based purely on observation and committing the observer to no theoretical hypotheses.

These generous concessions do not save the thesis that *all*[48] scientific discoveries reveal a gulf between essence and appearance. Science sometimes expands prescientific information without prejudicing it,

---

48. The quotations presented on p. 183 suggest this strong interpretation, but other passages point to a weaker thesis, e.g., *Capital*, I, 537, 499: "That in their appearance [Erscheinung] things *often* represent themselves in inverted form is pretty well known in every science except political economy" (italics mine). This is nevertheless compatible with the strong interpretation, since Marx might think that science is in order only when the inversion occurs.

It is probably impossible to establish exactly what he did think. Perhaps we should simply note, in his favor, that the thesis that an essence/appearance discrepancy is necessary for there to be a science of a domain does not entail that every assertion of the science reveals such discrepancy. Even so, the thesis seems too strong.

and sometimes confirms it without expanding it. The claim that the
work of socialist economics does not embarrass pretheoretical belief
simply does not entail that it is not science.

Some of the examples Marx uses in support of his dictum, rather
than illustrating it, confirm the point just made. While it may be a
"paradox that the earth moves around the sun," it is no paradox, in
the required sense, that "water consists of two highly inflammable
gases."[49] It is true that we do not expect it to be so composed, but the
discovery warrants no revision of our belief that water quenches fire,
and therefore involves no gulf between appearance and reality. Even
one who insists that reports of experience can be free of theoretical
commitment must grant that the statement "what extinguishes fire
is not composed of inflammable substances" is not a record of experience but a piece of elementary theory. The scientific picture of
the solar system did subvert beliefs which were innocent responses
to observation. The discovery of the constitution of water did not.[50]

Marx's dictum must be abandoned. If we accept his crude contrast
between observation and theory, we may say that scientific explanation always uncovers a reality unrepresented in appearance, but that
it only sometimes discredits appearance. Let us call science *subversive*
when it does the latter, and *neutral* when it does not.

I shall suppose that there is a need for a science of society if and
only if central social processes require theoretical explanation. I
shall now maintain that it is reasonable to find the need for a science
of society intrinsically regrettable. I shall present this claim first for
subversive and then for neutral social science.

The claim is easier to defend with regard to subversive social science. A gulf between social reality and its appearance is surely an
unfortunate state of affairs. But we must distinguish this contention
from others with which it might be confused.

One might deplore the gulf just because it entails that theory is
required to reveal reality. Then one is not deploring the gulf as such
but the fact that reality is not pretheoretically available. This is also

49. *Value, Price and Profit*, in *Selected Works*, I, 424.
50. Marx's example of the constitution of the air is also shaky. For it is at
least arguable that the air does not manifest itself as uniform, but simply fails
to manifest itself as multiform; in which case the discovery that it *is* multiform is not incompatible with something it *appears* to be.

true when neutral science is needed. Therefore this response to the gulf is not directed specifically against subversive science.

Suppose the gulf exists because it is necessary to conceal exploitation. Or suppose this functional explanation of the gulf is false, but that it does shield exploitation. In either case one might lament the gulf because by hiding exploitation it protects it. It is more difficult to wage battle against it when it is hard to see. This again is no objection to the gulf as such.

We may also set aside objections to the gulf on the ground that it leads men into error. For we have seen[51] that it can persist after they have been enlightened.

Is the gulf still objectionable, once we ignore unhappy conditions which may be associated with it? After all, mirages, which instantiate the gulf in nature, make desert journeys more interesting. But it seems unacceptably frivolous to excuse major gulfs between appearance and social reality on similar grounds. It is certainly reasonable to regret the fact that experience induces a propensity to believe falsehoods about important social matters, even when the propensity is restrained by theoretical knowledge.

But suppose Marx agreed that he was wrong when he declared that science is necessarily subversive. Would he continue to desire that socialism reduce the role of theoretical understanding, of neutral social science? I think he would, and reasonably so.

I believe that it is desirable for a person to understand *himself* without relying upon theory. For there is a sense, difficult to make clear, in which I am alienated from myself and from what I do to the extent that I need theory to reach myself and the reasons governing my actions.[52]

51. See p. 188.
52. Theory may be used to put someone in a position where he can understand himself without drawing upon it. Consider how psychoanalytic theory is employed in the therapeutic context. The analyst does not aim to supply the analysand with the theory and show him how it applies to himself. Rather, he employs the theory so as to enable the analysand to encounter directly the images and ideas influencing his behavior and feeling. In this respect the conclusion of the therapy resembles the attainment of Hegel's Absolute Knowledge. For though Absolute Knowledge replaces reasoning, it is possible only after prolonged engagement in it. In the psychoanalytical case too, the aim is

The need for a theory of the social processes in which I participate reflects a similar alienation from those processes. Hence a reduced reliance on social science is desirable. This does not, of course, make it possible. The yearning for transparent human relations can be satisfied in part, because we can specify removable social institutions, notably the market, which foster opacity. But it is futile to hope for the total transparency contemplated in the Hegelio-Marxian tradition.

Recent developments in linguistics, in communication theory, and in realms of economics which will outlive the market are sufficient proof of this. One cannot hope to eliminate neutral theory of human phenomena, though one can understand the desire to do so. The strongest realistic hope is that subversive theory will be unnecessary and that neutral theory will be generally accessible. Many would contend that if theory became generally accessible, observation statements would come to be cast in the theoretical vocabulary. I shall not explore that possibility. Its very formulation violates the crude distinction between observation and theory which has framed our discussion.

---

intuition, the means is discursion. The end state of a successful psychoanalysis counts as self-knowledge without theory in the sense relevant here.

THE CONTRIBUTORS

GEORGE G. BRENKERT is Associate Professor of Philosophy at the University of Tennessee. He has published articles on ethics and social and political philosophy.

ALLEN BUCHANAN is Associate Professor of Philosophy at the University of Minnesota at Minneapolis. He has published articles on the subjects of ethics, political philosophy, and epistemology.

G. A. COHEN is Reader in Philosophy at University College London. He is the author of *Karl Marx's Theory of History: A Defence* and has published articles on Marx and on political philosophy. He is currently preparing a book on *Marxism and Exploitation*.

ALAN GILBERT is Assistant Professor at the Graduate School of International Studies of the University of Denver. He is the author of *Marx's Politics: Communists and Citizens*.

ZIYAD I. HUSAMI, who holds a Ph.D. from the Department of Politics, Princeton University, has taught at the University of Pennsylvania. He has written on a number of topics in Marxian philosophy.

RICHARD W. MILLER is Assistant Professor of Philosophy at Cornell University.

STANLEY MOORE is Professor of Philosophy, Emeritus, at the University of California, San Diego. His latest book is entitled *Marx on the Choice Between Socialism and Communism*.

Jeffrie G. Murphy is Professor of
Philosophy at the University of Arizona.
He has published articles in moral,
legal, and political philosophy, and
is the author of *Kant: The Philosophy
of Right* and *Retribution, Justice and
Therapy*.

Allen W. Wood is Professor of
Philosophy at Cornell University.
He is the author of *Kant's Moral
Religion, Kant's Rational Theology*,
and a forthcoming study of the
philosophy of Karl Marx.